# Work and Welfare in Europe

**Series Editors**

Denis Bouget
University of Nantes
France

Ana Guillén Rodriguez
University of Oviedo
Spain

Jane Lewis
London School of Economics and
Political Science
UK

Daniel Clegg
University of Edinburgh
UK

Welfare reform in Europe faces an uncertain future. This series provides the essential data and analysis that scholars need to understand and debate current developments in work and welfare and to evaluate future trajectories of care-work, poverty, activation policies, retirement and work-life balance.

More information about this series at
http://www.springer.com/series/14386

Caroline de la Porte • Elke Heins
Editors

# The Sovereign Debt Crisis, the EU and Welfare State Reform

palgrave
macmillan

*Editors*
Caroline de la Porte
Department of Business and Politics
Copenhagen Business School
Copenhagen, Denmark

Elke Heins
School of Social and Political Science
University of Edinburgh
Edinburgh, United Kingdom

Work and Welfare in Europe
ISBN 978-1-137-58178-5       ISBN 978-1-137-58179-2    (eBook)
DOI 10.1057/978-1-137-58179-2

Library of Congress Control Number: 2016943490

Cover illustration: © Olga Yakovenko/Fotolia

Printed on acid-free paper

This Palgrave Macmillan imprint is published by Springer Nature
The registered company is Macmillan Publishers Ltd. London

# Foreword

## From Two to Three Tiers of European Union Socioeconomic Governance

Stein Rokkan, one of the founding fathers of comparative political research, famously argued that any adequate understanding of modern democratic governance had to take account of 'two tiers' of government: firstly, the so-called *parliamentary tier* of party politics and secondly, the *corporate tier* of the world of business and, in particular, nationally organized interests of employer and worker representatives influencing policy decision-making from outside parliamentary politics and public administration (Rokkan 1970). Ever since Rokkan's perceptive insight, the maturation of comparative political economy research from the corporatist debate of the 1970s and 1980s to the comparative study of welfare regimes of the 1990s, and the Varieties of Capitalism approach of the early 2000s, can be seen as one of perfecting the 'double edged' analytical toolbox. Its tools are used for uncovering the interconnections between the parliamentary and corporate tiers of representation and how they mutually shape processes of socioeconomic policy formation, implementation, the management of social order and conflict, and the significant consequences for performance outcome in terms of growth, price stability, (un)employment, welfare state generosity and redistribution, economic competitiveness, balance of trade and public finance. Exogenous shocks, such as the break-down of the Bretton Woods monetary system, the two oil shocks of the 1970s and the recessions and the currency crises of the 1980s and early 1990s, have been critically influential in the maturation of comparative political economy studies. These crises brought into the limelight how differently governed national economies responded in variegated ways to shocks as the consequence of especially path-dependent domestic institutional structures of parliamentary politics and corporate state–society relations.

The singular focus on domestic tiers of governance has always been both the strength and the weakness of comparative political economy and welfare state research. The lack of an explicit international or geopolitical dimension remained a distinctive blind spot, especially in light of the ongoing and intensifying changes in the international political economy in recent decades. Since the 1980s, ever-increasing world market interdependency, created by the liberalization of international finance, the rise of emerging economies, and the concurrent process of de-industrialization in advanced economies, undermined the weight and efficacy of domestic institutions of socioeconomic policy making. In the European Union (EU), the loss of domestic social and economic policy autonomy was proactively answered for by the completion of the Single Market process and the establishment of the Economic and Monetary Union (EMU), together with some transnational social policy integration. In the process, Europe entered an era of 'semi-sovereign welfare states'. This new reality, however, had little impact on the analytical toolbox of comparative welfare state and political studies and scholars' primary concern with domestic institutions and actor constellations. The traditional line of defence among students of comparative political economy research was that changes in the international economy, including accelerated European economic integration, affected national polities by acting on national political and corporate actor constellations. The issue was not so much whether the international economy shapes domestic politics and policymaking but how and through what types of political institutions and forms of legitimation, which remained tied to sovereign nation-states. The analytical blind spot, in particular for the intrusion of EU economic integration into domestic welfare state arrangements and industrial relations, was also based on the implicit and naïve belief that the Pareto-optimal success of EU economic integration (in terms of opening markets) would allow member states to organize their welfare systems and domestic strategies of economic adjustment as they saw fit, thereby reinforcing, rather than undermining, domestic policy autonomy.

Although the benign compromise between EU market integration and domestic social policy autonomy was precarious from the start, it took until the fallout of the Eurozone currency crisis in the wake of the sovereign debt crisis before the illusion of EU macroeconomic governance and national social policy 'non-interference' was undone.

Taking cue from Rokkan, it is fair to say that the major overhaul in fiscal surveillance in the Economic and Monetary Union (EMU) economic governance architecture, enacted in the wake of the 2010 sovereign debt crisis, and now supported by heterodox quantitative easing (QE) interventions of the European Central Bank (ECB) to counter inflation, conjures up an image of an intrusive 'third tier' of supranational governance, layered on top of domestic tiers of parliamentary politics and corporate interest representation. By deliberately breaking with the two-tiered tradition of methodological nationalism, this book, edited by Caroline de la Porte and Elke Heins, delivers a pioneering analysis of the new and intimate connection between EU macroeconomic crisis management and the reform momentum in European welfare regimes since the onslaught of the Great Recession in 2008. To some extent building on the equally important collection of Jon Erik Dølvik and Andrew Martin, *European Social Models from Crisis to Crisis* (2014), which traces how European monetary integration unfolded since the 1989 fall of the Berlin Wall, de la Porte and Heins reveal how deeply interconnected Europe has become in the wake of the Eurocrisis. As such, the volume offers one of the first collections in comparative welfare state and political economy studies that focuses explicitly on how third tier EMU socioeconomic governance impacts on the scope for crisis management of individual member states. In their co-authored chapter on EU socioeconomic governance, the editors incisively show how the European sovereign debt crisis, with deep aftershocks of mass unemployment and rising inequality, triggered a fundamental change in the formal nature of EMU economic governance. They demonstrate how through the layering of the Six Pact, Fiscal Compact, Two Pack, the European

Semester and the reinforced excessive deficit procedures (EDP) onto the existing institutional governance framework of EMU, extends (in terms of democratic legitimacy) far beyond existing EU-treaties. Individual country agreements with the Troika of the European Commission, the ECB and the International Monetary Fund (IMF), analysed in the empirical chapters of the book reveal how EU institutions today meddle in unprecedented ways with member welfare states. At the same time, the new EMU governance structure opened up avenues of unprecedented instances of 'backroom' diplomacy between the European Commission and governments in fiscal distress, as part of a parcel of the new 'third tier' of EU macroeconomic policymaking and politics.

European welfare states can no longer turn a blind eye to how EMU macroeconomic governance, including ECB decisions, affect national labour market and social policy. A more narrowly construed methodological nationalist perspective may continue to remain valid for studying domestic political reactions to the Great Recession with a focus on: political mobilization, social conflict, reform ownership, voting behaviour and government turnover. However, such an approach can no longer do justice to an adequate understanding of how domestic policy choices translate into macroeconomic, employment, and distributive outcome performance without delving deeper into third tier EU governance and the new power asymmetries that comes with it, as is highlighted by Stefano Sacchi (Chapter 8) in his contribution on 'conditional reform' in Italy.

## European Lessons from the Great Recession

In trying to extrapolate forward from the insightful and well-researched contributions of this book, four lessons loom large from the cautionary tales presented in the book on the recent interplay between reinforced EMU governance and domestic labour market and social policy reform. These include: (1) the EMU crisis management lesson; (2) the lesson that domestic policy choices continue to matter; (3) the political crisis lesson; and, finally, (4) the lesson, more implicitly alluded to in this book, of cognitive inertia and ideational capture.

First, the EMU crisis management lesson is that indiscriminate austerity undermines long-term economic consolidation and growth. This is convincingly brought out by: the chapters on Ireland by Fiona Dukelow, the comparative case analysis of bailout conditionality in Greece and Portugal by Sotiria Theodoropoulou, and the chapter on crisis-induced welfare reform in Italy and Spain by Emmanuele Pavolini, Margarita León, Ana Guillén and Ugo Ascoli. They are in the good company of the chief economists of the IMF and Organisation for Economic Co-operation and Development (OECD) and leading economists, such as Olivier Blanchard, Paul de Grauwe, Jean Pisani-Ferry and Paul Krugman, who, inspired by the 'expansionary consolidation' teachings of Alberto Alesina, have all come to criticize Europe's austerity turn after 2010 for prolonging the crisis. Fiscal consolidation has had a dampening effect on growth and has led to greater material deprivation and poverty through a massive increase of (youth-) unemployment. While future Eurozone economic developments are difficult to predict, the biased two-sided nature of fiscal consolidation, for the time being, implicates that the predicament of economic divergence, asymmetric competition, and social and intergenerational imbalances is unlikely to subside anytime soon. It therefore remains questionable whether the EMU can survive under the self-inflicting force of pushing EMU members further down the path of pro-cyclical asymmetric economic divergence and social imbalance in a highly heterogeneous regional economy.

The critical impact of EMU crisis management does not undermine the importance of national politics and policymaking. A second domestic policy lesson I draw from the comparative contributions to this book is that there remains ample scope for domestic policy innovation and reform (and by implication, policy failures). While levels of social spending have on average been relatively stable over the past decades and increased only slightly since the onslaught of the Great Recession, social policy repertoires have nonetheless transfigured in important ways. In this respect, domestic policymakers have not been the blind followers of the austerity-biased policy fashions in Brussels and Frankfurt. Two contrasting experiences stand out. The *positive* lesson is that assertive and active, non-segmented and family-friendly welfare states do better on practically all counts. By contrast, as a *negative* lesson, the problematic policy legacies of labour market dualization, pension-biased social insurance and perverse familialism have been exposed as unsustainable in terms of providing effective protection for the poor, the young and the less skilled. In hindsight, a coherent regressive macroeconomic policy paradigm of stable money and sound public finances, in combination with a powerful agenda of microeconomic structural social and employment reform was no guarantee of consistent enactment and implementation, before and after the onslaught of the Eurocrisis. Under the reinforced fiscal scrutiny, this book also reveals that some flexibility for national governments remains, required also for the purpose of reform ownership and legitimacy. In Ireland, Dukelow intimates, the Troika was 'pushing against' the 'open door' of neoliberalism. Also for Greece and Portugal, according to Theodoropoulou, the Memoranda of Understanding on Specific Economic Policy Conditionality (MoUs) did not trigger one-size-fits-all regressive national social and labour market reform. In their case comparison between Spain and Italy, Pavolini, León, Guillén and Ascoli bring out the novel and varied dynamics of Brussels 'backroom' diplomacy. This is also brought out by Sacchi. On recent French reforms under the European Development Funds (EDFs) in 2009 and 2013, Patrick Hassenteufel and Bruno Palier conclude that it remains difficult to claim that Brussels is the main driver of welfare state reform.

In hard economic times, politics and economics become inseparably linked. Where economic stagnation prevails, high unemployment and rising poverty and inequality become the breeding grounds for xenophobic anti-EU populism. This is the third political lesson of this admirable book. The inability to deliver on economic prosperity *and* social progress puts national governments under enormous pressure, as electorates continue to hold national leaders responsible for socioeconomic (mis-)fortune. Because political accountability is bound up with widely cherished national welfare states, it is little wonder that harsh austerity reform reinforcing economic and economic insecurity, employment instability, and income inequality, and double-digit unemployment, alongside additional failures to resolve the Eurocrisis, the refugee and immigration crisis, and the Jihadist terrorist threat, at the supranational level, is increasingly met with anti-establishment political mobilization and rising EU-sceptic domestic pressures to water down ruling governments' commitments to European solutions. A further complicating factor is that over the past half decade inter-governmental discord over fiscal policy degenerated into hostile frictions, locking the Eurogroup heads of state into a low trust 'joint-decision trap', which further undermines faith in EU institutions and policies. The new 'backroom diplomacy' of haggling over extended timelines and 'fiscal flexibility' does not bode well for popular legitimacy in the medium term.

The fourth and final lesson concerns *cognitive inertia* and intellectual capture. Established macroeconomic models have, against prevailing evidence, seemingly blinded EU economists from observing mounting disequilibria before the Eurocrisis and anticipating the threat of deflation thereafter. The low growth consequences of the new fiscal federalism seemingly have had little impact on macroeconomic policy thinking. The ECB's unconventional interventions are essentially meant to underwrite the liberalizing 'structural reform' agenda of the original SGP fiscal regime: a strategy that is not without risks of asset inflation and new financial bubbles. Neo-classically trained economists, working at the ECB, and Directorate-General for Economic and Financial Affairs (DG ECFIN) and DG Competition, apparently held firm to the neo-classical axiom that generous social provision inescapably reduces efficiency, productivity and economic growth by 'crowding out' private initiative and entrepreneurship. The cognitive re-assertion of the 'big trade-off' between equity and efficiency surely thwarts an assertive EU social investment strategy. Mounting evidence that social investment returns, reinforce economic competitiveness remains underexplored in the corridors of the EU, (with the exception of DG Employment, Social Affairs and Inclusion), precisely because of the staying power of prevailing ideas and perceptions informing mainstream economic modelling. Apparently, in times of great uncertainty, the unlearning of previous policy beliefs is the hardest part.

## Is Social Investment (with Teeth) Still the Answer?

Admittedly, the EU has entered a period of transition. Ultimately, the current schizophrenic posture of the European Commission as 'social investment cheerleader', espoused by the 2013 Social Investment Package, on the one hand, and 'fiscal austerity headmaster', anchored in the Fiscal Compact of the same year, on the other, will ultimately prove difficult to sustain- as de la Porte and Heins underscore in their conclusion. It is tempting to see the current policy mix of fiscal austerity, structural reform and quantitative easing, under the surveillance of the Troika of the European Commission, the European Central Bank (ECB) and the International Monetary Fund (IMF), as epiphenomena of the ultimate victory of 'single-market totalitarianism' over the democratic compromise of welfare capitalism between market liberalization and social protection: as Wolfgang Streeck provocatively intimates in his dark but impressive book *Buying Time. The Delayed Crisis of Democratic Capitalism* (2014). According to Streeck's reading of the delayed Hayekian revenge on Keynesian welfare economics, the crisis aftermath has put global financial elites, the ECB and the European Commission in an overpowering position to exploit an emergent political vacuum by re-invigorating EU market, currency and fiscal integration on the ticket of a particularly aggressive version of welfare state re-commodification. Although I share Streeck's appraisal of EU market and currency integration and subsequent crisis responses as having intensified regressive market-oriented reform pressures on national systems social protection, I take issue with his dour and deterministic conclusion that European welfare states are imploding under the 'winner-take-all' yoke of the high finance elites of Wall Street and the City of London, and supranational bodies like the IMF, ECB and European Commission. For Streeck, the EU's Social Investment Package, launched in February 2013 as a strategic vision for welfare state modernization for post-crisis Europe, based on forward-looking social policies to 'prepare' individuals and families to respond to the changing nature of social risks in the competitive knowledge economy, is no more than a foil, and really a pretext for a fully-fledged neo-liberalization of EU and domestic socioeconomic governance. In passing he argues that women, entering the labour market en masse since the 1990s, have served as handmaidens to employers in their political advocacy for labour market deregulation (by competing with men on lower wages and more flexibility required for work–life balance reconciliation). Consistent with the contribution of Jon Kvist to this book, my reading of social investment and more recent events is more positive- bearing on both the policy efficacy of social investment and a rapidly eroding popular support basis for fully fledged neo-liberalization across the EU.

The paramount importance of the 2013 Social Investment Package is that it officially endorses a socially inclusive and economically robust alternative to the less coherent fiscal austerity orthodoxy cum monetarist heterodoxy policy mix. Policy attention is shifting toward evidence of social investment reforms 'crowding in positive employment, productivity, equality and work–life balance returns. Also, the OECD and World Bank are increasingly distancing themselves from their former 'structural reform' prescriptions in favour of an agenda of 'inclusive growth', informed by new insights into the causes of inequality, the intergenerational transmission of poverty, gender change and family demography, and the paramount importance of lifelong education from early childhood on for the competitive knowledge-based economy. To be sure, the Social Investment Packages and the Youth Guarantee continue to be based on the voluntarist open method of coordination (OMC) with weak enforcement, surveillance and feedback monitoring procedures, as de la Porte and Heins highlight in Chapter 2.

On the other hand, the benefits of growth and employment and on welfare gains in social protection, intergenerational redistribution, gender equity, fertility, and social investment in the context of the aging population are now fairly well-established. The upshot is that the extent that individual European welfare states are able to shift to family services, early childhood education and care and active labour market policies, alongside a wider coverage of social protection-especially with respect to social assistance and universal public pension provision- as a more Pareto-efficient social contract again seems viable. From a political perspective, such a social investment edifice is also more feasible than the Hayekian nightmare that Streeck (2014) conjectures as inevitable, and which implies a far more intrusive and politically disruptive dismantling of national welfare states than currently on offer. Ultimately, as we know from the seminal writing of Peter Hall (1989, 1993) the political power of alternative policy ideas, experiences and insights only gains practical leverage if they provide answers to salient political problems. Two such political problems loom large. First, there is the political imperative to keep the single currency afloat. Current economic divergences and social imbalances may eventually undermine the sustainability of the EMU. The related second political conundrum is the rising anti-EU populist threat to the pro-EU political centre.

Regressive policy prescriptions triggering feelings of economic insecurity surely provide a fertile breeding ground for xenophobic anti-EU populism. Given the degree of political fragmentation, centrist European political families today face an inexorable dual challenge of legitimizing an EMU economic governance regime committed to market opening in the face of the populist temptation of national closure in their own ranks. The political dilemma is not merely an issue of policy feasibility but also one of legitimacy, in the sense of living up to the political commitment of enlarging the scope for a truly European 'social' market economy as laid down in the Lisbon Treaty. As economic and social realities seemingly renege on social justice and fairness, the implicit message to European voters has become that the 'social' market economy is suspended, at least until underperforming countries have done their 'structural reform' homework. Such a negative discourse plays into the hands of 'fringe parties', such as Martine Le Pen's National Front in France, Cinque Stelle in Italy, the True Fins, the Austrian Freedom Party, Geert Wilders' Freedom Party in the Netherlands, Alternative for Germany (AFD) or Golden Dawn in Greece, parties which already profit from European refugee crisis and the Jihadist terrorist threat.

Five years since the onslaught of the Eurocrisis, the new policy imperative for EME member states is to explicitly counter the dramatic social aftershocks of mass unemployment, inter-generational poverty transmission, and rising inequality and deprivation. The recovery is gaining strength, supported by lower oil prices and a weaker euro. The crisis has conclusively shown that welfare states providing adequate social protection and social investment for the poor are best able to secure fiscal sustainability. As growth is slowly picking up and labour market conditions are improving, (including declining levels of poverty and youth unemployment in most EU countries), it is time for more social investment leeway in EU fiscal governance. A fair assessment of the economic, social and political limits of austerity-biased reform, on the one hand, and a full recognition of the positive track record of social investment reform, on the other hand, are sine qua non for constructing an overlapping policy consensus of a currency union based on an employment-friendly macroeconomic framework that would allow the EMU and active European welfare states to prosper in tandem.

Together, negative anti-EU political feedback and positive social investment policy evidence open up a vista, contingent on political mobilization and EU administrative support, for explicitly anchoring a social investment menu in the European Semester exercise. A feasible proposal could be to establish a 'social investment protocol' in the Semester by discounting social investments, in the area of lifelong education, from the deficit rules in the reinforced Stability and Growth Pact (SGP) regime. This would bolster both the long-term economic stability and political legitimacy of the EMU and the European integration project writ large.

Discounting social investment in national accounts under a Social Investment Protocol comes with a double dividend. It is fully consistent with the self-image of Europe as laid down in the 2009 Lisbon Treaty and the Europe 2020 policy strategy of 'smart, inclusive and sustainable growth'. It would enable domestic policymakers to assertively take on reform ownership that may strengthen democratic legitimacy rather than being told by unelected EU authorities to speed up structural reform. To convince the European public, the social investment protocol should be tangibly based on a well-articulated normative vision of a 'Triple A social Europe', caring about the well-being of all Europeans in trying times.

Anton Hemerijck

# References

Dølvik, J.-E., & Martin, A. (Eds.). (2014). *European social models from crisis to crisis: Employment and inequality in the era of monetary integration.* Oxford: Oxford University Press.

Hall, P.A. (1989). The Political Power of Economic Ideas: Keynesianism across Nations', Princeton, NJ: Princeton University Press.

Hall, P.A. (1993). 'Policy Paradigms, Social Learning, and the State: The Case of Economic Policy-making in Britain', *Comparative Politics,* 25(3), 275–296.

Rokkan, S. (1970). *Citizens, elections, parties.* Oslo: Universitetsforlaget.

Streeck, W. (2014). *Buying time. The delayed crisis of democratic capitalism.* London: Verso.

# Preface and Acknowledgements

This book is based on a Special Issue in *Comparative European Politics* (Volume 13, Issue 1) published in 2015. We would like to thank the editors of *Comparative European Politics* and Palgrave Macmillan and the editors of the *Work and Welfare in Europe* series for agreeing to re-publish the original articles in this book. Some chapters have been slightly revised, but the main empirical analyses continue to refer to the period up until the middle of 2014. The foreword by Anton Hemerijck and a new introduction and conclusion by the editors address some of the more recent emerging issues in these fast-changing political times for European integration.

This book first took shape at the 2012 ESPAnet conference in Edinburgh, where initial drafts of many of the contributions were presented. A workshop in May 2013, financially supported by the Department of Political Science, University of Southern Denmark, gave us the opportunity to discuss subsequent drafts of all of the chapters. We would like to thank many colleagues for their valuable comments and advice, in particular, Anton Hemerijck, Jonah Levy, Nathalie Morel, Joakim Palme, Emmanuele Pavolini, Philippe Pochet, Ben Rosamond and Christilla Roederer-Rynning. For individual acknowledgments by the contributing authors, please see the notes in the respective chapters. We would like to thank Lynne Robertson for help with the final proof reading. We have presented this work at a number of conferences and workshops, most recently at the Council for European Studies in Paris (2015) and the Bremen International Graduate School of Social Sciences Summer School (2015). We would like to thank all session participants for their encouraging comments that give us some reason to believe that the European social dimension is more important than ever to preserve.

Caroline de la Porte
Copenhagen, Denmark

Elke Heins
Edinburgh, UK

# Contents

# Contributors

**Ugo Ascoli** is Professor of Economic Sociology and Social Policy at the Marche Polytechnic University (Ancona, Italy). His research focuses on the Italian Welfare State, the transformation of the Italian Welfare System in a comparative perspective and occupational welfare as well as third sector and voluntary organizations. Recent edited books include *Il Welfare in Italia* (il Mulino, 2011) and, together with Emmanuele Pavolini, *The Italian Welfare State in a European Perspective* (Policy Press, 2015).

**Caroline de la Porte** is Head of Department and Associate Professor at the Department of Business and Politics, Copenhagen Business School. Her research interests are centred on the EU and comparative welfare state reform, particularly in the areas of social inclusion, labour market policy and pensions. Her current research focuses on alterations to EMU governance after the crisis and European Court of Justice (ECJ) case law for atypical contracts as well as social investment. She is a member of the board of the Network for European Social Policy Analysis. She has recently contributed to various projects on the crisis and EU social policy in journals such as *West European Politics* and *Perspectives on European Politics and Society*.

**Fiona Dukelow** is Lecturer in the School of Applied Social Studies, University College Cork, Ireland. Her recent research focuses on the impact of the economic crisis on the Irish welfare state. She is co-author of *Irish Social Policy – A Critical Introduction* (Gill & Macmillan, 2009) and co-editor of *Mobilising Classics: Reading Radical Writing in Ireland* (Manchester University Press, 2010),

*Defining Events: Power, Resistance and Identity in Twenty-First-Century Ireland* (Manchester University Press, 2015) and *The Irish Welfare State in the Twenty-First Century: Challenges and Change* (Palgrave, 2016). She has also published recent articles in *Social Policy & Administration* and the *Journal of Sociology and Social Welfare*.

**Ana M. Guillén** is Professor of Sociology and Head of Department at the University of Oviedo, Spain. She has written extensively on welfare state development, comparative social policy, tensions between quality and quantity of jobs and Europeanization. She has published articles in journals such as *Social Science & Medicine, Social Politics, Journal of European Social Policy, European Societies, International Journal of Health Services, West European Politics and Social Policy and Administration*, among others. She has also acted as a consultant to the European Commission and several EU presidencies.

**Patrick Hassenteufel** is Professor of Political Science at the University of Versailles/Paris-Saclay since 2005 and Vice-Dean of the Faculty of Law and Political Science. His main research field is comparative health policy, and he also works more generally on the transformation of European Welfare States and on actor-centred policy analysis. He published in several international, French and German peer-reviewed journals. He is the author of a handbook on policy analysis, *Sociologie politique: l'action publique* (Armand Colin, 2011) and the co-editor-in-chief of the only French speaking political science journal specialized in public policy and public administration analysis (*Gouvernement et action publique*). Since 2004 he has been a member of the board of the French Political Science Association.

**Elke Heins** is Lecturer in Social Policy at the University of Edinburgh. Her research mainly focuses on labour market and social policy in comparative and European perspective. She is also interested in the politics of welfare, particularly in the United Kingdom. Recent publications in peer-reviewed journals such as *Socio-Economic Review, European Journal of Industrial Relations* and *Journal of Social Policy* dealt with the concept of flexicurity, the involvement of trade unions and third sector organisations in welfare policy delivery and the privatisation of welfare services.

**Anton Hemerijck** is Professor of Institutional Policy Analysis at VU University Amsterdam (the Netherlands) and Centennial Professor in the Department of Social Policy at the London School of Economics and Political Science (UK). Hemerijck has made important contributions to the comparative study of social policy with particular reference to theorizing changing (European) welfare states in times of intrusive social and economic restructuring. Seminal publications include *Changing Welfare States* (Oxford University Press, 2013). A new edited volume The *Uses of Social Investment* is forthcoming in autumn 2016 (also with Oxford University Press).

**Jon Kvist** is Professor of European Public Policies and Welfare Studies at the Institute of Society and Globalisation, Roskilde University. He was expert in the Danish Government Commission on Unemployment Insurance, June 2014–September 2015, and is national coordinator in the European Social Policy Network set up by the European Commission in 2014. He has published widely on the Nordic welfare model, European welfare states and Europeanization. Recently he has co-edited *Changing Social Equality* (Policy Press, 2013) and authored 'The post-crisis European Social model: developing or dismantling social investments' (*Journal of International and Comparative Social Policy*, 2013).

**Margarita León** is Senior Research Fellow at the Institute of Government and Public Policies (IGOP) of the Universitat Autònoma Barcelona. Her research interests include comparative welfare research, with a specific focus on processes of reform of welfare systems in Europe (Southern Europe in particular). She has co-edited with A.M. Guillén *The Spanish Welfare State in European Context* (Ashgate, 2011) and edited *The Transformation of Care in European Societies* (Palgrave, 2014). Her more recent publications include León, M. & Pavolini, E. (2014) 'Social investment or back to familialism? The impact of the economic crisis on family policies in Southern Europe' in *South European Society and Politics*.

**Bruno Palier** is CNRS Research Director at Sciences Po, Centre d'études européennes and Co-director of LIEPP (Laboratory for Interdisciplinary Evaluation of Public Policies). Between 2007 and 2011, he was the scientific coordinator of the European Network of Excellence RECWOWE (Reconciling Work and Welfare). He has published numerous articles on welfare reforms in France and Europe in *Politics and Society, Journal of European Social Policy, West European Politics, Governance, Socio-Economic Review, Global Social Policy, Social Politics* and various books. Recently, he co-edited *The Age of Dualization: The Changing Face of Inequality in Deindustrializing Societies* (Oxford University Press, 2012) and *Towards a Social Investment Welfare State? Ideas, Policies and Challenges* (Policy Press, 2012).

**Emmanuele Pavolini** is Associate Professor in Economic Sociology and Social Policy at the University of Macerata (Italy). His research interests are in two fields. The main one is comparative welfare state studies. He has extensively published in Italian and English on the Italian welfare state in comparative perspective; Southern European welfare states; specific social policies (family policies, elderly care/long-term care, childcare, social care and healthcare and, more recently, education); inequalities in the access to welfare state provision; occupational welfare; welfare mix and third sector organizations. A second field of research is related to the functioning of the labour market, economic development and enterprises' behaviours.

**Stefano Sacchi** is Associate Professor of Political Science at the University of Milan, Special Commissioner of ISFOL, Italy's national research institute on labour, training and social policy, and an economic adviser to the Italian Prime Minister's office. He has authored or co-authored more than fifty academic publications in the field of social and labour policy. In his former capacity as the special adviser to the Italian Labour Minister, he designed, drafted and politically negotiated several reforms, including the recent reforms of Italian unemployment benefits and short-time work.

**Sotiria Theodoropoulou** is Senior Researcher at the European Trade Union Institute in Brussels. Her current research focuses on the effects of macroeconomic policies on welfare states and economic performance in Europe, while she is more broadly interested in the interactions of institutions and economic policies in shaping economic performance in advanced economies. Recent publications in collective volumes published by Oxford University Press and Palgrave Macmillan have dealt with strategies for employment creation in the services sectors and the austerity programmes in Greece.

# List of Figures

# List of Tables

# 1

# Introduction: Is the European Union More Involved in Welfare State Reform Following the Sovereign Debt Crisis?

Caroline de la Porte and Elke Heins

This book analyses how the EU—through formal rules, informal pressure and new initiatives—has affected welfare state reforms in EU Member States following the sovereign debt crisis. The findings of the single and comparative country chapters in this book show that the nature of EU intervention into domestic welfare states has changed, with more focus on fiscal consolidation, and importantly, more constraints in terms of policy, politics and governance.

When our special issue entitled 'The Sovereign Debt Crisis, the EU and Welfare State Reform', on which this book is based, was in press, numerous other contributions were being written in parallel. In this introductory chapter we pick up on some of their insights to contextualize our contribution to this vibrant literature. This book builds

C. de la Porte (✉)
Department of Business and Politics, Copenhagen Business School, Denmark

E. Heins
School of Social and Political Science, University of Edinburgh,
Edinburgh, UK

© The Author(s) 2016                                                          1
C. de la Porte, E. Heins (eds.), *The Sovereign Debt Crisis, the EU and Welfare State Reform*, DOI 10.1057/978-1-137-58179-2_1

on at least three strands of partially overlapping literature. First is the burgeoning literature on what is dubbed the 'Great Recession' (Reinhart and Rogoff 2009) that focuses on ideologies and the relationship between states and markets in reform responses to the crisis (especially the euro crisis) in modern industrialized democracies. The second body of relevant literature is on welfare state reform in a comparative perspective that contextualizes policy responses in crisis situations with institutional alterations made over the last decades across European welfare states. The third strand of literature is on European integration and on Europeanization, respectively focusing on EU changes in policy areas associated with the crisis and in analysing the causal impact of the EU on reforms during the crisis. The literature on European integration in the context of the crisis focuses particularly on areas that have previously been considered to be of national competence only, such as banking, financial sector regulation and, not least, welfare state reform. The literature analysing the impact of these EU-level alterations, the subject of which this book mainly relates to, is just emerging (Matthijs and Blyth 2015; Wandhöfer 2014). There is a consensus among scholars that, compared to before the crisis, Europe has more leverage in areas linked to managing markets and states and, related to this, that these areas are more Europeanized.

Concerning the literature on the ideological and historical location of the Great Recession, Streeck (2014) focuses on the contradictions—between market principles and social rights—within democratic capitalism. He analyses how inflation, public debt and private indebtedness have successively been used by states over the last four decades to gain (not yet existing) resources for distributive policies. He further argues that high levels of debt, through increasing deregulation of the financial markets, have merely been 'temporary stopgaps' for governments that have supported gains on capitalist markets with continued welfare state development. The Great Recession has altered this situation, as public debt can no longer be used with as much elasticity as before 2007. As a result, austerity has become the dominant policy response, signifying that governments have now developed long-term plans of (public) savings to ensure that international creditors consider the governments' economies a safe investment. In the context of the sovereign debt crisis, national sovereignty has been surrendered to supranational institutions, which are 'deaf to democracy' (Streeck 2014, p. 96), to insulate 'the markets' from contradictory democratic demands for social justice. These democratic legitimacy problems notwithstanding, the EU measures taken in response to the crisis have helped prevent bankruptcy in some of the most heavily crisis-ridden economies, even if the austerity policies have been widely criticized (Scharpf 2011; Armingeon and Baccaro 2012a, b). In the Stability and Growth Pact (SGP)—set out to govern policies for a well-functioning Eurozone—more attention is now paid to public debt in both the preventive and corrective parts of the SGP. This turnaround in policy towards public debt is embodied in new initiatives layered onto the existing institutional framework of the EMU (Verdun 2015; de la Porte and Heins, Chap. 2).

Related to this, this literature highlights that the source of the asymmetrical impact of the crisis in Europe is due to distinct growth models and institutions of political economy between the periphery and the core of Europe. In particular, the demand-led model in the periphery does not square well with the EMU, which is implicitly tailored to the export-led models that are dominant in Northern Europe. There is a consensus that these distinct models were not built into the structure of the EMU or EMU membership conditions (Hall 2014; Regan 2015). Regan (2015), furthermore, argues that the institutionalization of this mismatch among the countries of the Eurozone exacerbates the imbalance of capitalisms in the Eurozone. Commentators and analysts argue that the future of the Eurozone should expand beyond a narrow understanding of 'Ordoliberalism'—state creation of market design to ensure 'optimal' functioning (Nedergaard 2013)—that underlies the policies in the EMU (Lechevalier 2015). The implication is that in the future the Eurozone should not reinforce a one-size-fits-all supply-side solution, implicitly expecting convergence towards the export-led model. Instead, it should shift towards transnational institutions flexible enough to support diversified social and economic models and, with it, broader and more diversified ideological paths within Europe (Hall 2014; Regan 2015). Thus far, the dominating one-size-fits-all model initially led to a rather narrow framing of the challenges at the EU level—seeing sovereign debt as the core problem. This is reflected in changes in the new institutional and governance framework linked to the EMU and in the bilateral agreements between European and international institutions with debt-ridden countries. The austerity policies prompted strongly by the EU/ International Monetary Fund (IMF) during the crisis—while preventing default of the crisis-hit economies—are criticized for exacerbating the differences between the core and the periphery in the crisis context (Armingeon and Baccaro 2012a, b; Hacker 2015; Regan 2015).

The second body of literature, comparative welfare state reform, points to reform responses in terms of policy, ideas, politics and institutional change. The authors note that despite a brief wave of Keynesian-type stimulus policies immediately after the outbreak of the financial crisis in 2007, governments have relied predominantly on austerity measures: tax cuts to stimulate the economy and spending cuts to achieve fiscal consolidation (Bermeo and Pontusson 2012; Farnsworth and Irving 2011, 2012; Greve 2012). Farnsworth and Irving (2012, p. 145) boldly argue that 'austerity' has become the new hegemon within a neo-liberal paradigm because 'for the first time in the modern history of the welfare state, austerity has come to unite politics and economics'. This chimes with explanations for 'the strange non-death of neoliberalism' (Crouch 2011) and the 'resilience of neo-liberalism' in Europe's political economy (Schmidt and Thatcher 2013). In this light, welfare reforms have been similar in direction—cost-containment—although within different institutional configurations (Farnsworth and Irving 2011, 2012). Overall, the responses of European welfare states are re-enforcing developments that were initiated before the crisis. This includes the use of flexible contracts to facilitate labour market participation but, biased to the advantage of employers, toughened access to unemployment and other benefits, as well as curtailing public expenditure in the areas of healthcare, pensions and education (Bermeo and Pontusson 2012; Bonoli and Natali 2012; Emmenegger et al. 2012; Greve 2012). The welfare state is still a key institution in modern capitalist democracies, but it has undoubtedly changed in character—more lean, more mean—following the sovereign debt crisis.

The third body of literature, that brings in European integration and Europeanization, analyses how the EMU focuses on public expenditure-shaped domestic reforms. The EU does intervene preventively or correctively on EMU members through the SGP in a two-level game (de la Porte and Natali 2014). Dølvik and Martin (2014) argue, in line with existing research, that the way European social models are institutionalized affects crises, and crises can, in turn, affect social models. Their edited volume focuses, from a historical perspective, on the intervening role of the EMU in changed patterns of employment and equality. The argument, which is novel compared to existing literature, is that macroeconomic conditions, and particularly budgetary requirements of EMU membership, are more important in determining employment and distributive outcomes in EU Member States than the social model institutions themselves. This is a point that has been on the margins of academic debate surrounding the construction of the EMU, although there have been warnings about the in-built asymmetry of the EMU and the dangers of centralizing monetary policy while leaving fiscal policy to be decided at the Member State level (Scharpf 2011). Earlier literature concluded that the EMU did present a theoretical threat to welfare states (Begg and Nectoux 1995). However, in-depth analyses have found that despite this asymmetry, there were only minor alterations to welfare states to meet EMU membership conditions, either because reform plans were not so ambitious to begin with or because the plans were altered in domestic political processes (Bolukbasi 2009).

Findings about welfare state change over the last two decades clearly indicate that EU Member States, which have incrementally responded to challenges of aging populations, globalization and the emergence of new social risks, have been better geared to meet the crisis that emerged in 2007. Germany has been a showcase example, where part of the success is due to changes to the labour market model *prior to* the crisis, embodied in the Hartz reforms—a series of reforms developed to make the labour market more flexible through atypical and fixed-term jobs. However, a side effect has been a change in the composition of the labour force with a growth of low-wage service sector jobs and a much higher degree of precariousness (Carlin et al. 2014). In France, by contrast, the social model and labour market regulation were not sufficiently adapted to meet challenges related to globalization and population aging although investments in childcare have enabled reconciliation of family and working life. The crisis was thus a lever leading to (necessary) welfare reforms that were undertaken in the shadow of EU and financial market hierarchy (Hassenteufel and Palier, Chap. 8; Le Cacheux and Ross 2014).

There is no literature specifically on the causal impact of the EMU on (welfare) reform efforts in this present crisis context, which this book focuses on. The literature thus far suggests that EMU countries are under more pressure with regard to budgetary constraints than non-EMU countries. Figure 1.1 shows that there is a more pronounced decrease of budget deficits in the 19 Eurozone countries, compared to the 9 countries that are not Eurozone members. This data needs to be interpreted with caution, as the development of budget deficits does not depend only on deliberate policy measures. However, the data does indicate that EU pressure for reform—through an excessive deficit procedure (EDP) and Memorandum of Understandings (MoUs)—has undoubtedly been higher in the Eurozone countries throughout the crisis, although the pressure of markets is likely to have been even more significant for Member State governments as a lever for reform. The crucial point, for all countries, is that the pressure to undertake reforms has been higher during the Great Recession compared to before the crisis, due to possible adverse reactions by markets (Fig. 1.1).

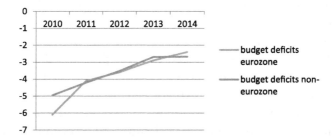

**Fig. 1.1** Budget deficits (as % of GDP) in Eurozone and non-Eurozone countries (2010–2014). *Source*: Eurostat, accessed 20 November 2015

This book analyses how EU policy affecting welfare states and labour markets has developed throughout the crisis and the mechanisms through which the EU has affected welfare state reforms in the Member States most severely hit by the crisis. Our comparative and single country analyses will show that radical welfare reforms have been undertaken as a consequence of the crisis and the resulting EU bailouts. These countries, mainly in the European periphery, have seen soaring rates of public debt, leading to a sovereign debt crisis in which it became difficult or impossible to re-finance public debt without the assistance of the EU and IMF. In the context of the sovereign debt crisis, the EU and the European Central Bank (ECB), together with the IMF, offered full or partial financial rescue packages to the most troubled countries through loans and other types of conditionality, starting with a bailout of Greece in Spring 2010. Ireland required financial assistance in late 2010 and Portugal in spring 2011. In late 2012, Spain sought a nearly €40 billion rescue package from the EU to stabilise its struggling banking sector but avoided a full state bailout. The next country to seek financial assistance from the EU was Cyprus in April 2013. At around the same time, new fears were sparked that Italy could no longer repay its public debt. In response the ECB bought up Italian government bonds on secondary sovereign bond markets with the condition implement a strict course of action, including welfare reforms, to promote growth and to balance the budget by the end of 2013.

Parallel to these developments, several successive decisions that aimed at strengthening the SGP were taken rapidly at the EU level, with a focus on correcting macroeconomic imbalances while also preventing future debt crises. In times of uncertainty, the EU institutions agreed on the new governance structure through ordinary legislative procedure, involving the Commission as well as the Council and the European Parliament. Potentially critical voices—such as the European Trade Union Confederation—did formulate alternative plans to austerity around (genuine) social investment, sustainable growth and quality jobs. However, since the new governance regime was developed primarily to avoid macroeconomic imbalances, with which the trade union movement agreed, it was not possible to mobilize pervasively against other aspects of the governance structure and underlying policies, even those implying long-term austerity for Member States (Erne 2015). There are, however, concerns about the renewed governance architecture around the SGP in the European Semester, since it puts indirect, but strong, pressure on welfare states with an emphasis on structural reforms (Pochet and Degryse 2012). The literature on the softer instruments of the European Semester, for aims such as fighting poverty, shows that hybrid solutions have been developed to support initiatives in Member States but that these have little formal leverage or political bite in the context of the challenges of poverty and unemployment facing EU Member States (Jessoula 2015).

The authors in this book examine welfare state alterations following the 2007 financial crisis at the EU and national levels. They shed light on the stronger causal role of the EU in welfare state reform through bilateral agreements with supranational institutions and on the ideas and policies underlying the EU's new governance architecture affecting welfare state and labour market reform.

In Chap. 2, 'A New Era of European Integration? Governance of Labour Market and Social Policy Since the Sovereign Debt Crisis', we develop a typology of EU integration to assess what kind of objectives as well as surveillance and enforcement mechanisms were used to assist in the development of new instruments affecting labour market and social policy throughout the crisis. It is shown that the governance of the EMU has been altered via a process of institutional 'layering', whereby new mechanisms are grafted onto the pre-existent institutional frameworks. Through these alterations the nature of EU intervention into domestic welfare states has changed, with an enhanced focus on fiscal consolidation, while other aims such as social equity and social investment have only recently re-gained attention on the EU agenda via softer governance methods. Furthermore, this strengthened governance regime is associated with increased surveillance and a higher degree of enforcement, which represents a radical alteration in EU integration. The potential for influencing European welfare states has thus increased substantially compared to the period before the crisis.

In 'A Framework for Social Investment Strategies: Integrating Generational, Life Course, and Gender Perspectives in the EU Social

Investment Strategy', Jon Kvist argues that the social investment strategy developed at the European level holds the promise of renewing the European Social Model in the aftermath of the crisis although the gender dimension has been overlooked in this context. Kvist offers a comprehensive life-course perspective on social investment that shows how the strategy is based on a generational contract combined with horizontal redistribution. The life-course perspective also focuses attention on the dynamic and multi-dimensional nature of social investments and cumulative effects over time. In an illustrative comparative study using the life-course perspective on social investment, Kvist points to some of the key gender dimensions that need to be addressed by appropriate policies to optimize the formation, maintenance and use of human capital in both economic and non-economic spheres by men and women. The comparative and single country analyses in this book show, sadly, that many austerity measures included re-commodification of labour and cost containment in areas such as early childcare as well as primary, secondary and tertiary education that are associated with social investment.

Fiona Dukelow, in her chapter '"Pushing Against an Open Door": Reinforcing the Neo-Liberal Policy Paradigm in Ireland and the Impact of EU Intrusion', argues that austerity measures demanded by the EU/IMF in return for large-scale financial support were drastic but that they did not constitute a change in social policy direction in Ireland. She shows that the recommendations made through the MoUs were welcomed by political elites and representatives of businesses and that paradoxically the EU/IMF-induced reforms even strengthened the neo-liberal paradigm that has been underpinning the Irish welfare state for decades. The empirical evidence is striking and the theoretical contribution highlights that paradigms can be re-enforced under crisis circumstances, rather than being altered.

Sotiria Theodoropoulou, in her chapter entitled 'National Social and Labour Market Policy Reforms in the Shadow of EU Bail-Out Conditionality: The Cases of Greece and Portugal', scrutinizes the intrusive role of the EU and the IMF—as well as the differences between them—in pensions, labour markets and collective bargaining in Greece and Portugal. In both cases financial assistance was provided conditionally, as detailed in MoUs, in exchange for structural reforms. The two cases show that, despite very high intrusiveness of MoUs due to tough conditionality and active surveillance in both countries, there were notable differences, with more radical policy intervention and more far-reaching reforms in Greece than in Portugal. The comparative analysis shows that the policy agenda embodied in the MoUs was to enhance fiscal consolidation via radical reforms under conditions of pervasive austerity, which has led to radical retrenchment of the Greek and Portuguese welfare states.

In their contribution 'From Austerity to Permanent Strain? The EU and Welfare State Reform in Italy and Spain', Emmanuele Pavolini, Margarita León, Ana Guillén and Ugo Ascoli analyse the altered impact of the EU on the two largest Southern European welfare states in the wake of the crisis. While the two countries avoided a formal bailout, they nevertheless came under the 'shadow of conditionality'. A longitudinal analysis across different policy areas highlights that both were following different paths pre-crisis, with Spain having made more investments to meet new social risks, whereas in Italy such reforms were envisaged but not enacted. From mid-2010 onwards, mounting pressure from the EU led to rapidly adopted reforms, which represents a retrenchment phase in both welfare states. The authors conceptualise this reform dynamic as a new 'age of permanent strain', characterized by extreme haste, intense tensions, growing anxiety among the population and growing public unrest.

In 'Conditionality by Other Means: EU Involvement in Italy's Structural Reforms in the Sovereign Debt Crisis', Stefano Sacchi focuses on the altered nature of conditionality in the Italian case. He argues that conditionality, although informal, can be extremely strong in terms of policy specificity as well as surveillance but weak along the enforcement dimension. He convincingly shows that market forces are the important causal factor intervening in the enforcement of policies prompted by the EU. He also shows that the use of ad hoc informal conditionality empowered the economically oriented actors, especially the Directorate General of Economic and Financial Affairs and the ECB.

In 'Still the Sound of Silence? Towards a New Phase in the Europeanization of Welfare State Policies in France', Patrick Hassenteufel and Bruno Palier analyse the EU influence on French welfare reforms.

Through a longitudinal perspective the authors find that reforms in the areas of pensions, healthcare and labour markets are increasingly made in line with EU prerogatives. The authors argue that there have been changes since before the crisis because the need for deficit reduction is now explicitly integrated into French political discourse and policies and the EU is able to demand evidence of reform. The authors also show that France has maintained leverage regarding the timing and content of the reforms. However, overall, the implication is that the EU is much more involved in welfare state reforms than before the crisis.

In our concluding chapter, 'Depleted European Social Models Following the Crisis: Towards a Brighter Future?', we discuss the core findings of reforms in European welfare states, especially in the areas of pensions and labour market policy. We also depict future research agendas in the context of changes in EU policy and politics following the crisis.

# References

Armingeon, K., & Baccaro, L. (2012a). Political economy of the sovereign debt crisis: The limits of internal devaluation. *Industrial Law Journal, 41*(3), 254–275.

Armingeon, K., & Baccaro, L. (2012b). The sorrows of Young Euro: The sovereign debt crises of ireland and Southern Europe. In N. Bermeo, & J. Pontusson (Eds.), *Coping with crisis: Government reactions to the Great Recession.* New York: Russell Sage Foundation.

Begg, I., & Nectoux, F. (1995). Social protection and economic union. *Journal of European Social Policy, 5*(4), 285–302.

Bermeo, N., & Pontusson, J. (Eds.) (2012). *Coping with crisis: Government reactions to the Great Recession.* New York: Russell Sage Foundation.

Bolukbasi, T. (2009). On consensus, constraint and choice: Economic and monetary integration and Europe's welfare states. *Journal of European Public Policy, 16*(4), 527–544.

Bonoli, G., & Natali, D. (Eds.) (2012). *The politics of the new welfare state.* Oxford: Oxford University Press.

Carlin, W., Hassel, A., Martin, A., & Soskice, D. (2014). In J.-E. Dølvik & A. Martin (Eds.), *European social models from crisis to crisis: Employment and inequality in the era of monetary integration* (pp. 49–104). Oxford: Oxford University Press.

Crouch, C. (2011). *The strange non-death of neoliberalism.* Cambridge, UK: Polity.

de la Porte, C., & Natali, D. (2014). Altered Europeanization of pension reform during the *Great Recession*: Denmark and Italy compared. *West European Politics, 37*(4), 732–749.

Dølvik, J.-E., & Martin, A. (Eds.) (2014). *European social models from crisis to crisis: Employment and inequality in the era of monetary integration.* Oxford: Oxford University Press.

Emmenegger, P., Häusermann, S., Palier, B., & Seeleib-Kaiser, M. (Eds.) (2012). *The age of dualization: The changing face of inequality in deindustrializing societies.* Oxford: Oxford University Press.

Erne, R. (2015). A supranational regime that nationalizes social conflict: Explaining European trade unions' difficulties in politicizing European economic governance. *Labor History, 56*(3), 345–368.

Farnsworth, K., & Irving, Z. (Eds.) (2011). *Social policy in challenging times: Economic crisis and welfare systems.* Bristol: Policy Press.

Farnsworth, K., & Irving, Z. (2012). Varieties of crisis, varieties of austerity. *Journal of Poverty and Social Justice, 20*(2), 133–147.

Greve, B. (Ed.) (2012). *The times they are changing? Crisis and the welfare state.* Chichester: Wiley-Blackwell.

Hacker, B. (2015). Under pressure of budgetary commitments: The new economic governance framework hamstrings Europe's social dimension. In A. Lechevalier & J. Wielgohs (Eds.), *Social Europe: A dead end. What the Eurozone crisis is doing to Europe's social dimension* (pp. 133–158). Copenhagen: Djøf.

Hall, P. (2014). Varieties of capitalism and the Euro crisis. *West European Politics, 37*(6), 1223–1243.

Jessoula, M. (2015). Europe 2020 and the fight against poverty—beyond competence clash, towards 'hybrid' governance solutions? *Social Policy & Administration, 49*(4), 490–511.

Le Cacheux, J., & Ross, G. (2014). France in the middle. In J.-E. Dølvik & A. Martin (Eds.), *European social models from crisis to crisis: Employment and inequality in the era of monetary integration* (pp. 105–143). Oxford: Oxford University Press.

Lechevalier, A. (2015). Eucken under the pillow: The ordoliberal imprint on social Europe. In A. Lechevalier & J. Wielgohs (Eds.), *Social Europe: A dead end. What the Eurozone crisis is doing to Europe's social dimension* (pp. 49–102). Copenhagen: Djøf.

Matthijs, M., & Blyth, M. (Eds.) (2015). *The future of the Euro*. Oxford: Oxford University Press.

Nedergaard, P. (2013). *The influence of ordoliberalism in European integration processes: A framework for ideational influence with competition policy and the economic and monetary policy as examples* (MPRA Paper No. 52331). https://mpra.ub.uni-muenchen.de/52331/1/MPRA_paper_52331.pdf. Accessed 23 Nov 2015.

Pochet, P., & Degryse, C. (2012). The programmed dismantling of the 'European Social Model. *Intereconomics, 4*, 212–217.

Regan, A. (2015). The imbalance of capitalisms in the Eurozone: Can the north and south of Europe converge? *Comparative European Politics*, 1–22. doi:10.1057/cep.2015.5. Accessed 2 Mar 2015.

Reinhart, C., & Rogoff, K. (2009). *Growth in a time of debt* (NBER Working Paper No. 15639). Cambridge, MA: National Bureau of Economic Research.

Scharpf, F. (2011). *Monetary union, fiscal crisis and the preemption of democracy* (Working Paper, Max Planck Institute for the Study of Societies). Cologne: MPIfG.

Schmidt, V., & Thatcher, M. (Eds.) (2013). *Resilient liberalism in Europe's political economy*. Cambridge: Cambridge University Press.

Streeck, W. (2014). *Buying time: The delayed crisis of democratic capitalism*. London and New York: Verso.

Verdun, A. (2015). A historical institutionalist explanation of the EU's responses to the euro area financial crisis. *Journal of European Public Policy, 22*(2), 219–237.

Wandhöfer, R. (2014). *Transaction banking and the impact of regulatory change: Basel III and other challenges for the global economy*. Basingstoke: Palgrave Macmillan.

# 2

# A New Era of European Integration? Governance of Labour Market and Social Policy Since the Sovereign Debt Crisis

Caroline de la Porte and Elke Heins

## Introduction: The European Union and Social Policy

The EU aims to safeguard and promote high social standards across the European Union, while respecting welfare state diversity (Scharpf 2002). However, since the EMU was institutionalised in 1992 in the Maastricht Treaty, the EU intervenes indirectly, as a functional spillover from monetary integration, in social and fiscal policy. In 1997, the Stability and Growth Pact (SGP)—a legally binding process of policy coordination with EU quantitative benchmarks, policies to support monetarism, national reports and EU surveillance as well as corrective mechanisms

C. de la Porte (✉)
Department of Business and Politics, Copenhagen Business School, Denmark

E. Heins
School of Social and Political Science, University of Edinburgh, Edinburgh, UK

© The Author(s) 2016
C. de la Porte, E. Heins (eds.), *The Sovereign Debt Crisis, the EU and Welfare State Reform*, DOI 10.1057/978-1-137-58179-2_2

in case of deviation from the benchmarks—was developed to ensure that the EMU would function optimally. More specifically, the SGP was designed to ensure that Member States pursue sound public finances under the EMU, especially through the EU limits for public debt (maximum 60 per cent of gross domestic product [GDP]) and budget deficits (maximum 3 per cent of GDP), but without direct intervention in social policy. As social spending makes up the biggest share of public expenditure in Member States (more than half of the total government expenditure was devoted to 'social protection' and 'health' between 2002 and 2012 according to Eurostat figures), the pressure on national welfare states exerted by the SGP has therefore been considerable, especially during economic recessions.

The core actors involved in EMU governance—that is, the Directorate-General for Economic and Financial Affairs (DG ECFIN), the Council for Economic and Financial Affairs, and the European Central Bank (ECB)—are economically oriented. These actors are concerned with upholding a monetarist paradigm and, with it, supply-side policies, such as labour market de-regulation as well as cost containment in areas such as pensions and healthcare (Barbier 2012; de la Porte and Pochet 2014; Scharpf 2011). The SGP and its underpinning monetarist paradigm have not been without criticism. McNamara (2005, p. 156) notes, 'Although the SGP has the word "growth" in its title, it is not likely to promote growth, but rather to be excessively restrictive at precisely the times that European states may need to stimulate their economies, as states are more likely to run up deficits in economic recessions.'

As a response to the EMU and the functional spillovers on (pressure to decrease) social expenditure, in the mid-1990s the development of a 'social dimension' to the EU and, in particular, the EMU was regarded as indispensable by left-of-centre political actors. The notion of a 'European Social Model' represents the idea that European welfare states are legitimately diverse but that they all aim to uphold high social standards, working conditions and well-being, which should be supported by the EU (Jepsen and Serrano Pascual 2005). In core welfare state areas, where Member States face similar challenges such as unemployment, aging populations and new social risks, the EU has promoted various ideas, for example 'flexicurity' (Viebrock and Clasen 2009), 'active aging' or a 'life course' approach to labour market participation—facilitating breaks from the labour market for education, parenting and care responsibilities without the potential loss of employment.

These policy ideas, many of them central in the emerging 'social investment' paradigm (Morel et al. 2012), have been promoted in the European Employment Strategy (EES) and the Open Method of Coordination (OMC), thereby contributing to the development of the European Social Model, albeit only through voluntary policy coordination. These policies are developed by 'socially oriented actors', that is, DG Employment and Social Affairs and the Employment and Social Affairs Council. Compared to the 'economically oriented actors', they have a weak legal basis for influencing welfare state reforms. Indeed, all decisions about the organization, financing and delivery of social security have thus far remained at the national level. While some countries have adopted common EU policy ideas through the OMC, its overall impact on welfare reforms has been weak (de la Porte and Pochet 2012).

However, even the treaty-based and thus much more enforceable SGP had its limitations. In the asymmetrical architecture of the EMU, monetary policy is pooled at the EU level, while fiscal policy remains uncomfortably caught between the EU and national level through EU pressure to curb public finances, but without direct or formal EU competency in this area (McNamara 2005; Scharpf 2002). While some Member States did undertake substantial reforms to comply with the Maastricht criteria—maximum 60 per cent public debt and 3 per cent budget deficit—prior to the 2007 financial crisis (see, for example, Hassenteufel et al. 2000; Jessoula 2012), the SGP was not sufficient to keep all countries within the set limits (De Haan et al. 2004; McNamara 2005). When the 2007 global financial crisis laid bare the asymmetries within the Eurozone and problems with the SGP's enforcement, it led to an incremental alteration of instruments and policies that affect welfare state reform, both indirectly, via the architecture of the EMU, especially regarding fiscal policy, and directly, aiming to affect welfare policy per se.

In this chapter, we analyse the way in which the instruments that were developed in response to the crisis alter the existing EU institutional framework with regard to labour market and social policy. In the next section, we develop the analytical framework, consisting firstly of a typology for detecting changes in EU integration and involvement and, secondly, of a clarification of concepts to analyse institutional change. In 'Analysing Governance of Social and Labour Market Policy Since the Crisis', we examine how new instruments have been developed since the onset of the crisis that affect the EMU and the social dimension. First, we analyse the development of instruments in the governance of fiscal and budgetary policy. We find that they have become more precise in terms of objectives and stricter in terms of surveillance and enforcement and that new instruments have been grafted onto existing institutional frameworks through a process of layering. Thereafter, we analyse the development of instruments more directly aimed at social and labour market policy. The findings show that the new initiatives have been layered onto the existing foundation in Europe 2020 but that they are weak in terms of surveillance and enforcement. This signifies that their potential impact is weak compared to the instruments governing policy via the EMU. In 'Assessing the Institutional Alterations of EMU and the European Social Dimension', we analyse the implications of the findings for European social policy. Overall, we find that the alteration of the EMU governance framework with its pressure on fiscal consolidation and, as an adjunct the social investment strategy developed in a weaker framework, penetrates deeper into welfare state policies than before the crisis. Finally, in the conclusion, we discuss the significance of the new EU governance instruments for welfare states and the process of European integration.

# Analytical Framework for Analysing Alterations in EU Integration in Labour Market and Social Policy

In this section, we develop a typology of EU integration to analyse the main new instruments since the crisis and their significance for labour market and social policy along three dimensions: objectives (policy aims), surveillance processes and mechanisms of enforcement. For each, there are four possible degrees of EU involvement (from low to very high).

Furthermore, a transversal issue we consider is the balance of actors involved in the devising of policy objectives, and the surveillance and enforcement processes. We argue that including employment and social policy actors (or other issue-specific actors) within a policy process provides a more comprehensive approach, for example, considering not only economic but also social sustainability aims, compared to processes driven exclusively or mainly by actors in economic and financial affairs, which are more narrowly focused on aims of fiscal consolidation. Secondly, to render this analysis dynamic and longitudinal, we analyse how these instruments and policies have altered the EU institutional framework governing economic, labour market and social policy over time, with the use of four key concepts from the literature on incremental institutional change. These are 'layering', which refers to creating a new policy grafted onto an existing institutional framework; 'revision', which refers to the formal reform, replacement or elimination of an existing policy; 'policy drift', which refers to the altered effect of a policy due to changed circumstances; and 'conversion', referring to the redirection of an existing policy framework for new purposes (Hacker 2004).[1]

The first dimension of integration is objectives (policy aims), that is, how precisely and to which magnitude policy change is suggested, which is a first indicator of the depth of EU involvement in Member States' social and employment policy, where EU competencies are marginal. We consider EU involvement as low if no change in objectives is required and only minor changes to existing policies are suggested. Medium EU involvement would be indicated by more alterations, but without changing the institutional set-up. High (and very high) levels of involvement signify alterations with the potential for undermining the existing institutional structure and fundamental principles of a policy area, thus indicating a high amount of external pressure. A policy aim such as enhancing social sustainability of pension systems would imply low involvement unless this aim were accompanied by

---

[1] In the framework developed by Hacker (2004), each type of change is associated with the types of political dynamics (coalitions and veto players) underlying the possible type of change. In this discussion, we merely use the concepts to assess and illustrate what types of changes have taken place in the European economic and social governance processes, without considering the political dynamics behind it.

specific measures. Some objectives, such as adjusting the levels of pension benefits, would represent a medium level of EU involvement, as it does not signify new principles of organising pension policy but just an alteration within an existing institutional set-up, whereas a policy aim suggesting reform of the existing pension system would signify high or very high EU involvement. In practice, and as we know from research on Europeanization of welfare policies, any policy objective would have a differentiated effect in Member States depending on a wide range of issues in the domestic arena, such as ideas, politics and markets. For example, in familialistic welfare states, the promotion of formal childcare policies (such as targets for the number of children in early childhood education) may be seen as high EU involvement because it challenges the existing male breadwinner/female career model and demands a significant change in policy objectives. In the Nordic welfare states, by contrast, such a policy merely confirms or re-enforces the existing policy paradigm that supports the reconciliation of work with family life; therefore, EU involvement would thus be low. However, to fully appreciate the impact of the EU on welfare states, it is necessary to consider not only domestic factors and the institutional fit with EU policy objectives but also which type of EU surveillance and enforcement Member States are exposed to.

The second dimension of EU integration is thus the surveillance of national policy by EU actors, which addresses the mechanisms the EU is endowed with to monitor whether Member States are implementing the agreed policies and moving towards EU benchmarks and/or national targets. The strength of surveillance is indicated by the frequency of policy monitoring and on whether the basis for surveillance is soft or hard law. It is also important to take account of which EU actors are involved in a particular surveillance process. Some EU actors, namely the economic and financial actors, operate in areas where the EU has strong jurisdiction so that these actors have more power than others, such as the employment and social affairs actors, where the EU has only weak legislative competence.

The third dimension of EU integration is enforcement, referring to the type of measures EU actors have at their disposal to ensure implementation and/or corrective action in the case of non-compliance with or deviation from EU policy. The most coercive measure consists of financial sanctions, although they have never been levied. Another form of enforcement consists of delineating a reform path and timetable to be followed to achieve an EU benchmark or aim, by issuing an 'excessive deficit procedure' (EDP) or 'country specific recommendation' (CSR). This may alter an institution in different ways depending on the specificity of objectives and how they fit with the existing institution. An EDP is treaty based and designed to ensure that a country effectively corrects a deficit, whereas a recommendation under an OMC is merely a suggestion for reform with no consequences in the case of non-compliance. In assessing enforcement, it is important to take account of the power balance between European institutions and Member States. In particular, the requirement of a qualified majority vote (QMV) gives more leverage to Member States since a qualified majority of Member States must agree to impose a sanction. By contrast, a reverse qualified majority vote (RQMV) gives more power to the European Commission because a qualified majority of Member States would need to agree *not* to impose a sanction. Up to the present, it is a mechanism that functions as a threat, as it has never been applied. A very high level of enforcement, combined with very strict surveillance, occurs in the case of countries that are under EU bailout and have to subject themselves to rigorous conditionality as a consequence of loan receipt in Memorandums of Understanding (see Theodoropoulou, Chap. 5). In such cases, very specific policy objectives, and a very high degree of surveillance as well as enforcement lead to what we would call 'intrusiveness' into domestic settings. This particular type of EU involvement would be captured in the Very High degree of involvement in our typology (see Table 2.1).

## Analysing Governance of Social and Labour Market Policy Since the Crisis

This section first presents the European Semester within which all new instruments are embedded and then examines the EU integration potential of each alteration to the governance architecture, in line with the

**Table 2.1** Typology of the EU integration of labour market and social policy

| Dimension of integration | Degree of involvement | | | |
|---|---|---|---|---|
| | Low | Medium | High | Very high |
| Objectives (policy aims) Note. This may differ according to welfare state type (and policy area). | Uncontroversial objectives, not challenging existent institutional arrangements, merely suggesting some minor adjustments in a particular policy area. | Objectives challenging some existing policies but not the underlying institutional structure of a policy area. | Objectives requiring comprehensive policy reform with the potential for undermining the existing institutional structure and fundamental principles of a policy area. | Objectives requiring far-reaching structural reform with a high potential for undermining the existing institutional structure and changing the fundamental principles of a policy area. |
| Surveillance | Infrequent ex post EU surveillance of national policy reports. | Frequent ex post surveillance of national reports that specify (country-specific) policy, which should meet common benchmarks and/or own national targets. | Regular ex ante and ex post EU surveillance of national policy reports. MS accountable to EU benchmarks or national targets and required to specify action plan to meet these targets. | Frequent ex ante and ex post EU surveillance of national policy reports. MS accountable to their own policies (which must aim to meet European targets and/or policy). |
| Enforcement | 'Naming and shaming' and/or soft recommendations (with a weak treaty base). | Treaty-based recommendations and possibility for sanctions in the case of non-compliance | Treaty-based recommendations *and* quasi-automatic financial sanctions in the case of non-compliance. | Conditionality (specified structural reforms) to receive financial assistance. |

*Source:* Own conceptualisation (see de la Porte and Heins 2014 for an earlier version)

framework delineated earlier. Figure 2.1 shows how the different instruments altering the EU governance architecture have been layered onto an existing institutional foundation.

The European Semester is a cycle of economic and fiscal policy coordination within the EU, agreed upon in 2010, which aims to increase coherence and effectiveness of economic and social policies. It is launched yearly by the European Commission via an Annual Growth Survey (AGS) that assesses the progress of the past year and sets out EU growth and job creation priorities for the coming year (European

| | Instruments of fiscal policy coordination | Mutual influence of the two sets of instruments | Instruments of social and labour market policy coordination |
|---|---|---|---|
| *Instruments and core objectives* | Two-Pack 2013 | | |
| | Fiscal Compact 2012 | | Youth Guarantee 2013 |
| | Six-Pack 2011 | ⇨ ⇦ | Social Investment Package 2013 |
| | Stability and Growth Pact 1997 | | Euro-plus Pact 2011 |
| | | | Europe 2020 (previously Lisbon Strategy, EES and social OMCs) 2010 |
| *Application of EU cycle* *Immediate objectives* | MIP, MTOs | | NRP, National Youth Employment Plans |
| | structural deficit rule, debt-deficit rule | | |
| | Convergence/Stability Programmes, DBPs | | |
| | ⇩ | Annual Growth Survey        ⇩ | |
| EU enforcement and surveillance | AMR, EDP, opinions on DBPs | | CSR, EPP commitments, Youth Employment Initiative, co-funding via ESF |

**Fig. 2.1**   Layering of instruments within the European Semester

Commission 2013c).[2] The European Semester, and in particular the AGS, is very powerful for the agenda-setting process as it gathers all policy aims, instruments and actors involved in economic, social and labour market policy. Furthermore, it is used to forward proposals for further strengthening the institutional architecture of the EU (European Council 2011).

## Altering the Governance of EMU Since 2010

The Maastricht Treaty introduced EMU pooled monetary policy at the EU level, while fiscal policy remained at the national level. The 3 per cent budget deficit criterion was closely monitored, and in the event of its breach by a Member State, an EDP could be launched. In an EDP, a plan has to be devised between the Member State and the Commission to exit the EDP, which could include reforms in pensions, healthcare or education. However, in 2005, this process was altered to take account of public investments. This rule change was controversial as it was put forward in the context on non-compliance with SGP criteria by France and Germany, which pointed to a politicization and thus a weakening of the process. In essence, however, the initial institutional architecture was not altered. Prior to the financial crisis of 2008, surveillance and enforcement of the SGP was medium, while the policy aims were highly specified (de la Porte and Heins 2014). After 2010, when the Euro was under threat, the EU instruments governing EMU and the oversight of Member States' budgets were reformed. The Six-Pack, the Fiscal Compact and the Two-Pack have radically altered the institutional framework through a process of institutional layering rather than a revision of the existing framework.

---

[2] Through the AGS, the EU Spring Council in March issues guidance covering fiscal, macroeconomic structural reform and growth enhancement for national policies on the basis of QMV. The policy priorities decided in the AGS should be included in Member States' Stability or Convergence programmes (concerning monetary policy) devised within the SGP and in National Reform Programmes (NRPs) concerning economic, employment and social policies devised within Europe 2020 that are to be submitted in April. Finally, the Commission proposes CSRs, which are then to be adopted/altered by the Council before the summer.

## Six-Pack

In December 2011, the Six-Pack[3] was adopted to increase the strength and scope of surveillance of all Member State economies with some specific rules for Eurozone Member States, especially regarding financial sanctions. The Six-Pack introduces several innovations that enhance European integration regarding fiscal and macroeconomic policy in terms of precision of objectives and mechanisms of surveillance as well as enforcement.

First, with regard to specifying and monitoring fiscal consolidation, Member States' budget balance should strive to reach country-specific Medium-Term Budgetary Objectives (MTOs), which previously did not hold Member States accountable. The MTOs are now more constraining in that the Six-Pack ensures stricter application of the fiscal rules by defining quantitatively 'significant deviation' from the MTO or the adjustment path towards it. Furthermore, an expenditure benchmark, that is, a rule which contains the growth rate of government spending at or below a country's medium-term potential economic growth rate, was introduced with the Six-Pack. Also, country-specific structural balances are specified: They can range from a structural budget deficit of 1 per cent of GDP to a budget in surplus. These MTOs embody a high degree of surveillance compared to the situation before the crisis. The structural budget deficit is a new benchmark that has been added on to the original provisions in the Maastricht Treaty. The structural deficit, together with the 3 per cent budget deficit, is seen as more accurate than the budget deficit criterion alone as it aims to filter out temporary fiscal measures and trends that are due to cyclical changes in the economy (Verhelst 2012). This preventative approach aims to keep Member State economies healthy in good times, rather than accumulating high deficits, and represents tighter integrated EU-Member State surveillance of budgets by making them accountable

---

[3] The legislation consists of these six parts: (1) the strengthening of surveillance of budgetary positions and coordination of economic policies, (2) acceleration and clarification of the EDP through a Council regulation, (3) enforcement of budgetary surveillance in the euro area through a regulation, (4) definition of a budgetary framework of the MS through a directive, (5) prevention and correction of macroeconomic imbalances through a regulation, (6) and enforcement of measures for correcting excessive macroeconomic imbalances in the euro area.

to their own MTOs. Furthermore, enforcement is high: The Commission can issue a warning to a Member State in case of significant deviation from its own adjustment path defined in the MTO. National governments may thus have less leverage in defining (or rather differentiating) their national political agendas (including welfare state reforms), due to the more constraining MTO, and the structural budget deficit, which constrains their budgets and thus plans for expansive fiscal spending, such as in social and labour market policy (European Commission 2013b).

A second novelty of the Six-Pack is the 'Macroeconomic Imbalance Procedure' (MIP) with accompanying indicators that is more far-ranging than the focus on public finances under the original SGP. In 2012, eleven indicators were selected for a scoreboard by the DG ECFIN to monitor the health of Member States' economies, including private debt, nominal unit labour costs and unemployment. This tool has enhanced the surveillance capability of the European Commission towards Member States. Although the Commission will take account of country-specific circumstances, the scoreboard represents a tool to quantitatively assess national economies. 'Alert Mechanism Reports' (AMRs) are designed to assess early on if there are risks of imbalances. If any risks are detected, the Commission can also request in-depth reviews of individual Member States to ensure the health of national economies. In the first AMRs, 12 Member States were subject to in-depth review, while in the second, 14 Member States were subject to in-depth review (European Commission 2012b).

Third, the Six-Pack increases enforcement of the SGP in case of non-compliance since an EDP can be launched if a Member State has breached either the deficit *or* the debt criterion, whereas previously only the deficit criterion was operational. Concerning enforcement, an EDP is launched, like before the crisis, through QMV in the Council. The level of enforcement is therefore only medium in this respect. However, in contrast to the situation before the crisis, the punitive aspect of enforcement has become very high for countries not complying with the correction of deficits or debts according to their plans. Indeed, if no effective action has been taken, quasi-automatic sanctions will be applied that could only be blocked by a RQMV in the Council. This means that a qualified majority of Member States (in Ecofin) must be against a Commission (DG

ECFIN) proposal for a sanction to be overturned. This represents a high level of enforcement. If the EU Council is satisfied with the implemented measures to counter the fiscal imbalance following the sanction, then the monetary sanction can be returned (Van Aken and Artige 2013). This measure is accompanied by a high degree of surveillance to verify that agreed measures to correct the imbalance are carried out. While a sanction has never been levied, it represents a strong shadow of hierarchy, compelling Member States to comply with EU aims to avoid fines.

In sum, fiscal consolidation objectives are highly specified and EU influence can be assessed as potentially high on this dimension as national governments have less leverage in defining (or rather differentiating) their national policy agendas (including welfare state reforms) due to the budget-restraining MTOs. The Six-Pack embodies a tighter and thus higher degree of integration on the surveillance dimension compared to the situation before the crisis, as a broader range of the economy is considered in the surveillance of Member State budgets through the MIP. In addition, with the new structural budget deficit criteria, a new benchmark has been added to the 3 per cent budget deficit criterion of the original Maastricht Treaty. Finally, the Six-Pack increases the enforcement of the SGP in case of non-compliance since an EDP can be launched if Member States have breached either the deficit or the debt criterion, where previously only the deficit criterion was decisive. The Six-Pack thus introduces benchmarks, mechanisms and processes through which to improve the plausibility of meeting the fiscal consolidation aims of the EMU and preventing future crises. This has an indirect but strong spillover on welfare policy, to which a large part of public expenditure is devoted.

### Fiscal Compact

The Fiscal Compact, added in 2012, is another legislative initiative that strengthens the aim of fiscal consolidation, together with surveillance and enforcement measures.[4] It complements and further reinforces the

---

[4] The Fiscal Compact was signed in March 2012 by all EU members except the United Kingdom and the Czech Republic and is the fiscal part of the Treaty on Stability, Coordination and Governance (TSCG).

SGP by including an automatic correction mechanism in the case of significant deviations from the MTO or the adjustment path towards it, and it renders the EDP almost automatic. It is binding for all eurozone Member States, while other Member States will be bound once they adopt the euro or, upon their discretion, earlier and with the possibility to choose the provisions they wish to comply with (European Parliament and European Council 2011).

The Fiscal Compact specifies the rules for curtailing public debt in case the limit of 60 per cent of GDP is exceeded.[5] It also requires that Member States converge towards country-specific MTOs with a limit of 0.5 per cent of GDP on structural deficits, also coined the 'golden rule' (Verhelst 2012). This can be extended to 1 per cent for Eurozone countries with a debt ratio significantly below 60 per cent of GDP. Economists recommend future MTOs to converge towards the 0.5 per cent benchmark, and to integrate this aim in Member State constitutions. This would force Eurozone countries to have balanced budgets in good times, which would render the likelihood of more than 3 per cent deficits less likely in economic downturns (Verhelst 2012). There is some flexibility, since the golden rule can be temporarily disregarded in exceptional circumstances. Nevertheless, the structural deficit targets enshrined in both the Six-Pack and the Fiscal Compact imply a high degree of enforcement and represent a further step in European integration by imposing Eurozone-fiscal discipline. However, even economists are concerned about the stringency of the golden rule, since it risks obstructing public investments that address long-term challenges such as aging and the shift towards a green economy. It seems, therefore, preferable that the implementation of the golden rule considers public investments. If not, Eurozone countries will, perhaps sensibly, be inclined to circumvent their golden rule' (Verhelst 2012, p. 3). In the case of circumventing the norms laid down by the Fiscal Compact, the European Court of Justice (ECJ) can impose financial sanctions of up to 0.1 per cent of GDP in case of non-compliance, which reinforces the corrective enforcement (ECB 2012, p. 83).

---

[5] The difference between the actual ratio and SGP limit shall be reduced by an average rate of one-twentieth per year as a benchmark.

Another novelty is that Member States must report on their national debt issuance to the Commission and the Council. This entails the expectation to discuss ex ante 'all major policy reforms', which suggests that it is negotiable bilaterally with each Member State, taking due account of circumstances. The Fiscal Compact strengthens the enforcement mechanism of the SGP, since all stages of the EDP should be implemented within a clearly defined time frame. When the Commission considers that an excessive deficit exists, this decision can only be overturned by RQMV. The Fiscal Compact thus strengthens the decision-making capacity of the Commission (compared to the Six-Pack) and reduces the political discretion of the EU Council. The measures for exiting an EDP and the timetable are negotiated between the Commission and the Member State, as was the case in the original SGP. Thus, there is some room for negotiation, although the threat of bad credit ratings from international rating agencies culminating in a sovereign debt crisis may incite Member States to follow reform paths developed with the Commission more closely. Furthermore, domestic politicians may use a breach of convergence criteria to implement sensitive reforms while conveniently shifting blame to the EU level (see contributions in this book; de la Porte and Natali 2014).

The Fiscal Compact, focused on fiscal discipline, builds on the Six-Pack but makes the aims with regard to structural deficits even more stringent. Surveillance is high, as Member States must discuss major reforms with the European institutions prior to their adoption. Ultimately, it reduces Member States' room for manoeuvre with regard not only to fiscal consolidation but also to structural reforms, such as in healthcare, pensions and labour markets. Moreover, the Fiscal Compact requires Member States to include the country-specific MTOs in national-binding law, preferably at the constitutional level. The instrument represents yet another initiative layered onto an existing institutional framework, rather than revision, since none of the previous instruments are replaced.

## Two-Pack

The Two-Pack, which came into force in May 2013, is a third initiative that has been layered onto the existent instruments governing the EMU

(European Commission 2013b). It specifies objectives in budgetary policy, together with high enforcement and surveillance mechanisms.[6] Its novelty is to introduce a common budgetary timeline and rules for all euro-area countries. The Two-Pack has a significant impact on 'sovereign' budgets—the basis for policy making—as it requires Member States to send their budget proposals to the Commission and the Eurogroup for approval before they are submitted to national parliaments.

The fact that national budgets, and thus details of policy reforms, are the object of close scrutiny—with strong potential for the EU to intervene in reform plans—implies that euro-area countries are now developing budgets in the shadow of EU surveillance. In their first assessment of Eurozone countries' draft budgetary plans[7] in autumn 2013, the Commission and the Eurogroup concluded that only two countries were 'compliant', three were 'compliant without any margin for possible slippage', three were 'broadly compliant' with 'some deviation from the adjustment path towards the MTO' and five were 'at the risk of non-compliance'. On this basis, recommendations were made to these countries. It is only in the case of 'particularly serious non-compliance' that the Commission may request a revision of the draft budgetary plan. It remains to be seen how effective enforcement will be and how precisely the Commission could require alterations in national budgets. Still, it represents much more interference in Member State budgets compared to before the crisis.

## Altering the Governance of the European Social Dimension Since 2010

In this section, we discuss how social policy aims and instruments have been altered in the wake of the crisis and what this signifies for the European social dimension. The coordination of European social and labour market policy was coordinated in the EES and various OMCs that have been insti-

---

[6] The Two-Pack consists of two regulations (based on Art 136 Treaty on the Functioning of the European Union [TFEU]) complementing the Six-Pack in euro-area countries to improve the transparency and coordination of Member States' budgetary planning and decision-making processes (European Commission 2013b).

[7] Applicable to those countries that are not under a macroeconomic adjustment programme.

tutionalised in the Lisbon Strategy in 2000 with the aim to achieve high levels of employment in combination with high levels of social protection. Pre-crisis, EU influence on setting policy objectives was medium, whereas the surveillance and enforcement of measures were low because the Lisbon Strategy was governed by the OMC (de la Porte and Heins 2014). The Lisbon Strategy, now Europe 2020, has been based on policy coordination that operates through policy learning with a strong emphasis on benchmarking policy performance. However, there have been some institutional innovations to enhance the use of EU funding for Europe 2020 aims, but these are accompanied by weak mechanisms of surveillance and enforcement. From the perspective of institutional change, this too represents an instance of institutional layering on an existing framework.

## Europe 2020

In June 2010, a new ten-year growth strategy coined 'Europe 2020' replaced the Lisbon Strategy as the main social and labour market policy instrument at the European level (European Commission 2010b). Like the new instruments governing the EMU, Europe 2020 firstly insists on fiscal consolidation in the crisis context. Beyond that, it is designed to deliver growth—if possible, socially and environmentally sustainable growth—that will require immediate investments but will pay off later in terms of economic growth, social well-being, equality and a greener environment. However, this strategy is dependent on significant government expenditure, which governments encumbered by a high public debt are hardly able to provide.

Europe 2020 is organised around five EU Headline Targets, which are supported by ten 'Integrated Guidelines' covering economic, environmental, employment and social issues, and seven 'flagship initiatives', which are novel institutional instruments. The policies adopted in these areas are to be reported in 'National Reform Programmes' (NRPs). Concerning the policy objectives, two of the Integrated Guidelines are devoted to employment policy and one to social exclusion, while there are no targets or guidelines for social protection issues. The aim to increase labour market participation stands stronger than ever—the previous benchmark of an average overall employment rate of 70 per cent was raised to 75 per cent (European Commission 2010b). The 'Agenda for new skills and jobs' is the flagship initiative that aims not only at supporting this aim but also at ensuring that workers are skilled and able to adapt to an altering labour market. Concrete proposals of this agenda are to improve flexicurity, to equip the workforce with appropriate skills for the modern labour market, to improve job quality and working conditions and, finally, to improve job creation. Employment subsidies or targeted reductions of non-wage labour costs as well as the promotion of self-employment—arguably of precarious character in the context of a crisis—are among the suggested measures for job creation (European Commission 2010a). These policies are, by and large, the same as those developed under the preceding Lisbon Strategy (2000–2010).

The social aim consists of promoting social inclusion, intimately linked to increasing labour market participation, and combating poverty. Under Europe 2020, Member States have committed to 'lift at least 20 million people out of the risk of poverty and exclusion' by 2020 (European Council 2011). Member States have to specify their own national targets in this area. These targets are not very ambitious, which suggests a lack of real political will to take the EU target seriously (de la Porte and Weishaupt 2013). Another flagship initiative—the 'European platform against poverty and social exclusion'—supports the social exclusion aim of the EU. The degree of EU involvement regarding the Europe 2020 objectives is low for poverty reduction, while it is medium for objectives such as activation and the raising of employment rates.

EU surveillance of Europe 2020 is medium, as it takes place ex post as part of an iterative policy cycle, now coordinated in the European Semester. On the basis of the NRPs, CSRs are made to Member States, suggesting policies to be adopted for reaching the broad policy aims delineated in Europe 2020. Enforcement of the CSRs is low, as the adoption of the suggested measures is voluntary. Existing evidence on CSRs on employment policies shows that they have at times been sources of inspiration for reform (de la Porte and Jacobsson 2012). However, the overall impact is low, particularly under conditions of fiscal constraint and low growth.

## The Euro-Plus Pact

The Euro-Plus Pact (EPP), adopted in March 2011, is based on the OMC between the 17 Eurozone members and 6 other countries (Bulgaria, Denmark, Latvia, Lithuania, Poland and Romania). Aiming at better economic policy coordination, it focuses on competitiveness, employment and financial sustainability, including a structured discussion on tax policy issues. It is a new initiative that has been layered onto the existing EU institutional framework. The EPP specifies objectives that primarily fall in areas that are under the competence of the Member States including wage monitoring, labour market reforms, tax reforms, pensions, healthcare and social benefits, fiscal rules and banking regulations.

In labour market policy, some objectives touch on core labour market issues, including decentralizing wage-setting agreements as well as revising wage indexation mechanisms (Barnard 2012). The EPP penetrates into sensitive national welfare state issues, specifying objectives to a high degree. It is integrated into the European Semester, where Member States should report on progress made towards the main aims: Surveillance is medium through the analysis of progress made to issues that are central in the EPP, alongside the assessment of progress made in other processes. The EPP is voluntary, using the OMC, and surveillance as well as enforcement is therefore as low as it is for Europe 2020. While each Member State has the discretion to select their own national measures to achieve the common goals—and to decide how far-reaching reforms should be—national commitments should be integrated in the NRPs that are central for Europe 2020 and Stability or Convergence Programmes in the framework of the SGP. The Commission then assesses implementation by Member States of 'Euro-Plus Pact commitments' together with the assessment of other CSRs. Compared to the new institutional architecture around the EMU—and even Europe 2020 with its headline targets and flagship initiatives—the EPP objectives are not likely to make headway via an OMC process, since they require domestic political commitment.

## Social Investment Package (SIP) and Youth Guarantee

Social investment is a comprehensive paradigmatic approach that emphasizes the need to invest in individuals and their skills throughout the life course so that they can participate in the labour market and combine work with other priorities, such as care responsibilities (European Commission 2013d). It implies investing in institutions for early childhood, schools, vocational training, upper tertiary education, activation and lifelong learning (see Morel et al. 2012). At the same time, temporary leave from the labour market should be facilitated without loss of employment. Social investment ideas build on the foundations of the universal welfare state, which is developed to meet these aims (see Kvist, Chap. 3).

Social investment, especially since a 2013 Commission Communication on the topic, provides an overarching policy framework to coordinate already developed economic, labour market and social policies. Member States can receive CSRs in the area of social investment through Europe 2020 (European Commission 2013d). The funding, especially from the European Social Fund (ESF), is intended to be better integrated with the SIP for the 2014–2020 period (European Commission 2014). However, the EES was also combined with European funding, and even where funding was linked to the EES aims, such as in the Central and Eastern European countries, the overall impact was weak (de la Porte and Jacobsson 2012). Policy objectives are defined to a medium degree, while enforcement and surveillance are both weak, although they are medium if co-funding is included in pursuing an aim under the SIP.

Parallel to the launching of the SIP, an initiative coined 'Youth Guarantee' was launched in April 2013 via a Council recommendation, due to the concern about youth unemployment. It was another instrument layered onto the existing Europe 2020 framework. The Youth Guarantee aims to ensure that all young people under 25 get a good-quality, concrete offer of employment or training within four months of them leaving formal education or becoming unemployed. This is a specific policy objective and is coherent with the supply-side aims of monetarism and with the main gist of social investment. The purpose is to avoid the inactivity trap among young people, as this could have negative consequences for their future participation on the labour market. The Youth Guarantee aims to enhance activation of young people, which was already part of the EES since the mid-1990s. Member State progress in this area is reported in 'National Youth Implementation Plans', which have started to be reported in 2014. The fact that €6 billion have been reserved in the 'Youth Employment Initiative' for the implementation of the Guarantee across Member States (co-funded with Member States) differentiates it from the EES that also focused on youth. If the initiatives are co-funded, then surveillance and enforcement will be medium; otherwise, they will be low.

## Assessing the Institutional Alterations of the EMU and the European Social Dimension

Altogether, the Six-Pack, the Fiscal Compact and the Two-Pack have incrementally, and in rapid succession, been grafted onto the existing institutional framework to achieve aims of fiscal consolidation and balanced budgets already present in the Maastricht Treaty. Although their overall aims are not novel, they represent a major leap forward in EMU integration due to new benchmarks requiring fiscal restraint, combined with high levels of surveillance and monitoring. Through these new instruments, especially the monitoring of Member State budgets as well as the reporting on structural reforms, Member States are under pressure to curtail expenditure in healthcare, pensions, early childhood programmes and elderly care. The AGSs highlight the need to keep public expenditure growth below the rate of medium-term GDP trends and to correct macroeconomic imbalances and decrease account deficits as well as levels of indebtedness (European Commission 2011, 2012a, 2013a, 2014). The necessary resources to facilitate investment in human capabilities and participation of women in the labour market, key elements in a sustainable social investment strategy, may not be prioritised or could be under-resourced.

Europe 2020, the main instrument to foster the European social dimension, aims to address the social and other non-monetary aspects of the EMU and the EU. However, Europe 2020 and the instruments grafted onto it, in particular the SIP, are developed under the monetarist paradigm. Thus, instruments addressing social consequences of the crisis—for example the Youth Guarantee—frame policy responses that lean on supply-side policies. This was the case before the crisis as well, but the instruments and aims for fiscal consolidation, structural reforms and structural deficits were not nearly as constraining, effectively allowing for legitimate diversity. Now, the possibilities for diversity have become more limited through the framework and aims around fiscal and budgetary constraint.

However, since the immediate effects of the crisis are receding, social aims that are not only at the service of the EMU are taking shape: Member States are encouraged to replace existing temporary or precarious contracts with open-ended contracts and to provide more security to workers on temporary contracts, while introducing more flexible conditions for workers on open-ended contracts—thus responding to dualization. Furthermore, there is a renewed emphasis on the need to develop childcare institutions to facilitate the entry of second earners into the labour market (European Commission 2014). However, the resources available from the EU are very limited, which means that Member States first need to have balanced budgets and healthy economies to be able to make such investments. One possible institutional alteration would be to consider these productive investments and not expenditure, thereby enabling Europe to improve and maintain its social model.

Table 2.2 summarizes our findings with regard to the typology on EU integration and involvement, which shows that since the crisis, the EU has been much more involved in fiscal policy, a core issue for welfare states, via the framework created for governing the Eurozone. It also shows that while there have been multiple initiatives integrated into and layered onto Europe 2020, these are governed by relatively weak instruments and processes, thus affecting welfare state reform only through voluntarism.

**Table 2.2** Analytical results: EU integration levels of instruments of fiscal and social governance

|  | Objectives | Surveillance | Enforcement |
|---|---|---|---|
| Fiscal policy coordination (to optimize the functioning of the Eurozone) | | | |
| SGP (pre-crisis) | High | Medium | Medium |
| Six-Pack | High | High | Medium |
| Fiscal Compact | High | High | High |
| Two-Pack | High | High | High |
| Social and labour market policy coordination (to address issues of economic growth as well as social sustainability) | | | |
| Lisbon Strategy (pre-crisis) | Medium | Low | Low |
| Europe 2020 | Medium | Medium | Low |
| Euro-Plus Pact | High | Medium | Low |
| Social Investment Package and Youth Guarantee | Medium | Low/Medium if co-funding | Low/Medium if co-funding |

# Conclusion

Since 2010, multiple new instruments have been created in the EU that affect welfare reform to an unprecedented degree. New instruments and policies have been grafted onto the existing institutional architecture to enhance the coordination of fiscal policy. The new norms, such as structural deficit rules as well as stricter enforcement and ex ante surveillance of Member State budgets, can be seen as a logical consequence of having more integration in monetary policy. These new rules have a significant impact on welfare states, as tight budgetary criteria makes expansionary public spending difficult even in healthy economies, let alone in crisis-ridden countries. The new instruments were agreed in unusually rapid succession in the context of an ongoing Eurozone crisis, leading to considerable institutional change in the EMU architecture in a short period of time. The resultant institutional architecture holds Member States accountable to the EU ex ante and ex post with regard to their budgets and public expenditure, including social expenditure.

Europe 2020, the framework designed to coordinate employment and social policy and further develop the European Social Model, is comparatively weak compared to the sharpened objectives, surveillance and enforcement mechanisms in the EMU. Although fostering social investment is on top of the EU social policy agenda, the extremely strict fiscal discipline and balanced budget rules that are highly institutionalised may undermine the implementation of Europe 2020.

In the current situation, social investment is needed to ensure a life course approach to labour market highly-skilled policy, aiming at improving skills and economic growth. This requires financing in the short-term to reap benefits in the future and in the long-term, such as alternative forms of taxation and co-funding from the ESF, although the effect of this is likely to be limited. The risk of missing the opportunity to develop social investment and only a limited supply-side and liberal agenda is particularly high in countries that are still struggling not only with the effects of the crisis. Some of these countries lack institutions geared to making social investment sustainable—starting with early childhood education and care through schools, higher education and life-long learning. Therefore, it is of utmost importance that EMU criteria and the new instruments developed for fiscal consolidation be altered to take account of investments made in such institutions if the social investment strategy is to meet its promises.

**Acknowledgements** We would like to thank many colleagues who have commented on different drafts of this chapter, including Susana Borrás, Jochen Clasen, Nathalie Morel, Joakim Palme, Maria João Rodrigues and Marion Schmid-Drüner.

# References

Barbier, C. (2012). La prise d'autorité de la Banque centrale européenne et les dangers démocratiques de la nouvelle gouvernance économique dans l'Union européenne. In B. de Witte, A. Heritier, & A. H. Trechsel (Eds.), *The Euro crisis and the state of European democracy* (pp. 212–241). Florence: European University Institute.

Barnard, C. (2012). The financial crisis and the Euro Plus Pact: A labour lawyer's perspective. *Industrial Law Journal, 41*(1), 98–114.

De Haan, J., Berger, H., & Jansen, D. (2004). Why has the stability and growth pact failed? *International Finance, 7*(2), 235–260.

de la Porte, C., & Heins, E. (2014). Game change in EU social policy: Towards more European integration. In M. J. Rodrigues & E. Xiarchogiannopoulou (Eds.), *The Eurozone Crisis and the Transformation of EU Governance*. Aldershot: Ashgate.

de la Porte, C., & Jacobsson, K. (2012). Social investment or recommodification? Assessing the employment policies of the EU member states. In N. Morel, B. Palier, & J. Palme (Eds.), *Towards a social investment welfare state? Ideas, policies and challenges* (pp. 117–152). Bristol: Policy Press.

de la Porte, C., & Natali, D. (2014). Altered Europeanisation of pension reform in the context of the Great Recession: Denmark and Italy compared. *West European Politics, 37*(4), 732–749.

de la Porte, C., & Pochet, P. (2012). Why and how (still) study the OMC? *Journal of European Social Policy, 22*(2), 336–349.

de la Porte, C., & Pochet, P. (2014). Boundaries of welfare between the EU and Member States during the 'Great Recession'. *Perspectives on European Politics and Society, 15*(3), 1–14.

de la Porte, C., & Weishaupt, T. (2013). The open method of co-ordination for social inclusion and social protection: Theoretical and empirical state-of-the-art. In J. Garcés & I. Monsonís Paya (Eds.), *Sustainability and Transformation in European Social Policy* (pp. 41–60). PIE-Peter Lang: Brussels.

European Central Bank (ECB) (2012). A fiscal compact for a stronger economic and monetary union. *ECB Monthly Bulletin, May 2012*, 79–94.

European Commission. (2010a). *An agenda for new skills and jobs: A European contribution towards full employment*. Communication from the Commission to the European Parliament, the Council, the European Economic and Social Committee and the Committee of the Regions, COM(2010) 682 final. Strasbourg: European Commission.

European Commission. (2010b). *Europe 2020: A strategy for smart, sustainable and inclusive growth*. Brussels: European Commission. http://ec.europa.eu/europe2020/index_en.htm. Accessed 20 May 2013.

European Commission. (2011). *Annual growth survey 2012*. COM (2011) 815 final.

European Commission. (2012a). *Annual growth survey 2013*. Brussels: European Commission. http://ec.europa.eu/europe2020/pdf/ags2013_en.pdf

European Commission. (2012b). *Report from the Commission on the Alert Mechanism Report 2013*. COM(2012) 751 final.

European Commission. (2013a, November 13). *Annual growth survey 2014.* COM(2013) 800 final, Brussels.

European Commission. (2013b, April 10). *Beyond the six pack and two pack: Economic governance explained.* Memo/13/318, Brussels. http://europa.eu/rapid/press-release_MEMO-13-318_en.htm. Accessed 30 April 2013.

European Commission. (2013c). *Strengthening the social dimension of the Economic and Monetary Union.* COM(2013) 690 provisoire. Brussels: European Commission. http://ec.europa.eu/commission_2010-2014/president/news/archives/2013/10/pdf/20131002_1-emu_en.pdf. Accessed 16 Oct 2013.

European Commission. (2013d, February 20). *Towards social investment for growth and cohesion: Including implementing the European Social Fund 2014-2020.* COM(2013)083 final.

European Commission (2014). *Policy roadmap for the 2014 implementation of the social investment package.* Brussels: European Commission.

European Council. (2011, March 25). *Conclusions of the presidency.* EUCO 10/11, Annex I.

European Parliament and European Council. (2011). Regulation (EU) No 1173/2011 of 16 November 2011, on the effective enforcement of budgetary surveillance in the euro area. *Official Journal of the European Union, L306,* 1–7.

Hacker, J. S. (2004). Privatizing risk without privatising the welfare state: The hidden politics of social policy retrenchment in the United States. *American Political Science Review, 98*(2), 243–260.

Hassenteufel, P., Delaye, S., Pierru, F., Robelet, M., & Serré, M. (2000). La libéralisation des systèmes de protection maladie européens. Convergence, européanisation et adaptations nationals. *Politique Européenne, 1*(2), 29–48.

Jepsen, M., & Serrano Pascual, A. (2005). The European social model: An exercise in deconstruction. *Journal of European Social Policy, 15*(3), 231–245.

Jessoula, M. (2012). *Like in a skinner box: External constraints and the reform of retirement eligibility rules in Italy.* Working Paper-LPF, 4/2012.

McNamara, K. R. (2005). Economic and Monetary Union: Innovation and challenges for the euro. In H. Wallace, W. Wallace, & M. A. Pollack (Eds.), *Policy-making in the European Union* (5th ed.pp. 141–160). Oxford: Oxford University Press.

Morel, N., Palier, B., & Palme, J. (2012). *Towards a social investment welfare state? Ideas, policies and challenges.* Bristol: Policy Press.

Scharpf, F. (2002). The European social model. *Journal of Common Market Studies, 40*(4), 645–670.

Scharpf, F. (2011). *Monetary Union, fiscal crisis and the preemption of democracy* (Discussion Paper 11/11). Cologne: Max Planck Institute for the Study of Societies.

Van Aken, W., & Artige, L. (2013). Reverse Majority Voting in comparative perspective: Implications for fiscal governance in the EU. In B. de Witte, A. Heritier, & A. H. Trechsel (Eds.), *The Euro crisis and the state of European democracy* (pp. 129–161). Florence: European University Institute.

Verhelst, S. (2012). *Will the national 'golden rule' eclipse the EU fiscal norms?* http://www.voxeu.org/article/what-will-golden-rule-mean-eurozone. Accessed 26 June 2014.

Viebrock, E., & Clasen, J. (2009). Flexicurity and welfare reform. *Socio-Economic Review, 7*(2), 305–331.

# 3

# A Framework for Social Investment Strategies: Integrating Generational, Life Course and Gender Perspectives in the EU Social Investment Strategy

## Jon Kvist

## Introduction

The European Social Model may come out of the economic crisis as the phoenix bird rising from the ashes: more economically sustainable and more socially just. At least the new European Union (EU) social investment strategy promises to "enhance person's capacities and support their participation in society and the labour market. This will benefit individuals' prosperity, boost the economy and help the EU emerge from the crisis stronger, more cohesive and more competitive" (European Commission 2013a).

The idea of investing in people's human capital, health and other capabilities is not new (Becker 1993; Kersbergen and Hemerijk 2012; Sen 1985). However, scholars, international organizations and governments show a growing interest in how to simultaneously curb inequalities and promote growth. Noble laureate James Heckman champions invest-

J. Kvist (✉)
Department of Social Sciences and Business, Roskilde University, Roskilde, Denmark

© The Author(s) 2016                                                    **43**
C. de la Porte, E. Heins (eds.), *The Sovereign Debt Crisis, the EU and Welfare State Reform*, DOI 10.1057/978-1-137-58179-2_3

ments in children with disadvantageous backgrounds (e.g. Heckman 2006). Professor Michael Marmot and his colleagues recommend a good start in life for all to improve health and reduce health inequities (Marmot et al. 2012). The World Health Organization (WHO) and the Organisation for Economic Cooperation and Development (OECD) both promote investments in persons to curb social, health and economic inequalities and to increase social cohesion and economic growth. Indeed, in the 2000s many governments expanded education and, especially, childcare.

Although many of the ideas behind social investments may not be new, it is novel for the EU to present them together as a coherent reform strategy embracing hitherto separate strategies and to swiftly incorporate the strategy in the European Semester. The President of the European Commission José Manuel Barroso noted in his State of the Union address in September 2012 that the Nordic countries have shown that effective social protection systems and strong partnerships make it possible to be both competitive and socially cohesive (Barroso 2012). The launch in February 2013 consisted of one Communication, a Recommendation plus eight staff working papers (European Commission 2013a, b). The separate strategies on health, social protection, long-term care and social inclusion were merged into one social policy reform strategy—that of social investments. In October 2013 the European Council (2013) agreed to integrate the social dimension of the European Monetary Union (EMU) into the European Semester, as suggested by the Commission (European Commission 2013c). As a result, 2014 was the first European Semester to be informed by the social investment strategy and the social objectives in the Annual Growth Survey.

In June 2014, country-specific recommendations asked member states to take action in 2014–15 in five areas connected to the social investment strategy, namely, pension and healthcare systems, labour market participation, active labour market policy, education and training and poverty and social inclusion. To these areas one may have added research and development (R&D), labour market segmentation, wage setting and sound finances. However, looking exclusively at the five areas and the 26 EU member states (Greece and Cyprus implement commitments under the EU/International Monetary Fund [IMF] financial assistance programmes), we get a maximum of 130 areas that the country-specific recommendations could cover. The Commission proposed recommendations in 99 of the 130 possible. All countries received country-specific recommendations. Three countries—Denmark, Sweden and the Netherlands—were given recommendations in two areas. Seven countries—Bulgaria, Croatia, Ireland, Lithuania, Poland, Portugal and Romania—received recommendations in all of the possible areas associated with social investments. The remaining countries received recommendations in three or four areas.

Social policy scholars have criticised social investment strategies for neglecting gender and class issues, children's well-being and the situation of the jobless poor and for having a too economic view of investments and returns (Lister 2003; Cantillon 2011; Nolan 2013; Pintelon et al. 2013). In relation to the EU social investment strategy, the critics are partly right and partly wrong. The focus on children is strong indeed; the only recommendation, "*Investing in children: breaking the cycle of disadvantage*", advocates reforms to dampen the impact of social class of origin for social risks. However, a closer look at the country-specific recommendations from June 2014 reveal that none of them mention social class, but they do address social mobility, female labour supply and Roma children as informed by the national experts on social inclusion (Frazer and Marlier 2014). The Communication, "*Towards Social Investment for Growth and Cohesion*", notes that gender disadvantages must be tackled in a more coherent manner including higher rates of female poverty, lower activity rates, part-time work and gender pay gap (European Commission 2013a, pp. 7–8). However, the country-specific recommendations do not show evidence of the new social investment thinking manifesting itself (yet) in gender issues beyond well-established ideas of improving female labour supply by reconciling work and family life through childcare provision.

The relative scarce attention to gender aspects in the current EU social investment strategy and in the majority of scholarly work on social investments is surprising for at least five reasons. First, gender matters for life chances: Families, education, the labour market, health and social relations are highly stratified arenas in gender terms. Second, inherent in the social investment strategy there are many gender issues such as reconciliation of work and family life. Third, gender issues, in particular questions of gender equality, have long been within the EU's legitimate sphere of social policy. Fourth, the Nordic countries that at the moment probably best represent the social investment approach have long been acknowledged for having some of the most gender equal societies and most expansive policies for families and children, the labour market and the socially disadvantaged. Finally, the remarkable increase of women's educational attainment, new gender roles and modern family types are all central components to take account of in ongoing reforms of labour market regulations favouring insiders and social policies based on male breadwinner models.

Paradoxically, there has also been little scholarly attention to gender aspects of the social investment strategy, despite many researchers emphasising that the strategy has important gender aspects (see contributors in Morel et al. 2012) and despite a multitude of gender studies on the causes and effects of the various policies making up the social investments. So far, no scholars have systematically examined how gender aspects come into play in a social investment strategy with regard to social investment policies and their social, health and economic returns. One reason may be that few social investment researchers have adopted the lifelong perspective that does justice to the core idea of social investments being about policies that, over time, benefit people and society.

The EU has gone one step in the right direction of adopting a framework that contains policies and returns over the whole life span as declared by László Andor (2013), Commissioner for Employment, Social Affairs and Inclusion: "We can restore and maintain prosperity in Europe if we invest in our human capital, from cradle to old age. This is what social investment is about." The three-stage life cycle approach with childhood, adulthood and old age was originally put forward by Seebohm Rowntree (1901) and informed poverty relief and social insurance in the 19th and 20th century. However, the life cycle perspective is problematic on two accounts. First, it assumes uniformity in our paths through life. However, due to social and structural change, generations' paths through life have become more complex and diverse across different socio-economic groups, including gender. Second, the perspective is problematic because many social issues and returns to social investments evolve over time. The significance of a life event or policy intervention in one life stage depends in part on what happened in the previous stage(s) and has consequences for what happens later. Hence, the life cycle approach cannot inform policymaking on social investments in the 21st century.

The aim of this chapter is to contribute to a more coherent framework, the life course perspective, on social investments that address the dynamic and multi-dimensional nature of social issues and social investment policies; contain multiple disciplinary approaches; emphasise differences between generations and diversity within generations—exemplified by gender—due to a dialectic relationship between human agency and contextual factors; and are high on policy relevance. The seemingly small change of focus from life cycle to life course dramatically changes our understanding of social issues and policies.

Arguments and evidence from economics, medicine, psychology, public health and sociology are used in this chapter to underpin how a life course perspective can inform social investment strategies. Cross-national institutional and statistical information for five countries representing different welfare regimes and corners of Europe—Denmark, Germany, Italy, Poland and the United Kingdom—is used to show the relevance and potential of social investments in the life course perspective.

How the social investment strategy serves an intergenerational contract through horizontal redistribution is explained in the first section. Also, how social and structural change form more diverse generations with (recurring) life events, especially in family, education and labour market trajectories, and lead to less fixed times of transition between life stages is discussed. A life course perspective on social investments explaining what policies and returns are characteristic for different life events, life stages and transitions is offered in the second section. In the third section gender is used to illustrate how the diversity view of the life course perspective can help inform social investments. The discussion is concluded in the final section.

## Social Investments from a Generational Perspective

We argue that the social investment strategy builds on an implicit contract between generations. The generational contract concerns production and reproduction. Those of working age finance welfare policies, including social investments, for children and youths and those who are retired. Those of prime age support children that, in due course, become the generation of workers supporting their parent generation in return.

Figure 3.1 illustrates how generations change position over time from being recipients in childhood and youth at Time, to being contributors in working age at $Time_{+1 \text{ generation}}$, to becoming recipients again in old age at $Time_{+2 \text{ generations}}$. This shifting of positions implies that the welfare state smooths resources over the life course and acts as a piggy bank for the individual (Barr 2001).

Indeed, Figure 3.1 thus shows how those individuals who are invested in are those same individuals who largely finance social investments—that is, a distribution of resources from myself to myself at different points of time in my life course. This horizontal redistribution of resources to oneself over the life course contrasts with the vertical redistribution of resources from the rich to the poor, from the healthy to the ill, from childless persons to families and from workers to workless.

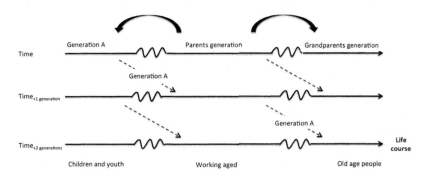

**Fig. 3.1** The intergenerational contract: horizontal distribution over the life course

The reproduction function of the generational contract has obvious gender aspects to it, as women of fertile age are bearing the main costs to maintain a stable replacement of generations. The current of the population in European countries can be explained by the 1968 generation not having as many children as their parents. Over time this means that there are fewer people to support and care for the larger population of the elderly. The reproductive elements of the generational contract can hardly be overestimated as evidenced by low fertility rates in many European countries.

Changing demographics influence national economies (see Lee and Mason 2011). Today, all countries face aging populations with large cohorts retiring at the same time as smaller cohorts enter working age. Social investment strategies are thus working on the backdrop of aging populations that makes it essential to design the best possible policies to form, maintain and use skills and enable individuals and families to have children and obtain an education and jobs.

At the same time social investment policies must take into account that generations themselves are changing. De-institutionalization and de-standardization of the family, education and work take place in all European countries. The postwar nuclear married couples and their children are giving way for more family types. More and more people cohabit, live alone, break up and enter new unions, perhaps with persons with children from their previous unions. Family trajectories no longer follow the same sequence of cohabitation, marriage and childbirth. Social investment policies facilitate transitions between family forms and avoid that belonging to any one family form hinders individuals' pursuits of their life chances in education and work.

The education trajectories themselves have changed. Personal development is no longer the reservoir of first the mother and then school but rather is becoming a lifelong process. Social investment in a life course perspective acknowledges that learning in any one stage must be seen in connection with what happened earlier and what is to happen.

The labour market has changed fundamentally since the heyday of the male breadwinner model in the postwar period. Women entered the formal labour market and increasingly work full-time. Work trajectories are made up by many jobs over the life course, often interrupted by reoccurring events of unemployment, sickness and education. In addition, education, family life and work trajectories intersect in new ways along the life course thereby replacing male breadwinner models with dual earner couples and single person households (Blossfeld and Drobnič 2001).

As a consequence of these social and structural changes, the view of uniform generations in the life cycle perspective must give way to an understanding of generations being more complex, amenable and heterogeneous. The life course perspective acknowledges that different generations have different possibilities and opportunities with diversity characterizing individuals' paths through life (Elder 1999). Social investment thinking aligns with the life course perspective on personal development in family, education and work as a lifelong process in which no life stage can be understood in isolation from other stages.

The life course perspective highlights that age is not simply biological or chronological and that transitions from one stage in the life course to another change over historical time and are diverse across individuals. Growing shares of generations take longer and more frequent education periods and make the transition to working age, on average, later than previous generations. The generation of the elderly today is generally more resourceful and less frail than 40 years ago, and individuals today retire at many different points of time in their lives. The social investment strategy aims in part to move and mold transitions from one stage to another. Sometimes the goal is to postpone the transition, for example, when preventing premature births or reducing involuntary early retirement. At other times the goal is to advance a transition, for example, from education or unemployment to work. In most instances the goal of social investment policies is to keep people on track in their life course, allowing them to form their own individual life trajectories without getting trapped in adverse situations. Typical goals are, thus, to reduce the rate of early school leavers and to support the unemployed and others to get them back into work.

In essence, the social contract between generations rests on the idea that each generation does its best, first, to acquire and maintain the skills needed to be productive and, second, to use these skills and have the number of children needed to keep the ratio between the working and non-working relatively stable. The goal of the social investment strategy is to help make this happen, acknowledging that generations are internally different.

# Social Investments in a Life Course Perspective

Social investments are made by different actors, including, most notably, families, firms and various state interventions. Public policies can thus be directed not only at the individual but also at the family and civil society and at firms and employers. There are two constitutive dimensions to the social investment strategy: the inputs or social investment policies and the outputs or the returns of social investment policies. Figure 3.2 shows that the type of policies and returns vary over the life course and extend far beyond education and activation policies and yield more than economic returns. Indeed, the social investment strategy contains a broad range of policies and returns from the start of life to the end of life.

Life starts in the womb. Adverse influences during fetal life, like undernutrition, prompt the fetus to adapt, which may cause persistent changes to organ structure and metabolism. Such changes were found to lead to problems such as issues with brain development as well as cardiovascular diseases and diabetes in adult life (Barker 1998; Hannon 2003).

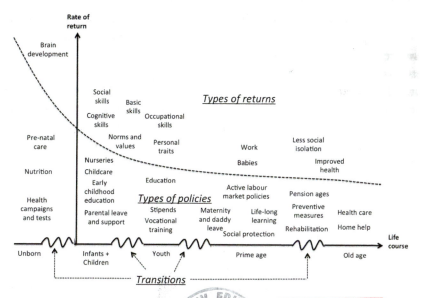

**Fig. 3.2** A life course perspective on social investment policies and their returns

From a social investment perspective, the social and economic costs of illness and under-development must, if possible, be avoided and, to the extent possible, replaced by healthier and more productive lives. To secure a healthy development of the fetus, health promotion campaigns, outreach, health checks, screening and other prenatal measures can be directed at pregnant girls and women in areas and situations where risk factors are high. Nurses and midwives may help guide the pregnant woman and her partner, if any, to adopt healthy lifestyles. After the birth, a variety of health professionals and community support workers can help the mother breastfeed and offer other parenting skills support.

Among others, James Heckman (2006) has pioneered studies of the effects of early environments on child, adolescent and adult achievement. Life course skill formation is a dynamic process in which early inputs strongly affect the productivity of later inputs (Burger 2010; Heckman 2006). Because skill formation is dynamic and skill demands increase, it is crucial to establish good cognitive and social skills in childhood.

Family investments in children can be boosted by leave schemes and family counselling that improve the amount and quality of child–parent interaction. Maternity, paternity and parental leave schemes give parents employment protection and, mostly, income support that extend the time children have with their parents. Mothers have postnatal maternity leaves of 12 months in Poland and the United Kingdom, which is far longer than 1.8 months in Germany, 3.2 months in Denmark and 3.7 months in Italy (figures for 2013) (Moss 2013), but the British scheme is the only well-paid maternity leave, as defined by the European Commission, as paying at least 66 per cent of previous earnings for 1.4 months. All countries run various forms of family counselling, but the data is too disparate to allow meaningful cross-national comparisons.

Policies making up state subsidized investments in children are child-care and early education. In short, early and high-quality childcare is key for social investments in children and has proven to have positive long-run consequences on academic and economic outcomes (Burger 2010; Havnes and Mogstad 2011). Heckman and colleagues found that high-quality early childhood programmes reduce crime, raise earnings, promote education and improve health (e.g., Campbell et al. 2014; Heckman 2000). Childcare gives returns for all children, but the largest returns come for children in families who are least likely to stimulate cognitive skills, such as those from dysfunctional families (Heckman 2006; Havnes and Mogstad 2011).

Childcare coverage rates vary with the age of children and between countries. The coverage rate for children between 3 years and compulsory school age in formal childcare is high in all countries, except Poland. In 2012, the Polish share of 35 per cent was much smaller than the 72 per cent in the United Kingdom, 91 per cent in Italy and Germany and 94 per cent in Denmark (Eurostat 2014). The coverage of children below 3 years in formal care is low in all countries, except Denmark. In 2012 the share was less than 10 per cent in Poland, up to 20 per cent in Germany, 22 per cent in Italy, over 35 per cent in the United Kingdom and 77 per cent in Denmark (European Commission 2013d). Childcare coverage is high for older children but lower for younger children, where it matters most.

To reduce the effect of intergenerational transmission of risks, children of less privileged families should get into childcare. In 2011, the share of children below 3 years who come from the poorest income quintile and are in formal care is 0 per cent in Poland, 17 per cent in Italy, 20 per cent in the United Kingdom, 21 per cent in Germany and 87 per cent in Denmark (European Commission 2013d). In comparison, the coverage rate for children in the richest families is 4 per cent in Poland, 23 per cent in Germany, 28 per cent in Italy, 53 per cent in the United Kingdom and 83 per cent in Denmark (European Commission 2013d). Thus, the coverage of young children from all income groups is negligible in Poland, low in Germany and high in Denmark. There are more children from middle and high income families in childcare than from poor families in Italy and the United Kingdom. No country succeeds in reaching out to all children in relatively poor families, but Denmark is performing notably better than other EU countries.

The quality of formal childcare is important for returns on investments and for the likelihood that families place their children in childcare. The quality of childcare depends on a lot of aspects like budget, pedagogy, staff qualifications and the ratio of staff to children. These aspects vary between different childcare institutions, making cross-national comparisons difficult. With this caveat in mind, there is general consensus that a good indicator of childcare quality is child–staff ratios. On average the child–staff ratio for pre-primary school education in full-time staff in 2010 was 10.0 in Denmark, 11.8 in Italy, 12.6 in Germany, 15.9 in the United Kingdom and 18.7 in Poland (European Commission 2013d).

The quality of interventions for children with social, learning and cognitive difficulties can be improved by professional specialists supporting regular staff. In Denmark and Germany such specialists include speech and language therapists, educational psychologists and experts on special educational needs (European Commission et al. 2014). Local governments in Italy and the United Kingdom decide which support staff is made available. In Poland, the staff gets support from educational therapists, and those working with older children also get support from speech and language therapists.

In adolescence, persons build on what they have learned in childhood and prepare themselves for early adulthood. Adolescents also engage in risk behaviour and may start unhealthy lifestyles like smoking and drinking. Policies include norm setting through information, taxes on tobacco and alcohol, combat on drug misuse and the promotion of good physical and dietary habits. Studies have shown that personal traits are amenable both in childhood and youth (Heckman 2008). This opens up the potential for measures that aim at instilling attentiveness and persistence and other traits that are helpful for success in life.

Education and vocational training aim at specific skills sets from basic to advanced or occupational. Study stipends and free or subsidised education reduce the disadvantage of coming from economically poor households. One EU2020 headline target is that at least 40 per cent of persons aged from 30 to 34 years in the EU obtain a tertiary degree or the equivalent (European Commission 2010). Countries can set their own targets in their national reform programs. Already in 2013, the United Kingdom had a share of 47.6 per cent and no national target, Denmark 43.4 per cent and a target of 40 per cent and Poland 40.5 per cent and a target of 45 per cent (Eurostat 2014). Germany had 33.1 per cent of persons with a tertiary degree (ISCED 5) and also boasts an extensive vocational training system (ISCED 4), which explains why the national target is 42 per cent, including ISCED 4. Italy trails far behind with a meagre 22.4 per cent actual rate and a target of 26–27 per cent.

The transition from education to work is an important life event and a litmus test of social investments. However, the crisis from 2008 onwards had a dramatic impact on youths becoming more excluded from society, and the cohorts that entered the labour market in the last few years are likely to become a "lost generation". Improvements started in Germany in 2011, but only later and to a lesser extent in the other four countries. In 2013 the youth unemployment rate for persons from 15 to 29 years was ranging from 4.6 per cent in Germany to 8.1 per cent in Denmark, to 10.0 per cent in Poland, 10.1 per cent in the United Kingdom and 12.4 per cent in Italy (Eurostat 2014). Youth long-term unemployment rates capture whether persons are brought off track in their life course. In 2013 the share of persons from 15 to 29 years with more than 12 months of unemployment stood at 1.5 per cent in Denmark, 1.9 per cent in Germany, 4.5 per cent in the United Kingdom, 6.8 per cent in Poland and 15.9 per cent in Italy (Eurostat 2014).

From a social investment perspective it is good to know if youths make returns on investments and if they are achieving further skills and competences. In 2013 the share of youths aged 15–29 years that were not in employment or training was 7.5 per cent in Denmark, 8.7 per cent in Germany, 14.7 per cent in the United Kingdom, 16.2 per cent in Poland and a staggering 26.0 per cent in Italy (Eurostat 2014). In short, almost one in six young Poles and one in four young Italians are currently off track.

Persons of prime age should, according to social investment thinking, ideally work, have babies and live active, independent and healthy lives. These aspects are interrelated: employment and good quality work are important not only for tax revenues and the sustainability of the welfare state but also for an individual's own well-being and health, parental investments in offspring and children's life chances. Health risks and precarious jobs and unemployment, especially long-term unemployment, are interrelated (Marmot et al. 2012).

Unemployment, economic insecurity and poverty negatively affect parental capacity as well as child well-being and later performance. Studies based on national longitudinal data have shown that the more severe, the longer and the earlier poverty occurs in the life of the child, the worse are the effects on school performance and adolescent well-being (Brooks-Gunn and Duncan 1997). Social protection, active labour market policies and lifelong learning that act to prevent adults from getting caught in a situation of no work or low income thus have a higher element of social investment than schemes in which these elements are in the background.

Social protection and other schemes ameliorating the impact of illness, loss of a job and other adverse life events reduce some of the associated anxieties. Social protection also makes adults take more risks such as changing jobs. Certain active labour market policies and lifelong learning help people out and in work to maintain existing skills and acquire new skills (Bonoli 2012).

For the overall assessment of social investment returns, the employment rate is an important benchmark. The EU has a 2020 headline target of 75 per cent employment of persons aged 20–64 years (European Commission 2010). The target is not differentiated according to age or gender, as was the case before the EU2020 strategy. Also countries can set their own targets. Hence, Denmark, with an employment rate of 75.6 per cent in 2013, has not reached its own goal of 80 per cent (Eurostat 2014). With a rate of 77.1 per cent, Germany just achieved its goal of 77 per cent. The United Kingdom has a rate of 74.9 per cent and has not set its own target. With rates of 59.8 per cent in Italy and 64.9 per cent in Poland, both countries are far from meeting their own targets of 67 per cent and 71 per cent, respectively.

All countries have problems with the employment of the older part of the prime aged. In 2013 the employment rate of persons from 55 to 64 years varied from 40.6 per cent in Poland and 42.7 in Italy to over 59.8 per cent in the United Kingdom and 61.7 per cent in Denmark to 63.7 per cent in Germany (Eurostat 2014). "Active aging" has become the catch phrase for social investment type policies for the elderly.

Active aging aims to move the transition from work to retirement to later in people's lives and to boost active, independent and healthy living and thus increase well-being and reduce care needs. Pension reforms raised retirement ages in all of the countries, but the real social investment approach is done in earlier stages. Early preventive measures can delay the onset of age-related mental and physical disabilities (Marmot et al. 2012). Early detection and quality care can help prevent or delay the development of chronic disease and minimise their consequences (WHO 2012).

# Social Investments from a Gender Perspective

Individuals have diverse life trajectories. However, the paths through life are not random. Family, education, work, health and social relations vary systematically by age, gender, migrant status, social class of origin and other socio-economic aspects. We use gender as an example of how social investment can help update the European welfare states.

Let us examine the issues at stake through a very simple, narrow and stylistic illustration of men's and women's net contributions to the public exchequer over their life course. Figure 3.3 shows that women consume more and contribute less to the public economy than men in strict economic terms. In the real world, gender differences depend on the socio-economic profile of the given groups, the sector of the labour market and the economic cycles, just to mention a few important dimensions.

Obviously the main focus of prenatal social investments should target pregnant women (see Area I in Fig. 3.3). That said, attention may also take into account the wider social and cultural context in which pregnancy takes place. Family interventions may be an idea, if the partner is present.

Early childhood education and childcare as well as primary schools are key institutions in secondary socialization. Primary socialization in families is more likely to conserve existing stereotypes. Hence, childcare and institutions can help combat stereotypes, if any, about gender roles (see Area II in Fig. 3.3). Being in childcare or schools is, of course, not a guarantee against gender stereotypes. For example, no countries provide gender-balanced provisions of childcare. There are simply very few male early years teachers and childcare givers. Even if the goal is not to achieve parity between men and women, there is still a very long way to go. Denmark is closest in the EU with 8 per cent of childcare givers being men (European Commission 2013d).

Fathers can be supported to invest more in their children through paternity leave schemes and through "daddy quotas" in parental leave schemes that can only be taken by men or otherwise forfeited (Hobson 2002). In 2013 fathers had 2 weeks statutory paternity leave in Denmark, Poland and the United Kingdom, 1 day in Italy and none in Germany

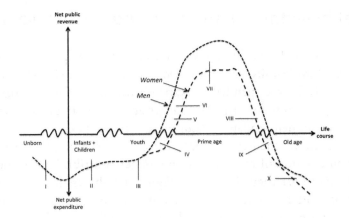

**Fig. 3.3.** Illustration of net revenue to the public sector over the life course

(Moss 2013). Although collective and individual agreements may supplement the statutory schemes, there is still a considerable scope to improve fathers' possibilities to invest time with their children in all countries.

Social investments during adolescence support individual performance in the educational system and general health. The EU2020 strategy operates with a headline target of a maximum 10 per cent of early school leavers (European Commission 2010), with no gender specific targets despite marked gender differences (see III in Fig. 3.3). Poland and Italy have set their own targets at 4.5 per cent and 16 per cent, respectively. Males in all EU countries fare worse than females in education. The rate of male early leavers from the educational system in 2013 was 7.9 per cent in Poland, 9.9 per cent in Denmark, 10.4 per cent in Germany, 13.7 per cent in the United Kingdom and 20.2 per cent in Italy (Eurostat 2014). The rate for females was 3.2 per cent in Poland, 6.2 per cent in Denmark, 9.3 per cent in Germany, 11.2 per cent in the United Kingdom and 13.7 per cent in Italy. Students' capabilities relate not least to early childhood development when the cognitive, social and language skills are established. More can be done in that stage to better prepare and equip children to excel in education. Also, the design of education could better take into account gender and other socio-economic differences.

Gender differences in educational attainment are large (see IV in Fig. 3.3). About half of women aged 30–34 years have tertiary education or the equivalent in Denmark (51.8 per cent), the United Kingdom (50.5 per cent) and Poland (48.4 per cent) in 2013 (Eurostat 2014). In Germany, the figure is 34.0 per cent, while women in Italy rank lowest with 27.2 per cent. Men's share stands at 44.6 per cent in the United Kingdom, 35.2 per cent in Denmark, 32.9 per cent in Poland, 32.2 per cent in Germany and at 17.7 per cent in Italy. The gender gap is biggest in Denmark and Poland and smallest in Germany. Since education is the best insurance against unemployment, ill health and other bad risks, the implication is to not reduce tertiary education for women but rather enable more men to take tertiary education.

Nevertheless, more women than men are side tracked during adolescence and young adulthood. Women have higher rates of Not in Employment, Education or Training (NEET) than men in all countries. The gender gap varies from 1.1 per cent in Denmark, over 3.3 per cent in Italy, 3.9 per cent in Germany and 5.7 per cent in both Poland and the United Kingdom. The area indicated by IV in Figure 3.3 thus covers a complex picture of more women doing better than men in education, but worse in being excluded.

Becoming a parent is a life-turning event that the social investment strategy supports. Policies aim to give the best conditions for good parenting and to prevent parenthood from becoming an obstacle for parent's, especially mother's, labour market participation. Nurseries, childcare and early childhood education enable parents to better reconcile work and family life so that women can have both children and careers (see point V in Fig. 3.3).

The growing number of single parents are particularly vulnerable in so far as there is only one potential income earner and only one person investing in children (mostly the child will be with both parents, just not at the same time). There are far more female single parents than male, and single fathers are, on average, better off in socio-economic terms. From a social investment perspective, the key is to get all parents into good quality work to avoid poverty and thus help boost parental investments in their children. Another goal is to enable parents to use their human capital, as discussed earlier.

Employment activity varies a lot between parents and non-parents and between countries. In Denmark, mothers aged from 25 to 49 years with children below 12 years work 1.6 percentage points more than women of the same age without children. In the other countries, mothers work considerably less than non-mothers: in Italy the difference is 8.6, in Poland 11.6, in the United Kingdom 16.4 and in Germany no less than 18.4 percentage points (European Commission 2013d). For men aged from 25 to 49 years the picture is a mirror image. The employment rate of fathers is considerably higher than for men without children, namely, 6.9 percentage points in Germany, 7.1 in the United Kingdom, 10.4 in Denmark, 10.6 in Poland and 11.4 in Italy (European Commission 2013d).

Availability, affordability and quality of childcare are the major reasons mothers give for not working or working only part-time. In Italy, of women aged 15–64 years with children up to the mandatory school age, 37 per cent report that they do not work or work part-time because childcare is not available, 57 per cent because childcare is too expensive and 5 per cent because the quality is insufficient. In Poland 35 per cent report lack of availability, 57 per cent that childcare is too expensive and 4 per cent that childcare is insufficient. Among British non-working mothers, the childcare availability is mentioned by 10 per cent, insufficient quality by 4 per cent and too expensive by 73 per cent (European Commission 2013d). One in four of similar mothers in Germany say that they do not work because of a lack of childcare and 31 per cent because childcare is too expensive. None of the Danish mothers gave the availability, price or quality of childcare as reasons for not working or working only part-time.

In light of relatively high childcare coverage of European children between 3 years and school age (except in Poland) as previously discussed, having children has a surprising impact on employment. However, the high coverage masks big differences in the number of hours children are in childcare. In Denmark, 87 per cent of children are in care 30 hours or more and 11 per cent are in care for 29 hours or less (European Commission 2013d). In Germany, the figures are 44 per cent and 46 per cent, respectively, and in the United Kingdom, they are 27 per cent and 66 per cent, respectively. In Italy, 17 per cent of children are in childcare more than 30 hours and 9 per cent 29 hours or less. There are no reliable figures for Poland. Low childcare coverage rates and the number of hours help explain the large cross-national differences in female employment rates.

Generally, men have higher employment rates than women (see VI in Fig. 3.3). With a difference of 20 percentage points, Italy has by far the biggest gender gap in employment rate and Denmark the smallest with 5.3 per cent (Eurostat 2014). Reducing employment protection legislation, reconciling work and family policies, training and making the tax system more friendly towards second earners are policies that have proven important to boost female employment (OECD 2012).

Women face both a gender pay gap and a glass ceiling in the labour market (see VII in Fig. 3.3). As existing EU legislation prohibits discrimination on the basis of gender, more measures are required at the national and local level. Ensuring fair returns on individual investments in education and in the labour market are crucial for the social investment strategy as it affects individual's incentives to learn and work as well as the financing of the system.

Employment among the elderly is generally higher and gender gaps smaller in Northern and Western European countries than in Southern and Eastern European countries. The area indicated by VIII in Figure 3.3 thus varies across countries. In 2013 the highest employment rate for persons aged 55–64 years in Germany was 69.8 per cent for men and 57.8 per cent for women, and in Denmark and the United Kingdom, it was 3–4 percentage points lower (Eurostat 2014). However, in Italy the employment rate is only 52.9 per cent for men and 33.1 per cent for women, and in Poland it was slightly lower at 51.3 per cent and 31.0 per cent, respectively. The gender gap is smallest in Denmark at nearly 10 percentage points and largest in Italy and Poland at around 20 percentage points. Women especially have care responsibilities again later in life; this time for frail elderly parents or parents-in-law.

Similar patterns can be found for retirement ages. In 2012 Italy had an official retirement age of 66 years and the other countries of 65 years. However, the effective average retirement age for men varied from 61.1 years in Italy to over 62.1 years in Germany and 62.3 in Poland to 63.4 in Denmark and 63.7 in the United Kingdom (OECD 2014). Similar figures for women were 60.2 years in Poland and 60.5 years in Italy to over 61.6 in Germany and 61.9 in Denmark to 63.2 in the United Kingdom.

The United Kingdom performs better in terms of retaining the elderly in the labour force for a longer time, albeit this may be caused by a multitude of aspects, not all of which are related to pensions and not all of which are positive, enabling factors. For example, difficulties in making ends meet may motivate the elderly to work longer.

Women draw out more than men in very old age (see Point X in Fig. 3.3), which can in part be explained by gender gaps in longevity and health. Women live longer than men but have more years of bad health. In 2012, for EU-28, life expectancy at the age of 65 years was 21.1 years for women and 17.7 years for men of which 12.6 and 9.3, respectively, were not healthy years (Eurostat 2014). Because of gender roles and women living longer than men, there is often no male partner to care for elderly women with care needs who thus have to resort to public schemes.

In turn, the gender gaps in longevity and health status are explained by the different psychosocial stress men and women have in earlier stages of the life course. Women face stress from paid work, balancing burdens of care to different generations and housekeeping (Marmot et al. 2012). Men's health is more influenced by working conditions (*ibid.*).

Many of the gender differences in old age derive from gender differences in the labour market. Women are more likely than men to spend periods working part-time and having career breaks due to caring responsibilities. The resulting gender pay gap can be found in all countries. Labour market inequalities translate into gender gaps in pensions and higher poverty rates of women, indicated by IX in Figure 3.3. Finally, gender stereotypes, for example, that women become old earlier than men, result in less demand for women in certain sectors of the labour market. In turn, all of this translates into women having lower income and consumption than men and thus worse housing quality, worse health conditions and higher social isolation.

According to a life course perspective, social investment measures should be taken at earlier stages to better share care and housework, to establish equal opportunities in the labour market, to live and work in more healthy ways and to alter norms and values in society about gender, care and work.

# Concluding Remarks

Taking the EU social investment strategy as its starting point, this chapter demonstrates how current social investment thinking can benefit from adopting a life course perspective to establish a more coherent framework. The chapter demonstrates five reasons for why the life course perspective is a good framework for a social investment strategy: The perspective allows multi-disciplinarity, is sensitive to social and structural change, addresses population diversity, acknowledges the dynamic and multi-dimensional nature of social issues and of social investments and, finally, has high policy relevance.

Substantively the chapter has three sets of findings. First, the generational perspective brings out that social investments involve horizontal redistribution over the life course through policies that enable the productive and reproductive functions that underpin the generational contract. The chief aims of social investments are thus to form, maintain and use human capital and maximise all people's life chances to get education, work and families.

Second, the life course perspective on social investments shows what policies and returns are characteristic in connection with different life events, life stages and transitions between stages. However, the life course perspective also focuses attention to the dynamic and multi-dimensional nature of social phenomena and social investments: advantages and disadvantages tend to accumulate over time and social investments at one point typically affect later policies and returns. The life course perspective points attention to when which policies may be particularly important in preventing, coping or promoting specific life events, turning points and transitions between life stages.

Third, the life course perspective insists that people's life trajectories are a result of human agency and context, both of which can be influenced by social investments. Using gender to illustrate this point in a cross-national comparison, we found that all European countries need more gender sensitive social investment policies. For example, male adolescents and young adults have greater difficulties than girls and young women in the education trajectory. Women do worse than men in work trajectories. Women live longer but have more years with bad health than men.

Finally, the analysis shows consistent cross-national differences. On almost all dimensions of social investment policies, the northern European countries—Denmark, Germany and the United Kingdom—do better than the Central and Eastern as well as Southern European countries represented, respectively, by Poland and Italy. On almost all dimensions on social investment returns the northern European countries do better than the Central and Eastern as well as Southern European countries (the non-trivial exception is longevity). This indicates a positive relation between social investment policies and returns on the macro-level that mirrors the positive relation found on the micro-level in many of the studies quoted.

Fortunately, social investment policies often kill two birds with one stone. For example, more gender equitable sharing of care may boost fathers' investments in children and reduce statistical discrimination of women in the labour market and the care burden on women. In turn, this may lead to smaller gender gaps in pay and pensions and better health for both genders.

The social investment strategy is fit to cope with many societal challenges. Because social investments can address the increased skill demand, less uniform labour markets and family types, labour supply and health, there is little doubt that all EU countries will look to social investment to guide their welfare reforms.

It is doubtful, however, that all countries can afford and implement all of the necessary institutional reform on the short and medium term to harvest the returns on the longer term. Indeed some of the countries most in need of welfare reforms are worst positioned to undertake reform due to the impact of the recent crisis on these countries (see contributions in this book). The EU social investment strategy is thus not likely to result in the resurrection of one common European Social Model from the ashes of the economic crisis.

# References

Andor, L. (2013). *Commissioner for employment, social affairs and inclusion speech*. In Conference on the Social Investment Package. Leuven, Belgium, 2–3 May.

Barker, D. (1998). *Mothers, babies and health in later life*. Edinburgh: Churchill Livingston.

Barr, N. (2001). *The welfare state as piggy bank: Information, risk, uncertainty, and the role of the state*. Oxford: Oxford University Press.

Barroso, J. M. (2012). President of the European Commission State of the Union 2012 Address Plenary session of the European Parliament. Strasbourg, 12 September.

Becker, G. (1993/1964). *Human capital: A theoretical and empirical analysis, with a special reference to education*. 3rd ed. Chicago, IL: Chicago University Press.

Blossfeld, H. P., & Drobnič S. (Eds.). (2001). *Career couples in contemporary societies*. Oxford: Oxford University Press.

Bonoli, G. (2012). Active labour market policy and social investment. In N. Morel, B. Palier, & J. Palme (Eds.), *Towards a social investment welfare state?* (pp. 181–204). Bristol: Policy Press.

Brooks-Gunn, J., & Duncan, G. J. (1997). Effects of poverty on children. *The Future of Children, 7*(2), 55–71.

Burger, K. (2010). How does early childhood care and education affect cognitive development? An international review of the effects of early interventions for children from different social backgrounds. *Early Childhood Research Quarterly, 25*, 140–165.

Campbell, F., Conti, G., Heckman, J. J., Moon, S. H., Pinto, R., Pungello, E., et al. (2014). Early childhood investments substantially boost adult health. *Science, 343*(March), 1478–1485.

Cantillon, B. (2011). The paradox of the social investment state: Growth, employment and poverty in the Lisbon era. *Journal of European Social Policy, 21*(5), 432–449.

Elder, G. (1999/1974). *Children of the great depression: Social change in life experience*. Chicago, IL: University of Chicago Press.

European Commission. (2010). Europe 2020: A strategy for smart, sustainable and inclusive growth. COM(2010) 2020, 3.3.2010.

European Commission. (2013a). Towards social investment for growth and cohesion. Commission Communication, COM(2013) 83 final, 20.2.2013.

European Commission. (2013b). Investing in children: Breaking the cycle of disadvantage, Commission recommendation, C(2013) 778 final, 20.2.2013.

European Commission. (2013c). Strengthening the social dimension of the Economic and Monetary Union, Commission Communication, COM(2013) 690, 2.10.2013.

European Commission. (2013d). *Barcelona objectives: The development of childcare facilities for young children in Europe with a view to sustainable and inclusive growth*. Brussels: European Commission.

European Commission, EACEA, Eurodyce and Eurostat. (2014). *Key data on early childhood education and care in Europe*. Luxembourg: Publication Office of the European Union.

European Council. (2013). Council conclusions, 24–25 October 2013.

Eurostat. (2014). *Statistics database*. Retrieved July 18, 2014, from epp.eurostat.ec.europa.eu

Frazer, H., & Marlier, E. (2014). *Investing in children. National policies. Synthesis report*. Luxembourg: Publications Office of the European Union.

Hannon, P. (2003). Developmental neuroscience: Implications for early childhood education. *Current Pediatrics, 13*, 58–63.

Havnes, T., & Mogstad, M. (2011). No child left behind: Subsidized child care and children's long-run outcomes. *American Economic Journal: Economic Policy, 3*(2), 97–129.

Heckman, J. (2000). Policies to foster human capital. *Research in Economics, 54*, 3–56.

Heckman, J. (2006). Skill formation and the economics of investing in disadvantaged children. *Science, 312*(5782), 1900–1902.

Heckman, J. (2008). Schools, skills, and synapses. *Economic Inquiry, 46*(3), 289–324.

Hobson, B. (Ed.). (2002). *Making men into fathers: Men, masculinities and the social politics of fatherhood*. Cambridge: Cambridge University Press.

Kersbergen, K. V., & Hemerijk, A. (2012) Two decades of change: The emergence of the social investment state. *Journal of Social Policy, 41*(3), 362–378.

Lee, R., & Mason, A. (Eds.). (2011). *Population aging and the generational economy*. Cheltenham: Edward Elgar.

Lister, R. (2003). Investing in the citizen-workers of the future: Transformations in citizenship and the state under New Labour. *Social Policy & Administration, 37*(5), 427–443.

Marmot, M., Allen, J., Bell, R., Bloomer, E., & Goldbladt, P. (2012). WHO European review of social determinants of health and the health divide. *The Lancet, 380*, 1011–1029.

Morel, N., Palier, B., & Palme, J. (Eds.). (2012). *Towards a social investment welfare state? Ideas, policies and challenges.* Bristol: Policy Press.

Moss, P. (Ed.). (2013). *International review of leave policies and related research 2013.* Retrieved April 20, 2014, from www.leavenetwork.org

Nolan, B. (2013). What use is 'social investment?'. *Journal of European Social Policy, 23*(5), 459–468.

OECD. (2012). *Closing the gender gap.* Paris: OECD.

OECD. (2014). *Average effective retirement ages.* Retrieved July 20, 2014, from www.oecd.org

Pintelon, O., Cantillon, B., den Bosch, K. V., & Whelan, C. T. (2013). The social stratification of social risks: The relevans of class for social investment strategies. *Journal of European Social Policy, 23*(1), 52–67.

Rowntree, S. (1901). *Poverty. A study of town life.* London: Thomas Nelson and Sons.

Sen, A. (1985). *Commodities and capabilities.* Amsterdam: Elsevier.

WHO. (2012). *Good health adds life to years.* Geneva: WHO.

# 4

# 'Pushing Against an Open Door': Reinforcing the Neo-liberal Policy Paradigm in Ireland and the Impact of EU Intrusion

Fiona Dukelow

## Introduction

Regardless of the diversity of explanations for how economic and social policy change occurs, during the early phases of the financial crisis there seemed to be a general expectation that change would occur. In particular, many predicted a turn away from faith in free markets and market competition (Peter Hall in Edsall 2008; Stiglitz 2011). Momentarily, it appeared that such expectations were being confirmed by 'an emergency reconversion' (Hemerijck 2012, p. 55) to Keynesianism. However, this opening in which Keynesianism regained some legitimacy and the balance between states and markets seemed to alter was short-lived. The ascendancy of austerity politics and policy marked the 'strange non-death of neoliberalism' (Crouch 2011), as the locus of the crisis, particularly in the Eurozone, was shifted from the problems of financialised capitalism to the fiscal problems of (some) welfare states. What began as a crisis for the financialised neo-liberal growth model became as much a crisis

F. Dukelow (✉)
School of Applied Social Studies, University College Cork, Cork, Ireland

© The Author(s) 2016
C. de la Porte, E. Heins (eds.), *The Sovereign Debt Crisis, the EU and Welfare State Reform*, DOI 10.1057/978-1-137-58179-2_4

for alternative paradigms, and focus has shifted from the strangeness of neo-liberalism's survival to exploring the reasons why it has survived (Peck et al. 2012; Schmidt and Thatcher 2013).

Ireland quickly became a source of support for rival paradigms in the austerity versus stimulus debate. Crucially, within the EU it was conferred exemplary status in policy responses that rested on a debt-based diagnosis of the countries in crisis and the necessity of fiscal consolidation. In 2010, Jean-Claude Trichet, then president of the European Central Bank (ECB), declared that 'Greece has a role model, and the role model is Ireland' (Trichet, 2010). Under the Programme for Financial Support, Ireland's adherence to fiscal targets and its (fragile) return to growth has been discursively deployed to affirm the design of the financial assistance model. According to the President of the European Commission, José Manuel Barroso (cited in Mackintosh 2013), the Irish case 'shows that the programmes can work. ... When there's a determination we can achieve results. This is a message that's valid for Ireland and other countries that are going through reforms'. Furthermore, Ireland is upheld as confirmation of the neo-classical economics idea of 'growth friendly fiscal consolidation'. This has been promoted by EU economic actors, such as the Directorate General for Economic and Financial Affairs (DG ECFIN 2012a), and promulgates the view that public expenditure cuts and limited tax increases attract positive market sentiment and enhance private sector investment and economic growth.

As the only liberal market economy in the Euro Area (Hay et al. 2008), Ireland's initial problems were symptomatic of the crisis-prone tendencies of its increasingly financialised and neo-liberalised growth model. Its property asset bubble was also facilitated by the structure of the EMU and macroeconomic imbalances across the Eurozone. In its early reaction to banking problems, the Irish government announced a near blanket guarantee of Irish banking liabilities in September 2008. This mirrored other nationally based responses to banking troubles within Europe at this time; however, no other country implemented as broad a guarantee (Dukelow 2015). Moreover, while fiscal stimulus was still the common mode of response across the Eurozone until early 2010, in Ireland, austerity was well advanced. When a loan was agreed with the EU/ECB/IMF in late 2010, the transition was clearly not the case of a recalcitrant state unwilling or unable to impose austerity. Austerity measures of 9 per cent of gross domestic product (GDP) were implemented between 2008 and 2010, and the loan agreement entailed adjustments of another 9 per cent of GDP between 2011 and 2014. Actions regarding fiscal consolidation and structural reforms contained in the Memorandum of Understanding (MoU) and the underlying ideas regarding budgetary discipline, market credibility and competitiveness, which were inspired by the dominance of German ordoliberalism in the EU's response to the Eurozone crisis (Schmidt and Woll 2013), reinforced and ramped up the thrust of many existing Irish policy objectives and changes already undertaken or planned. A close fit therefore prevailed between the dominant domestic policy paradigm and the paradigm underpinning the EU response to the Eurozone crisis. Consequently in the face of intrusive EU integration, particularly on the dimensions of surveillance and enforcement (de la Porte and Heins, Chapter 2), Irish political elites, notwithstanding some tensions and differences, responded, as the DG ECFIN (2012b, p. 3) observed, with a 'commitment to do "whatever it takes"' to reduce its deficit.

This chapter proceeds as follows. Drawing on the work of Hall (1993) and related authors, policy paradigms and ways in which they change are considered before reviewing developments in the Irish welfare state and the nature of Irish neoliberalism before the crisis. The construction and contestation of austerity among domestic policy actors in the early stages of the crisis are examined along with how the austerity imperative set out a path of retrenchment and reform, leading to an 'open door' with respect to increased EU intrusion. Particular focus rests on the nature and dynamics of first and second order changes to taxation and social protection policy and their role in the mutual reinforcement of the dominant policy paradigm by domestic and EU actors.

## Policy Paradigm Change, Ideas and Power

Although Hall's (1993) account of policy paradigms is perhaps more widely known for wholesale paradigm shift, revisiting the essay in light of how responses to the financial crisis have unfolded shows that it can also alert us to the quality of shifts within a dominant paradigm. Hall (1993,

p. 279) defines a policy paradigm as 'a framework of ideas and standards that specifies not only the goals of policy and the kind of instruments that can be used to attain them, but also the very nature of the problems they are meant to be addressing'. He delineates between three orders of paradigm change in the policy-making process and the components of policy involved at each level. First order paradigm change is typically associated with altering policy settings, such as the rate at which a benefit is paid, while second order paradigm change involves altering policy instruments, such as a particular kind of benefit or programme. Even if a great degree of change takes place at both of these levels, the paradigm will not break if the types of change 'preserve the broad continuities usually found in patterns of policy' (ibid.). In contrast, third order policy paradigm shift entails 'simultaneous changes in all three components of policy: the instrument settings, the instruments themselves, and the hierarchy of goals behind policy' (ibid.), thus breaking the hold of the existing paradigm.

Although located within historical institutionalism (Steinmo 2008), Hall's examination of the role of ideas in paradigm shifts also connects with the broader ideational turn in institutionalist accounts of politics and policymaking. Combining insights of historical and ideational or discursive institutionalism (Hay 2001; Schmidt 2010) helps balance the typical institutions-as-constraint view of historical institutionalism with the more dynamic orientation of a focus on ideas or discourse. Béland (2009, p. 703), for example, draws attention to how historical institutionalism, because of its focus on how institutions structure action, 'says relatively little about agenda-setting and the construction of the problems and issues policy actors seeks to address'. Moreover, when an outside shock upsets the coherence of institutional rules, the focus on ideas overcomes the historical institutionalist tendency to identify change in radical terms or in radical times only. Looking at change in this way might attune us only to third order paradigm change and to expect it to come from outside the paradigm. Focusing on the processes of ideational change at first and second order levels allows a more nuanced understanding both of change and of how shocks such as economic crises, which can also emanate from within a policy paradigm as in the case of the Irish crisis, are dealt with in an adaptive way within a paradigm. A paradigm can thus be 'stretched', sometimes in contradictory ways, by policy changes at first and second order levels, and third order change is not necessarily triggered. As detailed later, Ireland's response to the crisis encompassed first and second order policy changes. These were designed with the intention of aligning economic and, especially, social policy more closely with the goals of its policy paradigm based on the premise that social policy in particular veered off course in the years preceding the crisis.

In addition, rather than singularly drawing on Hall's account of how paradigms change at these levels, situating Hall's work alongside recent accounts of the role of ideas in the 'powering' of paradigms helps understand both the reinforcement of neo-liberalism in Ireland and the receptiveness to increased EU intrusion. Hall utilised Heclo's (1974) study of social policymaking as a matter of 'puzzling' and 'powering'. While Hall (1993) argued against 'a rigid distinction between powerbased and ideas-based models of politics' (p. 289), he emphasised the dynamics of puzzle-based paradigm change. Hall therefore placed significance in events that present as anomalies within the existing paradigm, which thereby becomes less consistent with reality. This may eventually lead to a loss of the paradigm's credibility and 'a shift in the locus of authority over policy' (ibid., p. 291), empowering a rival paradigm. More recent ideational approaches emphasise the social construction of economic and social policy problems and the ways in which policy change is driven not so much by puzzling over anomalies as by powering over how problems are constructed and how imperatives to change are framed (Cox 2001; Blyth 2013). Therefore, the success or otherwise of policy paradigms is not a matter of their degree of correspondence with economic and social realities but how they manage to frame a situation and what needs, in turn, to be reformed. This turns our attention to the relationship between power and ideas (Béland 2005) and entails an approach that is situated between historical institutionalism's more 'rationalistic' (ibid., p. 5) view of policy change and an overly constructivist account. Therefore, just as much as paying attention to discursive interaction is an exercise in observing how actors are trying to wield power through the ideas they use, it is equally important to attend to the relative positions of, and inequalities between, actors in terms of their ability to wield power. Existing institutional rules and norms can shape unequal power relations and empower or weaken the ideas and arguments of various groups of actors depending on how close they are to the dominant paradigm. This is an important point to be explored in the Irish context with respect to the weak position of domestic actors who opposed austerity. Moreover, in the case of EU actors, in particular DG ECFIN, the closeness between their ideas and the dominant domestic paradigm meant a relatively smooth transition from nationally driven efforts at deficit reduction to those taken under heightened external intrusion and ultimately the achievement of EU actor's powering over puzzling in promulgating the pertinence of growth-friendly fiscal consolidation.

## Economic and Social Policy Paradigms in Irish Welfare State Development

Ireland related unevenly to the post-World War II period of welfare expansion underpinned by a Keynesian paradigm. In the 1950s Irish economic policy underwent a significant paradigm shift after failure to achieve economic progress under a period of autarkic development. Ireland was re-conceived as a small state in a global world, dependent on external wealth and economic participation for its own prosperity. The state removed protectionist obstacles and committed to attracting foreign direct investment with a range of fiscal instruments. This stance, in which the state intervenes in the market and creates institutional settings conducive to international trade and investment, has had an enduring policy legacy, particularly in terms of the evolution of neo-liberalism in the Irish context. This policy departure did not extend to developing the welfare state to the same degree. The dominant belief was that economic growth would solve the pressing problems of unemployment and comparatively poor living standards. The Keynesian view that the welfare state would benefit the economy was not part of political thinking. A later brief 'social democratic turn' (Bew et al. 1989) saw the expansion of social services, but the policy paradigm informing the welfare state did not shift from poverty alleviation and relatively modest redistribution to something more egalitarian.

The international rise of neo-liberalism also meshed with local conditions in particular ways. A deep economic crisis during the 1980s, for example, saw a turn to social partnership by 1987. It enabled agreement around modest pay increases in return for taxation reductions, providing a non-conflictual route out of the crisis. Major economic growth followed in the 1990s as social partnership coincided with a number of other positive trends, including the creation of the single market at which point Ireland became an attractive investment site for non-European companies looking to trade in the EU. Within Ireland the imperative of cost competitiveness became more frequently articulated in political and policy discourse (Dukelow 2005). Greater emphasis was also placed on tax competition and light touch regulation. These imperatives were not accompanied by a particularly zealous or explicit articulation of neo-liberal ideology; neo-liberalism in Ireland presents itself as 'concealed, piecemeal, serendipitous, pragmatic, and consensual' (Kitchin et al. 2012, p. 1306) in a political system dominated by two conservative right-of-centre parties, Fianna Fáil and Fine Gael.

Unprecedented high growth rates meant that the state did not suffer from lack of revenue, and low unemployment rates meant that its most pressing problem in historical terms had abated. In these conditions, expansionary, drift-based change (Streeck and Thelen 2005) occurred in social protection, never contradicting the overall perception of economic policy and its goal of maintaining a competitive low-tax model. The notion of prudent economic management also prevailed, and with the exception of breaching Stability and Growth Pact (SGP) rules in 2001, Irish budgetary strategy appeared, as Scharpf (2013, p. 125) notes, a model of 'fiscal probity'. Real spending grew but declined as a proportion of the more rapidly growing GDP maintaining the pattern of below-average expenditure within the EU (an average of 18.6 per cent of GDP spent on social protection over the 2000s compared with an EU17 average of 27.6 per cent). Social protection rates were improved, new programmes were added and commitments were made to reduce poverty in reaction to both domestic pressure and EU social policy developments, but the overall goals of the welfare state were unchanged and poverty levels remained high. The Joint Report on Social Protection and Social Inclusion (DG EMPL 2007, p. 220) observed, for example, that while economic growth masked 'very significant investment in welfare benefits … the underlying high proportion at risk of poverty also reflects the structure of the Irish welfare system (based on flat-rate benefits) and points to a continued level of inequality in Irish society which must be a matter for concern'. Moreover, revenues from the booming economy covered expenditure increases while simultaneously allowing successive governments to reduce income, capital gains and corporate taxes and social insurance contribution rates and to enhance tax expenditures. Ireland thus maintained one of the lowest levels of revenue from tax and social contributions in the EU during the 2000s (31.3 per cent of GDP compared with an EU17 average of 41 per cent).

## Framing the Economic Crisis: The Influence of the Existing Paradigm

During the early stages of the crisis the existing economic policy paradigm, evident in the way third order policy goals and policy problems were debated, served to make sense of the economic instability. What were perceived as external problems were met with confidence in Ireland's growth model by the Minister for Finance, Lenihan (2008a): "[O]ur markets are flexible allowing us to respond quickly to difficulties; we have a dynamic and well-educated labour force; and the tax burden on workers and businesses is low. Not many countries anywhere in the world are facing the present global economic difficulties from such an enviable position."A new economic policy, Building Ireland's Smart Economy: A Framework for Sustainable Economic Renewal (Government of Ireland 2008), echoed these convictions. It was concerned with how to put the Irish economy in 'pole position' (ibid., p. 32) once the international downturn had passed. This meant applying the existing 'successful formula' to secure Ireland's position as 'a positive fiscal environment and a pro-business culture which secures it as a destination of choice for FDI and as a magnet for innovators and entrepreneurs' (ibid., p. 38).

By 2009 it was clear that Ireland's economic position was rapidly deteriorating. Emerging analyses and critique pointed to poor domestic policy choices such as procyclical fiscal policies and light touch regulation. This critique grew to include government handling of the banking crisis. The cost of the banking crisis significantly increased sovereign debt (adding 26 percentage points of GDP between 2007 and 2011 compared with a Euro Area average of 1.2; Weymes 2012) and ultimately led to the EU/IMF loan. However, such critique, articulated in particular by increasingly prominent economists and economic commentators, did not extend to questioning Ireland's overall economic model; blame focused on the incompetence of state actors and institutions rather than on market failures.

Government response to such criticism also displayed continued conviction in the economic model, which dictated the nature of the problems addressed, namely, that particular policy choices during the boom meant Ireland veered from the fundamentals of its growth model. The crisis was thus framed around three core problems: excessive growth in public expenditure, a related loss of competitiveness and loss of reputation. The Taoiseach (head of government) Cowen (2010) suggested, for example, that 'we ... badly overshot the mark. ... The general attitude was that we could afford to ramp up spending, while simultaneously being a low tax country, as if there were few hard choices to be made'. Although involving 'hard choices', this problem diagnosis was consistent with the goals of the existing economic paradigm; the problem was that expenditure policy was not fully compliant with them. The problem of a reputational crisis was articulated to convey the damage that both the banks and the debt crisis was doing to Ireland's image as a stable, competitive place to come and do business. Preserving financial market and investor confidence in the Irish economic model became a core part of the justification for deep austerity and for saving the banking system by whatever means and cost necessary. Saving the banks severely stretched and contradicted the notion of sound public finances yet was accommodated under the paradigm's overarching goals.

The response of economic actors, including employer organisations, displayed a great deal of similarity with the ideas of the political elite and their cognitive style of argumentation. The same faith in, and need for, renewal of the economic model was evident: 'Ireland must recreate its attractiveness for foreign investment. As a tiny trading nation this is the only way to survive' (McCoy 2008, p. 14). In diagnosing causes, similar emphasis was placed on the fiscal crisis being driven by 'unsustainable growth in current expenditure' (IBEC 2010, p. 14). Business leader commentary on banking problems, albeit rare, closely mirrored mainstream political arguments and concepts. The idea that the banking crisis was 'manageable' and the banking guarantee the right thing to do was evident in approval of state support for the banks: "Despite the huge public resources required, definitively addressing the banking crisis was always going to be necessary, though painful. The wider economy will remain in the doldrums without a vibrant, competitive banking sector" (McCoy 2010, p. 16). Contrasting with the shared interpretive framework of the government and mainstream economic actors, trade union leaders made the case for a major paradigm shift and employed both normative and cognitive arguments. The idea of the injustices and inequality caused by a 'redundant economic model' (Sweeney 2009) was fused with the idea that the crisis also proved the flawed logic of neo-liberalism. The latter point was made by arguing that the crisis revealed that 'privatised, deregulated and ultra-free markets' did not work and by highlighting the contradictions of the model in the way the state rescued the banks. A paradigm shift involving a 'fundamental realignment of our economy and society' (ibid.) was called for. The policy goals outlined therefore went against the grain of the dominant discourse. In reaction to Building Ireland's Smart Economy, the Irish Congress of Trade Unions (ICTU) thus argued that

> an agreement geared towards a relatively short period of recession followed by a bounce back to the high growth rates of recent years is not what is required. ... [S]ome kind of Social Solidarity Pact is required. ... It should be capable of being a bridge to a future that is more sustainable than the model upon which we relied for the last thirty years. (ICTU 2009, p. 7, original emphasis)

Challenging the dominant model also entailed challenging the detail of the problems identified by the dominant discourse. In rebutting the idea that the fiscal crisis was caused by excessive expenditure, the unstable, low tax model was highlighted as a cause of the problem with the public finances. However, this problem diagnosis held little sway in subsequent policy responses.

# Constructing and Contesting Austerity

The preservation of the dominant policy paradigm at third order level in how the problems posed by the crisis were framed followed through in how austerity was proposed and defended. Although some flexibility was initially acknowledged, austerity was asserted as the only sound policy option:

> While the strength of the economy in the past decade has given us some room for manoeuvre, we cannot put our reputation for fiscal responsibility in jeopardy. … A soft option of ignoring the budgetary challenge … would have grave consequences for the future of this country. … We must continue on a path of bringing spending into line with resources. There is no option. (Lenihan 2008b)

Dismissed as 'soft options', taxation and borrowing were both ruled out. Justifications for retrenchment also became tied to constraints imposed by rising borrowing costs as financial markets reacted to the growing scale of banking turned sovereign debt. Ultimately, retrenchment was tied to the underlying principle of 'sound public finances' (Government of Ireland 2010, p. 21), outlined as the 'clearest and most direct responsibility' (ibid.) of government in its relationship with the economy. Such reasoning did not differ among mainstream economic commentators and business leaders who promoted similar orthodoxies as to why austerity was necessary, why it had to be 'frontloaded', why it had to be deepened to respond to the worsening crisis and why expenditure cuts were preferable to tax increases.

Against this wave of debate on the necessity of austerity with contest largely circumscribed by questions of composition, scale and speed, trade union leaders and others on the left argued for a radically different set of policy instruments involving fiscal stimulus. Opposing the idea of 'no option' (Lenihan 2008b), the ICTU (2009, p. 39) argued that Ireland's low debt status during the early stages of the crisis meant that further borrowing to stimulate the economy was not the 'insurmountable problem' others claimed. As financial markets turned against Ireland, sovereign wealth funds were identified as alternative investment sources.

These arguments for economic stimulus were made in tandem with proposing that the SGP target of a 3 per cent deficit ceiling, initially set for 2013 under the EU EDP instigated in 2009, be extended to 2017. The rightness of a Keynesian strategy was contrasted with the 'nonsensical' neo-liberal response of trying to address debt by deflating the economy.

The limited impact and weak power base underpinning these ideas were not unrelated to the disintegration of the social partnership process. Attempts in early 2009 at negotiations to maintain a social partnership, which acknowledged union ideas in a framework for a pact for stabilisation, social solidarity and economic renewal (Department of the Taoiseach 2009), diverged significantly from the actual budgetary decisions taken. These included reductions in public sector pay and other retrenchment measures. Continued participation in social partnership, if it meant agreeing to retrenchment, placed the ICTU in a difficult position. Further attempts at negotiating a recovery plan fell through in December with a disagreement over how public sector cuts would be pursued in Budget 2010. The unravelling of partnership demonstrated the weakness of the union side being unable to bring its paradigm to power, and its limited institutional embedding in a polity also wedded to global neo-liberalist ideas (McDonough and Dundon 2010). The breakdown of social partnership combined with the congruence between the government's budgetary decisions and advocates of austerity further shifted the power balance from the unions to those who argued for austerity.

Evidence disconfirming the claims made for an austerity approach, including the absence of a return to growth, rising interest rates for sovereign debt and a fiscal deficit that was not shrinking, was not so much the source of puzzlement as proof that austerity efforts were not deep enough. By late 2010 this powering over puzzling at the domestic level was bolstered by the increased powering or coercion of the EU in imposing further austerity under the MoU. Thus, a €4 billion adjustment in Budget 2010, when it was claimed that it was 'the last big push' (Lenihan 2009), was followed by a €6 billion adjustment in Budget 2011, the first budget under EU/IMF conditionality. The Fianna Fáil/Green government in power since 2007 suffered enormous losses in the general election of spring 2011. However, its replacement with a Fine Gael/Labour coalition did not signal a different approach. In opposition, Fine Gael was highly critical of the role Fianna Fáil played in creating the crisis but did not adopt an anti-austerity position. Fine Gael's Programme for Government with Labour committed to re-negotiate the 'affordability' of the loan agreement and bore the influence of Labour in references to equality and solidarity. Overall, however, the Programme for Government affirmed the new government's support of the objectives of the MoU. By the time of the DG ECFIN's (2011) review visit in April 2011, it reported that the new government had taken 'strong ownership of the goals of the EU-IMF programme' (p. 3).

The MoU allowed for some flexibility 'in exceptional circumstances' on choice of budgetary measures that would yield 'comparable savings' (European Commission 2010, p. 1). However, yearly deficit reduction targets designed to see Ireland exiting the corrective arm of the EDP by 2015 remained at non-negotiable conditions. This led to some government revisions in relation to employment (job stimulus measures) and labour market regulation (reversing a cut in the minimum wage in return for greater flexibilities in other areas of wage regulation). A deeper adjustment in Budget 2012 than originally agreed (€3.8 billion instead of €3.6 billion) was pursued to meet the relevant deficit ceiling, and overall fiscal targets were met, as the DG ECFIN (2013, p. 45) notes, 'with ample margin'. For Budget 2014 the government negotiated a lower adjustment figure (€2.5 billion instead of €3.1 billion); however, this was still projected to reach a lower deficit ceiling than agreed in the MoU for 2014. Successive reviews by the IMF and DG ECFIN commented on the government's 'steadfast' commitment to meeting its obligations. At the same time, the necessity of complying with the MoU conditions, even in the face of disconfirming trends such as repeatedly downgraded economic forecasts and the growing problem of long-term unemployment, were emphasised: 'Resolute fiscal consolidation and implementation of the structural reform plans are essential to dispel doubts about debt sustainability and mitigate remaining risks. … Ireland's debt is sustainable, even under adverse scenarios, as long as the programme is fully implemented' (DG ECFIN 2011, p. 3). Therefore, not unlike the Irish governments' response to the lack of evidence for austerity's desired effect, a similar pattern of powering rather than puzzling over anomalies between the policy paradigm and policy outcomes was evident in the DG ECFIN's message about adhering to MoU conditions.

The concept of 'debt sustainability' also circumscribed both EU flexibility and Fine Gael/Labour's efforts to re-negotiate the costs of financial support. Against what were seen as more onerous terms imposed by the EU than the IMF in the original agreement, and ECB pressure in particular (Burke 2011), re-negotiations eased the re-payment of EU loans through lower interest rates and longer re-payment terms. Some banking debt was also restructured with longer-term loans. However, contrary to campaigns by civil society groups and politicians on the left, besides Labour who challenged the re-payment of banking debt, government aims were more modestly targeted at easing the cost of debt. This approach was seen as important to economic recovery and the maintenance of market confidence. It was also key to the government's aspiration of rebuilding Ireland's 'reputation as a reliable partner in Europe' (Gilmore 2013, p. 14), as the idea of lost reputation was extended to Ireland's status within the EU. By contrast Irish trade union criticism of EU institutions was more forthcoming, portraying the EU and ECB as 'driven by an absolute conviction about austerity' in contrast to the IMF, seen as 'a much more accommodating partner' (Begg 2013, p. 4).

## Austerity and Taxation Policy

The policy goal of maintaining a competitive low tax regime had significant influence on how changes to the taxation system were pursued and justified. Tax receipts fell from €47.2 billion in 2007 to €31.6 billion in 2010, and despite expressions of the reluctance to raise taxes, austerity measures were composed of approximately one-third tax increases and two-thirds expenditure cuts. Increasing tax revenue by changing rates and rules to existing taxes and by introducing new taxes conform to first and second order adaptations to Ireland's low tax model, and this approach remained consistent pre- and post-EU/IMF intervention. Changes were made that increased income, capital, inheritance and consumption taxes as well as social insurance contributions, and some tax expenditures were restricted. However, a property tax and a water charge, introduced in 2013 and 2014, respectively, were specific conditions contained in the MoU not previously seriously countenanced but were justified in the overall philosophy of broadening the tax base and keeping rates low in agreement with the notion of growth friendly fiscal consolidation. Ireland's 12.5 per cent corporate tax rate is, after Bulgaria's and Cyprus's 10 per cent rate, the lowest in the EU, and mention of it was noticeably absent in the MoU. Defended as 'a powerful expression of our pro-enterprise ethos' (Lenihan 2009), national autonomy in this area was strongly guarded against EU interference, particularly as pressure from larger member states to address the rate grew during loan negotiations and re-negotiations on the basis that it represents unfair competition.

While there was broad agreement with the concept of broadening the base, questions were raised with respect to how the burden has been shared between high and low income earners and between labour, capital and corporate sources. Tax increases fell heavily on income tax in the form of a new 'universal social charge', bringing a substantial group of low earners into the tax net. The tax net was also widened by reducing income tax bands and credits by 10 per cent in the 2011 Budget. Such changes were justified by applying the general concept of broadening the tax base to broadening the income tax base. Arguments that this placed a disproportionate burden of the tax changes on lower earners and counter proposals to introduce a new higher tax rate for higher earners were rejected with the argument that it risked dis-incentivising globally mobile high skilled workers (Cowen 2009). Advocates of progressive tax reform drew attention to the inequities of a vast range of tax expenditures that benefited the wealthy and the relatively low rates on capital taxes. Such arguments 'stretched' the paradigm somewhat. Rates on capital gains and inheritance were increased to 33 per cent from various lower levels, and the value of pension reliefs and other tax expenditures were restricted for high income individuals. Yet, as Collins and Walsh (2011, p. 6) note, the overall cost of tax expenditures remain 'a little-explored policy wilderness'.

Efforts to suggest that Ireland's low corporate tax rate undermined the broader competitiveness and stability of the Irish economy (Community Platform 2011) gained little attention as did a proposal to introduce a temporary levy on corporate tax payers. By contrast, business arguments about the need to increase 'tax offerings' to incentivise investment and maintain Ireland's competitiveness were reflected in decisions taken to introduce new tax expenditures and new employer subsidies, which have been deployed as job stimulus measures, agreed in consultation with the EU/IMF in return for savings elsewhere. A similar pattern is evident in how changes to pay-related social insurance (PRSI) were pursued. The employee contribution ceiling was removed and the income threshold lowered, while standard employer contributions went unchanged.

On the whole, civil society actors' efforts to make the case for a paradigm shift in tax policy so that it would eventually conform with European norms with respect to tax revenue and social expenditure had little political impact and little public support, while the impact of the MoU had the effect of introducing new types of tax but not conditions to reform corporate tax. Projections for 2015, the point at which the deficit is predicted to fall below the 3 per cent SGP ceiling, indicate total revenue of 36.3 per cent of GDP, which would remain below the Euro Area average (46.3 per cent in 2012). In 2013, 13 per cent of revenue was used to service debt (up from 2.8 per cent in 2007), which is calculated to have peaked at 124 per cent of GDP in 2013 (Department of Finance 2014). The nature of the rate and type of tax changes, both adopted and resisted, conform to a mix of first and second level paradigm changes, which has left the paradigm goals and problem diagnoses undisturbed. Competitiveness remained the guiding policy goal, setting restrictions on how much tax can be raised and who it can be raised from. In this way it represents the limit both to very high EU interference and enforcement and to the willingness of Irish political elites to do 'whatever it takes' in setting higher taxes.

## Austerity and Social Protection Policy

In contrast to the efforts to limit changes to taxation and to maintain the policy goal of a competitive, low tax regime, growth in public expenditure was believed to be one of the policy mistakes of veering from that formula. Social protection expenditure was thus the object of deeper domestic re-thinking to align its cost and purpose more closely with Ireland's economic model. This process gained urgency under EU/IMF conditionality, and very high intrusiveness, translating into coercive conditions, is evident, predicated on the belief that a more targeted system of social protection would assist in achieving growth- friendly fiscal consolidation and addressing long-term unemployment. Increased EU surveillance also highlighted the institutional stickiness of Ireland's policy-making culture of drift and procrastination, and reviews recorded concerns with the lack of speed with which reform targets were met, urging that the 'pace/ambition of reforms could be stepped up' (DG ECFIN 2013, p. 46).

Initial changes focused on more rapidly implementable first order changes in the form of payment rate cuts. Comprehensive rate cuts (cumulative average 10 per cent), announced under the mantle of the system's alleged generosity, were implemented in 2010 and 2011, with reductions to all payments except those for older people. Social insurance entitlements were deeply curtailed, particularly in the case of Jobseeker's Benefit. In 2009 the number of contributions required was doubled, and by 2013 the maximum claiming period was reduced from 15 to 6–9 months. Arguments that refuted the idea of the generosity, which made comparisons with rates across the EU and not just the government's comparison to the United Kingdom and with the risk of poverty rate (EAPN Ireland 2011), made little headway. In public discourse, political reference to generosity generated enormous debate about the cost of the social protection, sidelining the social purposes of the system and its role with respect to poverty.

Ideas about generosity fused with ideas about the dis-incentive effects of social protection, contributing to an individualised, voluntarist narrative about unemployment. The unemployment rate rose from 4.5 per cent in 2007 to a peak of 14.7 per cent in 2012, and long-term unemployment also became a significant problem, with 60 per cent of those unemployed being unemployed for more than 1 year and 30 per cent for 2 years (IMF 2013). Dis-incentive concerns focused on arguments about high replacement rates and an overly passive social protection system that had not kept pace with activation developments elsewhere (Department of Finance 2009; Department of Social Protection 2010). Consequently, deep rate cuts were applied to young people in receipt of Jobseeker's Allowance and Supplementary Welfare Allowance in 2010 (51 per cent for those aged 18–21 years, 30 per cent for those aged 22–24 years) to incentivise training and employment, while all others who refuse employment or activation faced sanctions of a 30 per cent reduction in payment.

While not specifically mentioned in the initial MoU, successive updates specified the need to 'better target social support to those on lower incomes, and ensure that work pays for welfare recipients' (European Commission 2011, p. 13). Thus, initial rate cuts and ideas circulating in domestic debate led to much deeper and unprecedented rapid structural reform under the coercive conditions of the MoU. Puzzling about the cost of social protection and the related rise in unemployment was thus heavily circumscribed by imposing solutions that conformed to the idea of growth-friendly fiscal consolidation. Both DG ECFIN and IMF reviews increasingly drew attention to what were considered inefficient and outdated design features of the social protection system including its flat structure, the unlimited duration of assistance payments and the rarity of sanctions for the unemployed and 'a host of universally provided benefits linked to age' (DG ECFIN 2012c, p. 26). Comparatively, greater emphasis was placed on reforming what was problematised as a weak system of activation with insufficient conditionality, cited as one of the reasons for Ireland's growing problem of long-term unemployment (DG ECFIN 2012c). Conditions were ramped up in MoU updates, including more effective monitoring of both the unemployed and the performance of the activation system.

Two areas in particular illustrate the comparatively greater mutually reinforcing effect, in contrast with taxation policy, between Ireland's efforts to reform its social protection system and the impact of increased EU intrusion. The first relates to the application of sanctions. As the rarity of sanctions and their lack of enforcement came to light under external surveillance, later MoU updates included the condition that the Department of Social Protection would 'ensure appropriate incentives through the implementation of sanctions' (European Commission 2013a, p. 2). In addition to the 30 per cent penalty introduced in 2010, a further sanction of the full suspension of payment for 9 weeks for claimants who continue to refuse engagement was introduced in 2013, along with extending the 51 per cent rate cut to young people up to 24 years of age in 2014. The enforcement of sanctions also increased: in 2013, 3000 sanctions were applied out of a total of 5000 overall since their introduction (Department of Social Protection 2014). The second area relates to more far-reaching second order institutional change through the privatisation of some activation services. This is occurring in the broader context of activation policy developments involving the major re-organisation of the delivery of social protection services to integrate them with employment supports through individualised case management, which includes activation obligations in return for social protection. While MoU conditions instigated these changes in broad terms, the design detail remained within the national domain. In this regard privatisation was first mooted in national policy in 2011, with the United Kingdom and Australia being considered as countries to emulate in terms of an efficient payment-by-results model of private delivery of activation services (Department of Social Protection 2011). As an actual programme condition, the procurement of private providers of activation services was not included in the MoU until 2013 in an effort to accelerate the pace of reform (European Commission 2013b). A programme for private provision of activation services for the long-term unemployed, called JobPath, was eventually put out for tender at the end of 2013.

Overall, Irish social protection policy moved from expansionary drift to a system more tightly aligned to neo-liberalism, evident in the problem diagnosis discourse of national actors and re-inforced by the increased surveillance of IMF and DG ECFIN actors, which exposed what are seen as major weaknesses in the Irish system. Besides first order rate cuts, which were more wholesale in the period of austerity before EU/IMF intervention, the major impact of conditionality was to accelerate and intensify the pace and scope of second order changes to programmes and services. Intrusion pushed Irish policy proposals to a much faster implementation stage than normally seen in the Irish context, even though the quickened pace of reform was still considered slow and the progress of activation reforms remains in the spotlight of European Commission and ECB post-programme surveillance.

## Concluding Remarks

Analysis of the ideas that framed the diagnosis of Ireland's crisis and policy response demonstrated the powering of dominant political actors and economic interests in contrast to the weaker position of advocates of an alternative paradigm and response to the crisis. That domestic balance of interests and ideas was not altered by the increased intrusiveness of EU and IMF policy actors, and the conditions imposed, framed by the notion of growth-friendly fiscal consolidation, did not represent a major departure from the prior ideational framing of the crisis and how to solve it. Analysis of subsequent changes to taxation demonstrates efforts to reinforce the policy goal of a competitive low-tax regime with first and second order policy changes consistent with that policy goal but which place a higher burden on ordinary income earners, while the low corporate tax regime is protected and corporate welfare enhanced in some cases. Deeper change and policy goal re-alignment is evident in social protection policy, with substantial first order changes and, under the influence of increased EU intrusion, deep second order changes, which aim to transform the means of poverty alleviation from relatively ungenerous income support to relatively ungenerous activation.

Under new instruments of economic and financial policy integration, EU surveillance and fiscal conditionality will remain higher than in the pre-crisis period though not as high as during the 2010–2013 period when the Programme for Financial Support was in place. Ireland remains under the corrective arm of the SGP and a post-programme surveillance mechanism as well as the new budgetary surveillance under the Six-Pack and Two-Pack. The 2012 Fiscal Compact means that further debt rule reduction rules will come into effect for Ireland in 2019.

The Fiscal Compact's emphasis on Member States being accountable to medium-term budgetary plans suggests that the EU is in the shadow of a national budgetary setting and, thus, also of social spending. There appears little room in Ireland for expanding social policy in the direction of social investment, or otherwise, in this more tightly controlled future. Moreover, political debate in Ireland since the Programme for Financial Support ended has been dominated by the potential for tax cuts. Notwithstanding the current failure of 'growth-friendly fiscal consolidation' to deliver improved economic and social outcomes, and possible future tensions between increased EU intrusiveness and national policy preferences, for the present, at least, Ireland's neo-liberal policy paradigm remains firmly in place.

# References

Begg, D. (2013, February 22). The implications of the crisis for European integration and democratic legitimacy, address to EU heads of mission. Retrieved June 4, 2014, from http://www.ictu.ie/download/pdf/address_to_ eu_heads_of_mission_db_feb_22_2102.pdf

Béland, D. (2005). Ideas and social policy: An institutionalist perspective. *Social Policy & Administration, 39*(1), 1–18.

Béland, D. (2009). Ideas, institutions, and policy change. *Journal of European Public Policy, 16*(5), 701–718.

Bew, P., Hazelkorn, E., & Patterson, H. (1989). *The dynamics of Irish politics.* London: Lawrence and Wishart.

Blyth, M. (2013). Paradigms and paradox: The politics of economic ideas in two moments of crisis. *Governance, 26*(2), 197–215.

Burke, M. (2011). Who benefits from the crisis in Ireland? *Soundings, 47*(Spring), 130–142.

Collins, M., & Walsh, M. (2011). *Tax expenditures: Revenue and information forgone – The experience of Ireland* (Working Paper No. 1211). Dublin, Ireland: Trinity Economics Papers.

Community Platform. (2011). *Paying our way.* Dublin: Community Platform.

Cowen, B. (2009). Statement on the budget by the Taoiseach Mr. Brian Cowen T.D., Dáil Éireann, Thursday, 10 December 2009, at 11.00 a.m. Retrieved October 20, 2013, from http://www.taoiseach.gov.ie

Cowen, B. (2010). Speech by the Taoiseach, Mr. Brian Cowen TD on the 2011 Budget, Dáil Éireann, Wednesday, 8 December 2010, at 10.45 a.m. Retrieved October 20, 2013, from http://www.taoiseach.gov.ie

Cox, R. (2001). The social construction of an imperative: Why welfare reform happened in Denmark and the Netherlands but not in Germany. *World Politics, 53*(3), 463–498.

Crouch, C. (2011). *The strange non-death of neoliberalism.* Cambridge: Polity Press.

Department of Finance. (2009). *Replacement rates and unemployment.* Dublin: Department of Finance.

Department of Finance. (2014). *Draft Ireland's stability programme update April 2014.* Dublin: Department of Finance.

Department of Social Protection. (2010). *Report on the desirability and feasibility of introducing a single social assistance payment for people of working age.* Dublin: Department of Social Protection.

Department of Social Protection. (2011). *Project plan for the development and implementation of the national employment entitlements service.* Dublin: Department of Social Protection.

Department of Social Protection. (2014). *Annual report 2013.* Dublin: Government of Ireland.

Department of the Taoiseach. (2009). *Framework for a pact for stabilisation, social solidarity and economic renewal.* Dublin: Department of the Taoiseach.

DG ECFIN. (2011). *The economic adjustment programme for Ireland: Spring 2011 review.* Brussels: European Commission.

DG ECFIN. (2012a). *Annual growth survey 2013.* Brussels: European Commission.

DG ECFIN. (2012b). *Economic adjustment programme for Ireland: Winter 2011 review.* Brussels: European Commission.

DG ECFIN. (2012c). *Economic adjustment programme for Ireland: Spring 2012 review.* Brussels: European Commission.

DG ECFIN. (2013). *Economic adjustment programme for Ireland: Autumn 2013 review.* Brussels: European Commission.

DG EMPL. (2007). *Joint report on social protection and social inclusion 2007.* Luxembourg: Office for Official Publications of the European Communities.

Dukelow, F. (2005). A path towards a more 'employment friendly' liberal regime? Globalisation and the Irish social security system. In B. Cantillon & I. Marx (Eds.), *International co-operation in social security: How to cope with globalisation* (pp. 125–154). Antwerp: Intersentia.

Dukelow, F. (2015). State to the rescue: The bank guarantee and Ireland's financialised neo-liberal growth model. In R. Meade & F. Dukelow (Eds.), *Defining events: Power, resistance and identity in twenty-first-century Ireland* (pp. 143–160). Manchester: Manchester University Press.

EAPN Ireland. (2011). *Budget 2012 – Pre-budget submission.* Dublin: EAPN Ireland.

Edsall, T. (2008, October 13). Global economic crisis likely to have profound consequences for US politics, world relations. *Huffington Post.* Retrieved October 20, 2013, from http://www.huffingtonpost.com/2008/10/13/global-economiccrisis-li_n_134393.html

European Commission. (2010, December 30). Ireland memorandum of understanding on specific economic conditionality. Retrieved September 14, 2014, from http://ec.europa.eu/economy_finance/articles/eu_economic_situation/pdf/2010-12-07-mou_en.pdf

European Commission. (2011, July 28). Ireland memorandum of understanding on specific economic conditionality. Second update. Retrieved September 14, 2014, from http://www.finance.gov.ie/sites/default/files/EUimfJul2011.pdf

European Commission. (2013a, June 3). Ireland memorandum of understanding on specific economic conditionality. Ninth update. Retrieved September 14, 2014, from http://www.finance.gov.ie/sites/default/files/moujun2013search.pdf

European Commission. (2013b, April). Ireland memorandum of understanding on specific economic conditionality. Eight update. Retrieved September 14, 2014, from http://www.finance.gov.ie/sites/default/files/mousearch-march2013.pdf

Gilmore, E. (2013, June 28). Our task in EU is to build on what we have achieved. *Irish Times.*

Government of Ireland. (2008). *Building Ireland's smart economy: A framework for sustainable economic renewal.* Dublin: Stationery Office.

Government of Ireland. (2010). *The national plan for recovery 2011–2014.* Dublin: Stationery Office.

Hall, P. (1993). Policy paradigms, social learning and the state: The case of economic policy making in Britain. *Comparative Politics, 25*(3), 275–296.

Hay, C. (2001). The 'crisis' of Keynesianism and the rise of neoliberalism in Britain: An ideational institutionalist approach. In J. Campbell & O. Pedersen (Eds.), *The Rise of neoliberalism and institutional analysis* (pp. 193–218). Princeton, NJ: Princeton University Press.

Hay, C., Riiheläinen, J. M., Smith, N. J., & Watson, M. (2008). Ireland: The outlier inside. In K. Dyson (Ed.), *The Euro at ten, Europeanization, power and convergence* (pp. 182–203). Oxford: Oxford University Press.

Heclo, H. (1974). *Modern social politics in Britain and Sweden: From relief to income maintenance.* New Haven: Yale University Press.

Hemerijck, A. (2012). Two or three waves of welfare state transformation? In N. Morel, B. Palier, & J. Palme (Eds.), *Towards a social investment welfare state?* (pp. 33–60). Bristol: The Policy Press.

IBEC. (2010). *IBEC pre-budget submission 2010.* Dublin: IBEC.

ICTU. (2009). *Building Ireland's smart economy. A framework for sustainable economic renewal. Preliminary observations by the Irish congress of trade unions.* Dublin: ICTU.

IMF. (2013). *Ireland IMF country report no. 13/93.* Washington DC: IMF.

Kitchin, R., O'Callaghan, M., Boyle, M., Gleeson, J., & Keaveney, K. (2012). Placing neoliberalism: The rise and fall of Ireland's Celtic Tiger. *Environment and Planning A, 44,* 1302–1326.

Lenihan, B. (2008a, July 4). Government and the financial services sector Minister's speech at PAI conference on financial regulation. Retrieved October 20, 2013, from http://www.finance.gov.ie

Lenihan, B. (2008b, October 14). Financial statement of the Minister for Finance Mr. Brian Lenihan, T.D. Retrieved October 20, 2013, from http://www.budget.gov.ie

Lenihan, B. (2009, December 9). Financial statement of the Minister for Finance Mr. Brian Lenihan, T.D. Retrieved October 20, 2013, http://www.budget.gov.ie

Mackintosh, J. (2013). Ireland: Poster child for austerity. *Financial Times*. Retrieved October 20, 2013, from http://blogs.ft.com/ft-long-short/2013/03/04/ireland-poster-child-for-austerity/

McCoy, D. (2008, June 25). Pay pause in public sector would be in national interest. *Irish Times*.

McCoy, D. (2010, April 16). Cost of banking crisis is a manageable burden. *Irish Times*.

McDonough, T., & Dundon, T. (2010). Thatcherism delayed? The Irish crisis and the paradox of social partnership. *Industrial Relations Journal, 41*(6), 544–562.

Peck, J., Theodore, N., & Brenner, N. (2012). Neoliberalism resurgent? Market rule after the great recession. *The South Atlantic Quarterly, 111*(2), 265–288.

Scharpf, F. W. (2013). Monetary union, fiscal crisis and the disabling of democratic accountability. In A. Schäfer & W. Streeck (Eds.), *Politics in the age of austerity* (pp. 26–58). Cambridge: Polity.

Schmidt, V. (2010). Taking ideas and discourse seriously: Explaining change through discursive institutionalism as the fourth 'new institutionalism'. *European Political Science Review, 2*(1), 1–25.

Schmidt, V., & Thatcher, M. (Eds.). (2013). *Resilient liberalism in Europe's political economy*. Cambridge: Cambridge University Press.

Schmidt, V., & Woll, C. (2013). The state: The bête noire of neo-liberalism or its greatest conquest? In V. Schmidt & M. Thatcher (Eds.), *Resilient liberalism in Europe's political economy* (pp. 112–141). Cambridge: Cambridge University Press.

Steinmo, S. (2008). Historical institutionalism. In D. della Porta & M. Keating (Eds.), *Approaches and methodologies in the social sciences: A pluralist perspective* (pp. 118–138). Cambridge: Cambridge University Press.

Stiglitz, J. (2011, July 7). The ideological crisis of Western capitalism. *Social Europe Journal*. Retrieved June 4, 2014, from http://www.social-europe.eu/2011/07/the-ideological-crisis-of-western-capitalism/

Streeck, W., & Thelen, K. (2005). *Beyond continuity – Institutional change in advanced political economies*. Oxford: Oxford University Press.

Sweeney, P. (2009, January 31). What we need for recovery is a major Keynesian-style stimulus package. *Irish Times*.

Trichet, J.-C. (2010). ECB annual report for 2008 – Report on the 2009 annual statement on the Euro area and public finances (debate), European Parliament, Thursday, 25 March, Brussels, Belgium. Retrieved June 4, 2014, from http://www.europarl.europa.eu

Weymes, L. (2012). Fiscal consolidation does it deliver? Dublin: Central Bank of Ireland. *Economic Letter Series, 12*(7), 1–14.

# 5

# National Social and Labour Market Policy Reforms in the Shadow of EU Bailout Conditionality: The Cases of Greece and Portugal

Sotiria Theodoropoulou

## Introduction

The global financial crisis that broke out in 2007 triggered sovereign debt banking and balance-of-payments (Pisani-Ferry et al. 2013) crises in the Euro area. Caught unprepared, the EU member states eventually organised and financed, jointly with the International Monetary Fund (IMF), crisis management mechanisms to prevent disorderly sovereign debt defaults in Eurozone member states. Greece, Ireland, Portugal and Cyprus received financial support (bailouts) in exchange for implementing programmes of economic adjustment described in the Memorandums of Understanding (MoUs). These documents, devised and revised by the Troika and the government of the member state receiving support, shape the decisions of the Euro area member states and the EU on whether or not to grant and continue financial support to a bailed out government (ibid.).

S. Theodoropoulou (✉)
European Trade Union Institute, Brussels, Belgium

© The Author(s) 2016
C. de la Porte, E. Heins (eds.), *The Sovereign Debt Crisis, the EU and Welfare State Reform*, DOI 10.1057/978-1-137-58179-2_5

The MoUs spell out the policy strategy, detailed targets to be met within the limits of the available funding and comprehensive action plans. As the main pillars of the adjustment strategy have been fiscal austerity and improving competitiveness through structural reforms, the measures in the MoUs have touched on national social and labour market policies, even though these policy areas fall outside the EU competence. The questions that are asked in this chapter is whether the MoUs have changed the potential of the EU to intrude into the reform of national social and labour market policies and, if so, how. How has the European response to the crisis affected national social and labour market policies?

Indirect EU pressure on national social and labour market policies resulting first from the conditions for joining the European Monetary Union (EMU) and then from complying with the rules of the Stability and Growth Pact (SGP) has been present since the first stage of the EMU (Leibfried and Pierson 1995; Ferrera 1996; Featherstone 2001). It could be thus argued that any current pressure from new instruments such as the MoUs is similar in origin to what went on before. However, up until the bailouts, EMU conditionality emphasized fiscal outcomes (e.g., budget deficits) rather than the means of achieving them (cf. Blavoukos and Pagoulatos 2008), while enforcement of the SGP rules had been patchy. As will be shown in this chapter, the MoUs prescribed in much greater detail the policies to be carried out. If member states failed to comply, financial support could be suspended, provoking a disorderly default on their public debt, which could arguably force them to abandon the euro and might even, via a domino effect, lead to the dissolution of the Eurozone (Buiter 2011).

Moreover, the EU member states currently have to reform their welfare states in a context of 'pervasive austerity', which differs in two important respects from the 'permanent austerity' (Pierson 2001) under which they have been modernising their welfare states since the 1990s. Firstly, pervasive austerity has been the direct outcome of policy choices, from the adoption of the euro to the response to the crisis, rather than long-term societal and economic trends. Secondly, the recession and high and lasting unemployment that it has led to (IMF 2012; in t'Veld 2013; Wren-Lewis 2013) creates extra pressures on welfare states, beyond those of aging societies and low productivity growth that underlay permanent austerity. This is an important change in the economic and political context of reforms, the implications of which have to be investigated.

To explore these questions, the measures taken in Greece and Portugal until June 2014, following the adoption of their MoUs, with a focus on the areas of pensions, labour market policies and collective wage bargaining are compared. It will be argued that the capacity of the EU to intrude in national social and labour market policy reforms has increased, in the context of the crisis and through the use of MoUs, to reach very high levels. Moreover, intrusiveness has varied across countries and policy areas, depending on the difficulty of implementing the MoU reforms, the extent to which the macroeconomic adjustment has been seen to be stalling, the degree to which a given policy area is directly relevant to the adjustment in question and the urgency of the financing need. While steps have been taken, in the context of the reforms, that would have been, in principle, akin to modernisation of aspects of their welfare states, the budget cuts, combined with the increased needs for welfare support, have led to a weaker safety net.

The rest of this chapter is structured as follows. The concepts of EU integration and intrusiveness used in the chapter and the empirical approach and case selection will be introduced and explained in the next section. In Concepts and Case Selection the intrusiveness of the MoUs and its variation across countries will be examined, while in Intrusiveness in Practice: A Horizontal View of the Greek and the Portuguese Memoranda of Understanding, intrusiveness and its effects across the areas of pensions and labour market policies in the two countries will be examined. The discussion will be concluded in the final section.

## Concepts and Case Selection

### Conceptualising the Integrative Capacity of the MoU Instrument

To examine whether and, if so, how and how far the EU has, through the MoUs, been affecting national social and labour market policies, we use the typology of EU integration proposed by de la Porte and Heins

(Chapter 2) in relation to which the MoUs appear to be in a league of their own to the point that integration becomes intrusiveness in terms of objectives, enforcement and surveillance. The objectives refer to the precision of policy aims—in other words, to what extent the EU interferes in shaping policy aims (henceforth, 'objectives' will be interchangeably used with the term 'interference'). Surveillance refers to how the EU can monitor the implementation of agreed national policies, and enforcement refers to which measures the EU has at its disposal to ensure implementation in case of non-compliance. The MoUs are intrusive because they are associated with very specific objectives with detailed measures and timetables to meet these (thus, high interference), very high surveillance and very high enforcement. By comparing the MoUs across policy areas within and across countries, we attempt here to establish the priorities guiding the adjustment strategy of the MoUs.

## Empirical Strategy and Case Selection

To gauge whether the capacity of the EU to intrude in national social and labour market policy reforms has changed, we have studied the MoUs and their evolution from their adoption and through their regularly scheduled revisions up until the summer of 2014. We are interested not only in how EU integration under MoUs is different from the other reinforced instruments of EU economic governance (see de la Porte and Heins, Chapter 2, for a detailed analysis) but also in whether EU involvement varies across countries and policy areas. Moreover, we look into *how* the EU has been influencing the social and labour market policies of member states via the MoUs.

The cases of Greece and Portugal present similarities and differences that allow us to explore these questions. The two countries, like all bailed out member states, have had to sign two Memoranda to receive their funding: one with the IMF authorities, called the Memorandum of Economic and Financial Policies (henceforth, MEFP) and one with the EU authorities called the Memorandum of Understanding on Specific Economic Policy Conditionality (MoU). The adjustment policy strategy that has been a condition for receiving financial support and its operationalization has been the same in relation to both types of Memoranda. The level of detail and prescription has, however, been systematically different. The requirements of the MEFPs, in line with a relatively recent revision of the IMF's statutes in accordance with the principle of 'parsimonious conditionality', have been, in general, limited to areas of direct relevance for adjustment (Pisani-Ferry et al. 2013). The MoUs, by contrast, have gone into much greater detail about the measures required to implement the guidelines of the policy strategy agreed between a government and the Troika. To take one very simple indicator illustrating the difference between MoUs and MEFPs, the former have always been longer (cf. Sapir et al. 2014).

The nature of the problems that the economic adjustment programmes sought to correct was similar in Greece and Portugal, although their magnitude was greater in the case of Greece. Both countries saw their public finances deteriorating substantially in the aftermath of the global financial crisis of 2008 although Greece's fiscal balances were already severe, as successive governments had failed to reduce the Greek public debt/gross domestic product (GDP) ratio, which remained very close to or above 100 per cent from the launch of the euro until the crisis (see Figs. 5.1 and 5.2). In 2009, a similarly large proportion of their public debt—75 per cent for Portugal and 79 per cent for Greece—was held abroad (Cabral 2010). Their financial sectors were quite robust, especially compared to Ireland's, at the beginning of the global financial crisis, although, as the public debt crisis and the subsequent recession unfolded, their banking systems too were drawn into it.

Both countries had high current account deficits in 2008—16.5 per cent of GDP for Greece and 12.6 per cent of GDP for Portugal (AMECO data)—which had been growing steadily since 2000. They had both suffered price and cost competitiveness losses during the first decade of the euro, although the extent of these losses varied depending on the indicator of relative prices or costs used to measure it. Figure 5.3 shows the evolution of two Harmonized Competitiveness Indicators for Greece and Portugal from 1999 to early 2010, when the sovereign debt crisis broke out, illustrating real effective exchange rates vis-à-vis the other Euro area members, using as a relative price indicator the GDP deflator and unit labour costs for the whole economy. An indicator greater than 100 shows relative price or cost competitiveness losses. In Greece, the losses were

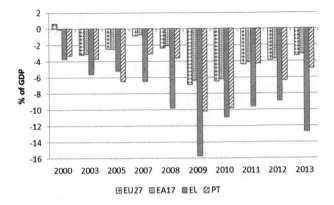

**Fig. 5.1** General government budget deficit as share of GDP, EU27, EA17, Greece, Portugal, 2000–2013. *Source*: Eurostat Government Finance Statistics Database

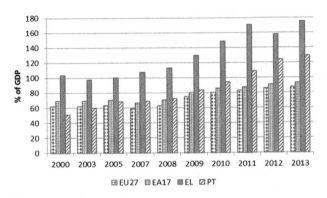

**Fig 5.2** Gross public debt as a share of GDP, EU27, EA17, Greece, Portugal, 2000–2013. *Source:* Eurostat Government Finance Statistics Database

more pronounced when the real effective exchange rate was calculated on the basis of the relative GDP deflator than when calculated on the basis of relative unit labour costs. Greece had gone through several years of high nominal output and public spending growth, which had fuelled labour cost increases in excess of productivity growth. In Portugal, on the other hand, we see an opposite picture, which is consistent with the fact

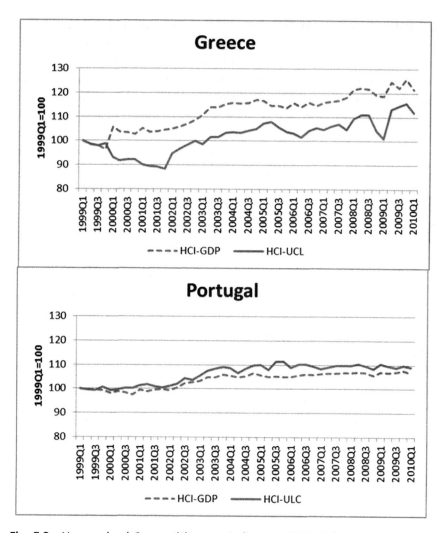

**Fig. 5.3** Harmonized Competitiveness Indicators, GDP deflator, Unit Labour Costs, Greece and Portugal, 1999Q1–2010Q1. *Source:* ECB Exchange Rates statistics

that labour productivity had slowed down significantly since 2000, pushing unit labour costs upwards (OECD 2010).

Greece and Portugal displayed similarities in their welfare states too, most notably their weakness, which has been associated with high inequality, high poverty (see Table 5.1), a strong division between insiders and outsiders, limited redistribution and inefficient welfare spending. In both countries, policymakers had used the EU to promote modernisation reforms in areas such as pensions, active labour market policies and income support in the 1990s and the 2000s, although Portugal had arguably gone further in this respect, having undertaken in 2007, for example, a pension system reform that addressed its sustainability problems and having also established a Minimum Income scheme. Be this as it may, neither of the two welfare states had yet caught up with the EU average public spending on social transfers per head when the crisis hit (Zartaloudis 2014), and the divergence became even more pronounced from 2009 onwards, especially when considering the much steeper increases in unemployment in the two countries (see Fig. 5.4).

The success of the adjustment programmes in meeting their stated objectives has varied distinctively between the two countries, with the two Greek programmes having been by far the least successful in restoring the country's affordable access to the financial markets and in moving forward along the lines of forecasts of crucial macroeconomic variables on which the terms of the programme were spelled out (Pisani-Ferry et al. 2013; Sapir et al. 2014). In fact, in July 2015, the Greek government requested and received a third bailout. The Portuguese programme, by contrast, was completed in June 2014 with Portugal returning to the financial markets, albeit with a very fragile economy beset with problems, such as higher than anticipated public debt and unemployment rates,

Table 5.1 Inequality and poverty, EU, Greece and Portugal, 2010, 2012

|  | Gini coefficient (0–100) | | Risk of poverty (60 per cent of median equivalized; per cent of population) | | Risk of poverty anchored at 2008 (60 per cent of median equivalized; per cent of population) | |
|---|---|---|---|---|---|---|
|  | 2010 | 2012 | 2010 | 2012 | 2010 | 2012 |
| EU27 | 30.5 | 30.6 | 16.4 | 16.9 | 16.4 | 18.2 |
| EU15 | 30.5 | 30.7 | 16.3 | 16.8 | 17.0 | 19.0 |
| EA17 | 30.2 | 30.4 | 16.2 | 17.0 | 16.2 | 18.7 |
| EL | 32.9 | 34.3 | 20.1 | 23.1 | 18.0 | 35.8 |
| PT | 33.7 | 34.5 | 17.9 | 17.9 | 16.1 | 19.4 |

Source: Eurostat EU-SILC database

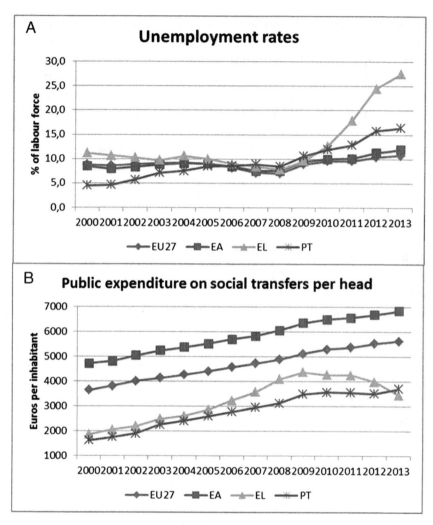

**Fig. 5.4** (a) Evolution of unemployment rates, EU27, Euro area, Greece and Portugal 2000–2013. (b) Evolution of public expenditure on social transfers per head, EU27, Euro area, Greece and Portugal 2000–2013. *Source:* Eurostat Labour Force Statistics and Government Finance Statistics Databases

which will take a long time and sustained efforts to repair (Sapir et al. 2014).

Various reasons have been provided for the successes and failures of the adjustment programmes (see, e.g., Theodoropoulou and Watt 2015, for Greece). Some of the explanations were common to both countries, most notably the adverse external environment created by pervasive austerity (Krugman 2013), and some were different insofar as they related to different problem loads (greater in Greece), administrative capacities to implement reforms (weaker in Greece) and so forth (Pisani-Ferry et al. 2013). Moreover, the first Greek programme was implemented at a time when the EU approach to crisis management had not yet crystallised, thus leading to contradictions that made 'Grexit' a probable event (ibid.).

Interestingly for our comparative study, the government parties of the two countries had different attitudes towards the programmes. In Portugal, parties of the centre-right and centre-left generally agreed that austerity and adjustment were necessary. In Greece, on the other hand, up until 2010 when the bailout was sought, significant factions within the main parties on the centre-right and centre-left had been questioning the necessity of any fiscal austerity for adjustment, while the leftist SYRIZA party, which after 2012 became the constitutional opposition in the Greek parliament, eventually won the January 2015 general elections on the promise of getting rid of the MoUs.

Thus, while the two countries present similar economic problems, the extent of these problems varied, as did the willingness and capacity of national policymakers to implement the adjustment programmes. This variation will allow us to explore whether EU intrusiveness has varied from one case to the other and, if so, along which dimensions. Moreover, the similarities in welfare states allow us to see how and to what extent the twin objectives of fiscal savings and modernisation achieved practical balance in the context of the programmes and of pervasive austerity.

## Intrusiveness in Practice: A Horizontal View of the Greek and the Portuguese Memoranda of Understanding

The level of interference associated with the MoUs has been very high. Measures and reforms had to be agreed with an unprecedented degree of specificity. Both fiscal and structural measures touched on social and labour market policy areas. Structural reforms were aimed at ensuring that fiscal and current account adjustments would be sustainable through alteration of the structures (e.g., export base, fiscal management mechanisms), which, according to the Troika, underlay the budget and current account deficits in the first place. However, insofar as the EU policy response to the crisis has not facilitated the sustainable adjustment of macroeconomic imbalances due to its effects on the demand side of the economies (DeGrauwe 2011; Pisani-Ferry et al. 2013; Wren-Lewis 2013), the more the targets were missed, the more the interference in setting policy objectives increased to administer ever larger doses of structural reform on the supply side.

Interference has varied over time and across the two countries. Taking as a proxy thereof the number of words devoted to measures related to social and labour market policies in the rolling versions of the MoUs, we are in a position to make some interesting observations (see Fig. 5.5), akin to findings reported by Sapir et al. (2014). First, the number of words on social and labour market policy measures in Greece rose steeply between the first and the second Greek programme, with only a slight subsequent decline in the most recent revisions of the second programme. Secondly, the first Portuguese MoU started out with a much higher number of words on welfare state measures than did the first Greek programme. As Portugal had a relatively lighter problem load (see also the discussion of policy areas later in this chapter), this may simply suggest that the 'technology' of bailout conditionality evolved as its implementation advanced. In other words, the Troika probably learned from its experience of applying the MoU in Greece and, therefore, in Portugal, started out more dynamically. This is also visible in the gradually streamlined structure of the MoUs.

The MoUs have been characterized by very strong surveillance, with their policy content being controlled (negotiated and agreed) ex ante and ex post. Every version of the MoU has been accompanied by a detailed timetable of actions that had to be taken by various government departments. Under the conditionality programme, there is a provision for the Troika to visit the country every three months to monitor whether or not the agreed measures have been implemented according to the schedule laid down in the MoU and to assess the impact of measures taken

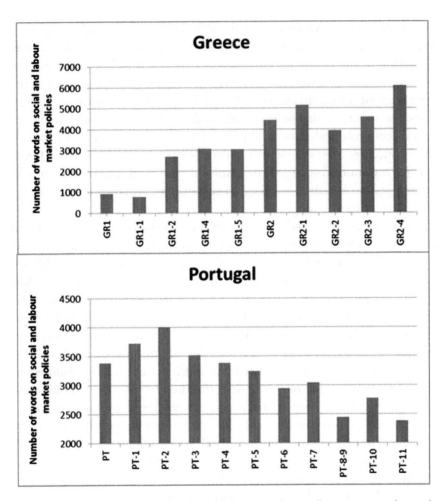

**Fig. 5.5** EU interference in social and labour market policy measures through the MoUs, Greece and Portugal. *Source:* Author's calculations based on the MoU texts; no reliable data available for the third review of the first Greek programme-GR1-3

against the fiscal targets. In the event of inaction, delay or undershooting of targets, new and/or complementary remedial measures are supposed to be agreed on with the national government as a condition for a recommendation by the Troika to the Eurogroup that it continues financially supporting the member state. Our study of the MoUs has suggested that surveillance became tighter and lengthier whenever the implementation of the programme either stalled or failed to deliver the desired results (see Table 5.2). This has been the case more frequently in Greece. On the one hand, after the launch of the second programme, the

**Table 5.2** European Commission-DG ECFIN for MoUs and review dates

|  | Date of review publication | Important events |
|---|---|---|
| Greece |  |  |
| GR1 | May 2010 | Adoption of first MoU |
| GR1-1 | August 2010 | Programme implementation on track |
| GR1-2 | November 2010 | Programme implementation on track |
| GR1-3 | February 2011 |  |
| GR1-4 | July 2011 | Sharp deterioration in growth recession relative to programme forecasts since spring 2011; first decision about Greek PSI; Greek authorities' commitment to reform 'stalled' in late spring |
| GR1-5 | December 2011 | Papandreou resigns; Papademos government takes office; recession deepens; Lagarde states programme 'in a difficult phase' |
| GR2 | March 2012 | Adoption of second MoU-PSI-Restructuring of privately held Greek debt to take place; shift in emphasis in MoU towards structural reforms to achieve internal devaluation as a priority |
| GR2-1 | December 2012 | Two closely spaced elections in May and June 2012 that failed to give majority to any party and saw massive electoral losses for the two major parties; following long deliberations and months of government immobilization, a coalition centre-right/centre-left government is formed; negotiations with Troika resumed in August to break down in October over disagreements on proposed measures |
| GR2-1, milestone 1 | January 2013 |  |

(continued)

**Table 5.2** (continued)

| | Date of review publication | Important events |
|---|---|---|
| GR2-1, milestone 2 | February 2013 | |
| GR2-1, milestone 3 | March 2013 | |
| GR2-2 | May 2013 | |
| GR2-2, milestone 1 | June 2013 | |
| GR2-3 | July 2013 | |
| GR2-4 | April 2014 | Negotiations with Troika suspended at the end of 2013; delay in approving voted Greek 2014 budget |
| Portugal | | |
| PT | June 2011 | Adoption of MoU |
| PT1 | September 2011 | |
| PT2 | December 2011 | |
| PT3 | April 2012 | |
| PT4 | July 2012 | |
| PT5 | October 2012 | 2013 budget approved in the Parliament; largest tax increases ever |
| PT6 | December 2012 | Large protests about labour law changes |
| PT7 | June 2013 | Constitutional court rejects several key measures leading government to miss expenditure cutting targets; anti-austerity protests mount-Minister of Finance/'personification of austerity' and leader of smaller coalition party resigns in July |
| PT8-9 | November 2013 | Eight reviews postponed following government initiative; demonstrations continue |
| PT10 | February 2014 | |
| PT11 | April 2014 | |

European Commission services started reporting in between the regular quarterly reviews of the MoU on the compliance with 'milestones' in the programme. These assessments were used to authorise the disbursement of 'sub-tranches' of the tranche of financial support that the Eurogroup had already approved. Surveillance was thus stepped up in excess of the already tight controls established in the MoUs. On the other hand, the ex ante evaluation of the programme to be followed became more meticulous and protracted in both Greece and Portugal whenever the results of adjustment were such as to suggest that the programme might become subject to a financing gap.

The MoUs and their explicit references to social and labour market policies entailed an unprecedentedly strong enforcement dimension insofar as progress achieved in these policy areas feeds into the EU decision-making process concerning financial support for member states as well as the national banking systems by the European Central Bank (ECB). A further indication of the MoUs' very strong enforcement clout is the fact that, in spite of alternate parties with contrasting policy stances having taken office in both Greece and Portugal, the compliance with the MoU conditions did not change. In fact, in early 2012, following the requirement of the lenders and immediately before the adoption of the second Greek programme, both the PASOK (centre-left) and New Democracy (centre-right) parties were compelled to sign letters to the lenders in which they undertook to stick to the agreements signed (cf. Pavolini et al., Chapter 6, for the cases of Spain and Italy). In July 2015 the Greek SYRIZA-led coalition government performed a massive U-turn and accepted measures in, among others, the areas of pensions and labour market policies, which it had been opposing for months in its negotiations for the conclusion of the final review of the second bailout.

Last but not least, the more apparent any implementation difficulties became, the more the enforcement dimension was geared up. During the second Greek programme, the phrase 'prior to disbursement' started appearing with increasing frequency before particular measures, invariably those of direct relevance to the public budget and/or competitiveness (e.g., pensions, labour costs, healthcare systems, employment protection legislation), thereby stressing the urgency of their implementation.

No such mentions of specific measures were to be found in any of the Portuguese MoUs.

The events that preceded the agreement on a third bailout for Greece in July illustrate how the combination of surveillance and enforcement have acted as a powerful leverage for increasing interference in the Greek policymaking. The final ex post review of the second bailout had been pending since September 2014, which meant that the Greek governments had not received any funding since August 2014. By June 2015, the Greek government coffers had completely dried up, as the newly elected Greek government kept up with the repayments to its official creditors by using the cash reserves of the broader public sector in Greece. In spite of the SYRIZA-ANEL coalition government being staunchly opposed to measures involving pensions and labour market reforms and an impressively high share (62 per cent) of Greek people having voted against such measures in the July referendum, the Greek government eventually capitulated in exchange for a new bailout.

## Intrusiveness in Pension and Labour Market Policy Reforms in Greece and Portugal

We turn now to the measures actually taken in the context of conditionality in the two countries in a number of key policy areas, such as pensions and labour market policies. This allows us to reflect on the three dimensions of EU intrusiveness through the MoUs and particularly on interference in policy objectives.

There are certain caveats in gauging the EU effect on national social and labour market policies through an analysis of the content of the MoUs alone. First of all, there is the question of identifying the extent to which the Troika members and the national government respectively influenced the negotiated measures included in the MoUs. Strictly speaking, accurately identifying the influences of each actor from the texts alone is difficult. However, from the available information, we may deduce some points about the role of the different actors.

There are some indications that national governments would be allowed to choose among functional equivalents of measures that would achieve similar adjustment in terms of macroeconomic variables but would have differing implications in terms of distribution of the adjustment costs. The media have regularly reported on negotiations and disagreements between the Troika and government officials in the member states before agreeing on the measures to be taken (see, e.g., Hope 2012, 2013a, b; Wise 2013a, b). However, such 'choice' does not alter the pressures for or overall magnitude of adjustment but rather the distribution of specific measures across policy areas and different sections of the population. Thus, it is not possible to attribute the evolution of policy outputs in the areas that will be examined entirely to the EU. Yet, as the experience of the latest Greek government showed, as long as a government has to rely exclusively on official funding of its financing needs, time spent on coming up with alternatives and negotiations does not work in its favour because the release of funds is conditional on an agreement over measures.

Given that the Troika also included the IMF, the question arises of whether it was the EU members of the Troika or the IMF, or possibly both, that pushed for a given measure. Insofar as the MoUs were actually more detailed than the MEFPs (Sapir et al. 2014), it is fairly safe to assume that the EU pressure on member states has been at least as strong as, if not stronger than, the IMF's.

A second aspect concerns the specific direction of reforms. The comparison of the two types of Memorandum suggests that, in general, the Troika members concurred on the areas in which measures would need to be taken. There are indications, however, that the MoUs promoted an even harder line than the MEFPs in favour of fiscal austerity and of a strengthening of market adjustment mechanisms, especially in the labour markets, rather than of a strengthening of socio-economic institutions that could support non-market coordination for reversing losses in competitiveness (cf. Hall and Soskice 2001). Olivier Blanchard, chief economist of the IMF, has, for example, on more than one occasion highlighted in his research, including with the IMF, the importance of quality of labour relations, itself an outcome of 'trust' among social partners for facilitating the adjustment of an economy to macroeconomic shocks

(Blanchard and Philippon 2004)—an argument that has also informed IMF advice to Greece and Portugal (Blanchard et al. 2014). The research publications of the Directorate-General for Economic and Financial Affairs (DG ECFIN) and the ECB, on the other hand, have consistently highlighted the importance of improving market flexibility in the context of the EMU (Degryse et al. 2013). This is consistent with the economic policy assignment under the EU economic governance, which has embedded in it the notion that labour and product market flexibility should take the main role in supporting adjustment to country-specific shocks, and this is why they should be as flexible as possible, while the main objective of fiscal policies should be to maintain public finances on a sustainable path by limiting fiscal discretionary actions.

## Pensions

Greece and Portugal have had similar pension systems, with a mandatory public contributory, pay-as-you-go pillar and other non-mandatory pillars. Under the mandatory pillar, pensions have been provided in both countries by social insurance funds. In Greece, the system has been highly fragmented across sectors and professions with a large number of social insurance funds, a situation that has not only translated into relatively high administrative costs but also led to substantial differences and inequality in coverage and provisions (Petmesidou 2010). In Portugal, the main provider has been the Social Security System, although there were, until recently, other smaller funds covering specific groups of employees (e.g. public servants, banking sector employees) (Ribeiro Mendes 2010). Both countries also had special public targeted and minimum pension schemes with redistributive aims and funded by state transfers (OECD 2005). The risk of poverty or social exclusion has nevertheless been consistently high among the elderly (65+) in both Greece (28 per cent) and Portugal (27 per cent) compared to 21 per cent of elderly people at risk of poverty in the EU15 (Eurostat 2014a).

Prior to the crisis, the long-term projections on the sustainability of the pensions systems in both Greece and Portugal looked alarming. It was projected that by 2060 Greece would be spending about 24.1 per cent of its GDP on pensions (European Commission 2009, p. 128) compared to 20.8 per cent in Portugal (European Commission 2006, p. 155) and 12.4 per cent on average in the EU (ibid.). Unlike Greece, however, Portugal had taken more effective action prior to the crisis to tackle unsustainability while maintaining adequacy, solidarity and fairness among and within generations (ibid.; Ribeiro Mendes 2010). By the time Greece adopted the MoU, there was substantial scope and need for rationalisation in the Greek system.

Old-age pensions were affected by measures included in the MoUs in both Greece and Portugal, although to differing extents and at different points in the programmes. In both countries, the value of pension benefits was reduced on several occasions as part of the fiscal policy measures aimed at meeting budget balance targets. The cuts were progressive and often took the form of freezes, the suspension of indexation and the elimination of the thirteenth and fourteenth annual instalments thereof (European Commission 2010a, 2011b). This last measure was cancelled in 2013 by the constitutional court in Portugal as anti-constitutional. Following the MoUs, the Portuguese authorities also introduced more means-testing and more focused targeting of some pension benefits (Ribeiro Mendes 2012).

In Greece, a comprehensive reform of the system was required from the early MoU versions of the first programme with the aim of controlling the increase in pension spending. Interference was very high. The original MoU laid down several specifications for the reform package that the Greek parliament subsequently adopted; these touched on crucial features of the system both for primary and auxiliary pensions, such as reducing the fragmentation of the pension funds; remedying the lack of transparency in rules and the large differentials in benefits and conditions of entitlement; amending the calculation of benefits and eligibility rules, including the retirement age, which was raised and equalised for men and women; and tightening the rules governing early retirement (European Commission 2010c). There was provision also for the automatic introduction of a mechanism for adjusting the retirement age to ensure sustainability, while the calculation of benefits changed from benefit-defined to contribution-defined. Among the requirements of the MoU was the establishment of a means-tested minimum guaranteed income for elderly people (above the statutory retirement age) designed to protect the most vulnerable groups in a manner consistent with fiscal sustainability (European Commission 2010a).

In that sense, the reforms that were required introduced several long overdue elements of modernization into the Greek system, although the Greek government in 2010 allowed certain occupational categories to keep their pension funds outside the new system (Matsaganis 2013). In spite of these reforms and cuts, the cost pressures on the pension system did not ease, notably because of waves of early retirement among employees aged 55 years and above that were made redundant (Petmesidou 2013).

In terms of surveillance, the Greek MoUs explicitly mentioned that the pension reforms would be designed 'in close consultation with European Commission, IMF and ECB staff', while their 'estimated impact on long-term sustainability would have to be validated by the EU Economic Policy Committee' (European Commission 2010a, p. 63; 2012a, p. 133). The choice of the Economic Policy Committee (subordinate to the Economic and Financial Affairs Council) as a validating authority suggests that the primary aim of the proposed reforms was their cost-containing effects on public budgets rather than social protection considerations, such as equity or income replacement in old age. Moreover, pensions was one of the policy areas for which enforcement was tightened in Greece after the adoption of the second programme, with some of the required measures being preceded by the phrase 'prior to the disbursement of the next tranche'.

In Portugal, by contrast, a demand for 'comprehensive reform' of the system was first introduced only in the seventh revision of the MoU, published in June 2013 (European Commission 2013a), almost two years after the adoption of the original MoU. The reform was presented as part of the fiscal consolidation strategy with no mention of any deterioration in the sustainability of the pension system itself. The emphasis in the MoU was on the progressive distribution of the costs of reforming the system. Considered against the stated objectives of the 2007 framework law for social security, which included adequacy in addition to fairness (Ribeiro Mendes 2010, p. 7), the proposed reforms are a manifestation of very high interference as they proposed changes likely to undermine the adequacy principle applicable to the pension system.

Overall, the evident emphasis of the pension-related measures has been on sustainably reducing their cost for the government budget both in the long run through reforms and with immediate effect through ad hoc cuts that were decided in the face of worse than expected performance in meeting fiscal targets. Reducing inequity among beneficiaries affiliated to different funds was also promoted by the MoUs and, in the case of Greece where fragmentation was greater, it was partly achieved, albeit at less generous levels of benefit than previously. Changes could not be characterised as a 'paradigm shift' in either of the two countries (cf. Hall 1993).

## Labour Market Policies

### Unemployment Benefits

The unemployment benefit (insurance and assistance) systems in Greece and Portugal have not been among the most effective in supporting the unemployed. A common characteristic has been the rather low coverage of the unemployed (Matsaganis 2013; OECD 2014) due to demanding eligibility conditions. A notable difference between the two systems has related to the significance of the unemployment assistance benefits—that is, those granted to unemployed people not qualifying for unemployment insurance—which have been more generous in Portugal and, up until recently, rather insignificant in Greece. The Portuguese system, in comparison with the Greek one, has thus been considered more likely to create unemployment and inactivity traps (Stovicek and Turrini 2012).

The first Greek adjustment programme, in its quest for 'rationalisation' of the country's social benefits systems, led, through several channels, to a decrease in the generosity of the unemployment insurance benefits and a consequent reduction in their fiscal costs. The targeting of beneficiaries was tightened through means-testing and the abolition of certain special benefits targeting geographical areas and sectors (e.g., tourism; European Commission 2010a). Furthermore, a limit was placed on the maximum amount of time, within an overall four-year period, for which an unemployed worker was entitled to claim a contributory unemployment benefit. What is more, the level of this benefit was reduced from 454 to 360 euros per month due to changes in the minimum wage to which it is linked (Matsaganis 2013, p. 20).

Concurrently, the MoU sought to expand the coverage of the Greek system by the targeted extension of unemployment insurance to the self-employed from 2012 onwards (Matsaganis 2013). The first programme also contained provisions for the introduction of two new assistance benefit schemes. First, a Minimum Income Guarantee was to be applied in two pilot areas of the country, with a total available expenditure capped at €35 million euros. By June 2014, At the time of this writing (June 2014), this pilot scheme had yet to be implemented due to technical difficulties. Secondly, an income-tested benefit equal to €200 per month was to be established, extending support for up to another 12 months to long-term unemployed persons who had exhausted their entitlement to unemployment benefits (12 months) provided they did not qualify for other training schemes. Total expenditure of this benefit was capped at €20 million (European Commission 2011a), a restriction that can hardly fail to limit its coverage.

In the area of unemployment benefits, interference of the MoU is assessed as very high. In addition to providing specific guidelines for cuts and reforms, there was an evident impulse towards enhancing the poverty alleviation function of the system at the expense of previously protected labour force categories, typically those with well-established previous employment records. It is noticeable, however, that enforcement in relation to this aspect has been less stringent, for the reform of one of the two schemes planned as a move in the aforementioned direction has been delayed, seemingly without any tightening of surveillance and enforcement by the Troika.

In principle, the attempts to extend coverage would have represented a positive development had the whole initiative not been so constrained by fiscal considerations. The actual coverage rate (benefit recipients/unemployed) for contributory unemployment benefits fell between 2010 and 2013. Meanwhile, in the non-contributory unemployment benefits for the long-term unemployed, coverage increased between 2010 and 2012 but was expected to fall in 2014 due to the increase in long-term unemployed and the aforementioned cash limit (Matsaganis 2013). For the same reasons, the generosity of the system was reduced even for Greek labour market 'insiders', thereby weakening the safety net at a time when job losses have also been hitting prime age, previously securely employed, males.

In Portugal, the reform of the unemployment benefits under the MoU aimed to reduce long-term unemployment and to strengthen the social safety net (European Commission 2011d). Reforms were introduced in 2011 in an attempt to limit any unemployment and inactivity trap effects by reducing both the duration and the level of the benefits. An attempt was made, similar to the measure implemented in Greece, to extend coverage of the system by lowering the length of the contributory career required for eligibility from 15 to 12 months and by including certain categories of self-employed people; and yet, in 2013, six out of ten unemployed persons in Portugal had no access to unemployment benefits (OECD 2014). Here too, the level of interference has been high, but the result has fallen short from a third order policy change.

## Active Labour Market Policies

Up until 2010, spending on active labour market policies as a share of GDP in Greece was 0.2 per cent, less than half of the EU28 and EU15 average, having registered an increase of 0.08 percentage points since the beginning of the crisis in 2008. The largest shares of this expenditure were devoted to employment and business start-up incentives. In Portugal, by contrast, in 2010 public spending on active labour market policies (ALMPs) was 0.6 per cent of GDP, equal to the EU average, while the available data estimates a marked decrease of about 0.010 percentage points in 2011 (Eurostat 2014b). Most of the expenditure in 2011 was used for training programmes.

In this policy area, the aims of the MoU measures in Greece and Portugal would appear to be very similar, namely, to improve the matching of workers and vacancies and to promote the employability of the unemployed with a particular focus on the long-term unemployed and the disadvantaged, while ensuring optimal effectiveness of the resources committed. The Portuguese MoU prescribed an evaluation of the effectiveness of existing policies in tackling long-term unemployment, improving the employability of youth and disadvantaged categories and easing labour market mismatch, as well as an action plan for further improvements (European Commission 2011c). In Greece, the first adjustment programme stipulated that the policies aimed at supporting the unemployed should be designed to, among other things, facilitate the mobility of workers across sectors and occupations, promote the employability of disadvantaged groups and improve the quality of training services. To these ends, the government was to adopt an action plan by the first quarter of 2013. The MoU specified the means through which these goals should be pursued and called on the government to provide an overview of the programmes already in place, together with plans for their rationalisation and an indication of the sources of funding.

This proposal was expanded and became more specific in the second review of the second MoU. By that time (spring 2013), unemployment rates had soared to alarming levels in Greece and new emphasis was placed on measures that could help prevent long-term unemployment and the inevitable accompanying erosion of skills. At that point, the MoU suggested an expansion of the short-term public works programmes for the long-term unemployed and the young not in employment or training as 'a measure of emergency and temporary nature', alongside the provision of a youth voucher scheme to private sector employers to promote the training and re-skilling of young unemployed people (European Commission 2013c). It must be open to doubt whether—given the massive increases in unemployment, especially in Greece, and the tight budget constraints—this targeting provided sufficient support for those who lost their jobs. The level of interference represented by the Greek programmes has been high, given the specificity of the goals.

In the case of Portugal, where the previous record of ALMPs was apparently better, the MoU prescriptions tended rather to emphasise evaluation, monitoring and some correction of the inefficiencies. Again, the notion of a targeting of available resources to those most in need was present. In Portugal, accordingly, intrusiveness was not exceptionally high by MoU standards and in contrast to the Greek case.

## Employment Protection Legislation

Up until the global financial crisis and in spite of some far-reaching reforms undertaken from the 1980s onwards (Venn 2009), Greece and Portugal had been among the Organisation for Economic Co-operation and Development (OECD) countries with the most restrictive Employment Protection Legislation (EPL) (OECD 2004). In fact, given these countries' weak and fragmented welfare states, the EPL has been one of the most important pillars of social protection in both of them (Emmenegger 2011).

Reforms in the Greek EPL were requested already in the first MoU. In the course of the two programmes, three types of measures were stipulated. First, measures were to be taken with the aim of reducing the costs of, and other restrictions associated with, the dismissal of workers on regular contracts; these related to matters such as severance payments, the length of notice of dismissal and probationary periods for new recruits or definition of threshold of collective dismissals. Provision was to be made at the same time for harmonisation of these measures across blue- and white-collar workers. Secondly, reforms were to be devised to facilitate greater use of temporary and fixed-term contracts, including at sub-minima wages for young people, temporary work agencies and part-time work (European Commission 2010 b, c). Thirdly, the MoU promoted measures to increase flexibility in working time arrangements (European Commission 2014b). Greater flexibility in labour utilisation was thus promoted not only for regular contracts and working time arrangements but also for flexible and atypical forms of employment, potentially further increasing their attractiveness to employers. However, greater flexibility did not suffice to moderate the rise—that proved explosive beyond any forecasts—in unemployment in Greece. In fact, the second MoU suggested further reforms in the same direction of reducing firing costs, in spite of the high unemployment rate and the deepening recession. Meanwhile, the notion of security was sacrificed on the altar of the need to reduce expenditure on unemployment benefits.

According to the Portuguese MoU, the EPL reforms were to be aimed at reducing labour market segmentation, fostering job creation and easing labour market adjustment (European Commission 2011d). The focus of the measures adopted has been on severance payments and on individual dismissals. Severance payments were redesigned to reduce their cost and to align them across different types of contracts, in particular fixed-term and open-ended ones, as well as between Portugal and the EU average. The new legislation also brought into being two compensation funds (European Commission 2013b), which essentially shifted the financing of severance payments to the newly recruited by imposing a sort of insurance payment. The definition of fair dismissal was relaxed in the summer of 2012 with the elimination of a number of obligations formerly incumbent on employers. However, most of the measures in question were ruled 'unconstitutional' and overturned by the Constitutional Court in 2013 (European Commission 2013b).

The MoUs of both countries have been highly intrusive in the field of EPL, not only because of the specificity of the measures required but also due to the important role played by EPL for purposes of social protection in the two countries (Emmenegger 2011). Still there has been no 'paradigm shift', as in both countries EPL remained relatively strict (cf. OECD 2013). It is not clear why the EU average would be the most appropriate benchmark for the Portuguese economy if the aim was to facilitate the regaining of competitiveness. In 2008, the OECD ranked Germany, arguably the most competitive member state in the Eurozone, only slightly below Portugal and well above the middle of the distribution of restrictiveness of EPL (Venn 2009).

The pattern of intrusiveness and the reforms undertaken in the areas of EPL and policies to support the unemployed (income support and activation) suggest a de facto evolution from the principle of flexicurity to the notion of 'flexilience', that is, flexibility for resilience (cf. Canton et al. 2014). As mentioned earlier, the effectiveness of reforms in the unemployment benefit systems that were supposedly designed to achieve modernisation was restricted by public budget constraints, while the pressure for enhancing active labour market policies has been strictly limited to measures designed to assist those most disadvantaged. Thus, massive fiscal adjustment, taking place in a context of pervasive austerity in the Eurozone, would appear to have given precedence to shock resilience over and above a concern for security.

## Collective Bargaining and Minimum Wages

Insofar as one of the main objectives of the adjustment programmes was to restore reverse internal real exchange rate appreciations and rebalance the current accounts of Greece and Portugal, reforms in wage-setting procedures, most notably collective wage bargaining and minimum wages, have been an important pillar of the MoUs in both countries. Both Greece and Portugal have been traditionally characterised by fragmented industrial relations systems that have not supported a growth model reliant on exports and competitiveness (Regan 2013). The MoUs in both countries sought to change collective wage bargaining structures in favour of a decentralised system, on the principle that wage agreements should reflect the productivity developments and ultimately the competitiveness needs of individual firms. To that end, measures were foreseen and adopted in both countries to restrict the extension of collective agreements to non-signatories. In Greece, the hitherto practice of automatic extension was eliminated as was the practice of prolonging the validity of a collective agreement after its expiry date in the event that no new agreement had been reached yet. In Portugal, the similar administrative practice was henceforth limited to a small number of cases and, under certain conditions of limited representativeness, was actually abolished, while any potential extension was required to take account of the potential implications for the competitiveness of the firms in the sector. The MoUs also advanced reforms allowing work councils at the firm level to negotiate wages, regardless of their trade union membership (Greece) or of conditions such as geographical and functional mobility and working time (Portugal).

In Greece, the conditions for recourse to arbitration were also changed by requiring the consent of both employers and workers, instead of workers alone as before. Moreover, the scope of the national collective wage agreement was fundamentally reduced by making the determination of minimum wages statutory rather than collectively agreed. The minimum wage was in this way reduced from €750 to €€80, while for workers aged under 25 years it was set at €511. The Portuguese MoUs included a commitment by the government that, for the duration of the adjustment programme, it would not change minimum wages unless labour market and economic conditions so permitted, and it was always subject to an agreement with the Troika (European Commission 2011c).

Intrusiveness in this area has been unprecedented, which is not surprising given the importance of wage developments for the internal devaluation that was being pursued in both member states. In that context, interference was very high in both countries and its evolution has been particularly interesting with regard to the role of social partners who have been mentioned regularly in the MoUs as parties to be consulted about reforms.

This seems to be a case of mere window dressing. For example, in Greece, the MoU of the second programme, unlike the MEFP, stipulated as a matter of urgency that the government would, in consultation with the Troika, legislate measures that would deliver the necessary adjustment in labour costs, following the 'failure' of the social partners and the government to come up with measures that could help in a timely manner (European Commission 2012a). This happened following major reforms in collective wage bargaining, a drop in private-sector wages of 20 per cent characterized as 'unprecedented in any developed countries' (European Commission 2012b) and the absence of any of the expected sizeable effects of such 'cuts' on the country's economic performance. In other words, the failure of the adopted strategies to deliver the intended outcomes for reasons that clearly cannot be blamed on the lack of implementation are seen to lead to more interference in the form of blatant bypassing of the social partners.

Similarly in Portugal, the social partners were to be consulted in devising an action plan that would effectively decentralise wage setting by work councils at the firm level. This stipulation was eventually dropped and replaced by a report that would allow the government 'to assess the options for ensuring more effective decentralization of wage bargaining and promoting wage flexibility' (European Commission 2014a).

In Greece, moreover, enforcement became particularly high with the phrase 'prior to disbursement' preceding measures as early as the fifth review of the first programme (European Commission 2011b) and even more in the early MoU versions of the second programme, when the difficulties of implementation had mushroomed (European Commission

2012a, b). Overall, intrusiveness in the reforms related to wage setting was higher in Greece than in Portugal, with the changes that took place in the former constituting a paradigm shift (cf. Hall 1993).

## Conclusions

Our analysis has suggested that the potential of the EU to intrude in national social and labour market policy reforms has increased, in the context of the crisis, to reach unprecedentedly high levels through the use of the MoUs in the bailed out member states. Due to their institutional set up, the MoUs have represented a major advance along the road of surveillance and enforcement. The degree of their interference has indeed been particularly high in the cases of Greece and Portugal, as evidenced by the wealth of detail displayed in the specifications for action in the areas of social and labour market policy.

However, the extent of this overall intrusiveness has varied. The more difficult, politically and/or technically, the MoU reforms have been to implement, the greater the level of intrusiveness; the more the adjustment with regard to fiscal or competitiveness variables has failed to take place according to plan, and the more direct the relevance of a policy area for the adjustment in question, the more insistent the intrusiveness has become. The events that led to the conclusion of the adjustment programme attached to the second Greek bailout and the agreement on the third in January–July 2015 suggest that the more urgent the need for financial support is, the stronger the hand of the EU has been in imposing particular measures. The function of a positive ex post implementation assessment as a necessary condition for the disbursement of funds as well as the choice of the ECB to make its support to the Greek banking system conditional upon an agreement with the Troika (Whelan 2015) have shown that time for protracted negotiations or even the deliberation and study of different policy options is not on the bailed out government's side.

In a nutshell, it can be argued that, faced with the difficulties of implementing the conditionality agreements—difficulties that have arguably not always been due to the lack of political will in persevering with their one-size-fits-all adjustment strategy (Pisani-Ferry et al. 2013)—the response of the EU has been to step up its intrusiveness rather than to envisage any reconsideration of the strategy itself (cf. Ladi and Graziano 2014).

The aforementioned factors that are associated with variations in intrusiveness are by no means exogenous. Instead, they are likely to be linked to domestic politics and institutions, which we have treated here as given. Further research should seek to illuminate how domestic factors have shaped the negotiated measures and the EU intrusiveness. The effects of the reforms induced by the MoUs have often taken, in principle, steps towards the modernisation of the pension system (in Greece) and of labour market policies (in Greece and Portugal)—'modernisation' here being taken to mean a process of extending protection to sections of the population not hitherto covered by the system, as well as the rationalisation of resources. Examples include extension of the social safety net to cover areas that were not previously reached (e.g., in pensions and income support for the unemployed in Greece) or attempts to alleviate inequity within systems (e.g., pensions in Greece). At the same time, however, the need to cut public expenditure on these policies to meet challenging adjustment targets and the increase in demand for social and labour market policies due to the deep recession and mounting unemployment rates have borne down on and detracted from the efficacy of such attempts. The adequacy of benefits has suffered; the labour market policy reforms promoted seem to have privileged flexibility and resilience over security while further weakening the industrial relations systems. The analysis of these policy areas does not claim to provide a complete picture of the direction in which social and labour market policies in the two countries change, insofar as other important areas such as healthcare and the public sector have been left out. Tight budget constraints inevitably involve cuts; however, it is an open question whether, how and how soon any of these savings will be reinvested in other areas.

This increased potential of EU intrusiveness through the MoUs does not necessarily mean that the same possibility for imposing such a strategy exists for all Eurozone or EU member states through the reinforced economic governance tools. After all, it has been the dependence on official funding and continued ECB support for the national banking system that ultimately reduces the bargaining power of national government vis-à-vis the lenders. While MoUs are clearly more intrusive, it remains to be seen how the country-specific recommendations will be implemented in practice and what will happen if they are not implemented (cf. Degryse et al. 2013). Even so, the strategy pursued through the MoUs provides a flavour of the priorities promoted by the economic actors in the EU, namely, the DG ECFIN and the ECB. As mentioned earlier, flexibility for resilience ('flexilience') seems, at the present time, to be overruling flexibility and security in the context of the EMU.

Might the Eurozone members have been better off without the bail-outs and the conditionality programmes that came attached to them and that were implemented through the MoUs? The bailouts were crucial in preventing disorderly defaults, which could have very plausibly led to the dissolution of the Eurozone in the form that we knew it until 2010 and again in 2015, when the possibility of Grexit was put on the negotiation table of the Eurogroup. The economic consequences of such a default and exit for the bailed out member states would have been grave and immediate and would have most likely involved much sharper cuts in public social spending and losses in real wages. Instead, the financial support packages bought time for the EU to contemplate the options for addressing the shortcomings in the institutional architecture of the EMU. Yet, the bailouts have certainly not resolved the crises.

The evidence suggests (Sapir et al. 2014) that the adjustment programmes implemented through the MoUs have not even managed to ensure the sustainable adjustment of macroeconomic imbalances in the countries where they have been implemented. As such, Greece and Portugal will have to deal with the consequences of this strategy, including significantly higher than predicted public debt/GDP ratio and unemployment rates for many years, while it appears that their production capacity has also been damaged through hysteresis effects (Ball 2014). The conditions of pervasive austerity that have been spreading through Europe will make any resolution of these problems both fraught and protracted.

In other words, it would seem very difficult to claim that the heightened EU intrusiveness in national social and labour market policies is a necessary evil that is justified insofar as it has led to desirable macroeconomic outcomes. In the longer run, and contrary to intentions, the outcome of this approach may jeopardise the sustainability of the EMU itself.

**Acknowledgements** I am grateful to Caroline de la Porte, Elke Heins, Nikos Koutsiaras, Maria Jepsen, the referees of this chapter and the participants of the international seminar, 'The sovereign debt crisis, the EU and welfare state reform', held at the Centre for Welfare State Research, University of Southern Denmark, Odense, on May 2, 2013, for their constructive feedback on earlier versions of this chapter; to Kathleen Llanwarne for editorial help; and to Kristian Krieger for his support. The usual disclaimer applies.

# References

Ball, L. (2014). *Long-term damage from the great recession in OECD countries.* Baltimore, MD: Johns Hopkins University and Mimeo.

Blanchard, O. J., Jaumotte, F., & Loungani, P. (2014). *Labor market policies and IMF advice in advanced economies during the great recession* (IMF Research Department Staff Discussion Note). Washington, DC: IMF.

Blanchard, O. J., & Philippon, T.. (2004). *The quality of labor relations and unemployment* (Working Paper No. 4-25). Cambridge, MA: MIT Department of Economics.

Blavoukos, S., & Pagoulatos, G. (2008). The limits of EMU conditionality: Fiscal adjustment in Southern Europe. *Journal of Public Policy, 28*(2), 229–253.

Buiter, W. (2011, December 7). The terrible consequences of a Eurozone collapse. *Financial Times.* http://www.ft.com/intl/cms/s/0/6cf8ce18-2042-11e1-9878-00144feabdc0.html#axzz34nHieBt0. Accessed 23 June 2014.

Cabral, R. (2010, May 8). The PIGS' external debt problem. *VoxEU blog.* http://www.voxeu.org/article/gips-external-debt-problem. Accessed 20 June 2014.

Canton, E., Grilo, I., Monteagudo, J., Pierini, F., & Turrini, A. (2014). *The role of structural reform for adjustment and growth.* Brussels: DG ECFIN Economic Brief.

de la Porte, C., & Heins, E. (2016). A new era of European integration? Governance of labour market and social policy since the sovereign debt crisis. In de la Porte, Caroline and Elke Heins (Eds.), *The sovereign debt crisis, the EU and welfare state reform* (pp. 15–42). London: Palgrave Macmillan.

DeGrauwe, P. (2011). *The governance of a Fragile Eurozone* (Economic Policy, CEPS Working Document No. 346). Brussels: CEPS.

Degryse, C., Jepsen, M., & Pochet, P. (2013). *The Euro crisis and its impact on national and European social policies* (Working Paper 2013.05-advance online version). Brussels: ETUI.

Emmenegger, P. (2011). Job security regulations in Western Democracies: A fuzzy-set analysis. *European Journal of Political Research, 50*(3), 336–364.

European Commission. (2006). *The long-term sustainability of public finances in the European Union* (European Economy No. 4/2006). Brussels.

European Commission. (2009). *Pension schemes and pension projections in the EU-27 Member States—2008-2060, Volume I-Report* (European Economy Occasional Paper No. 56). Brussels.

European Commission. (2010a). *The economic adjustment programme for Greece* (European Economy-Occasional Papers 61/2010). Brussels.

European Commission. (2010b). *The economic adjustment programme for Greece, second review* (European Economy-Occasional Paper No. 72). Brussels.

European Commission. (2010c). *The economic adjustment programme of Greece* (European Economy-Occasional Paper No. 61). Brussels.

European Commission. (2011a). *The economic adjustment programme for Greece-third review* (European Economy-Occasional Paper No. 77). Brussels.

European Commission. (2011b). *The economic adjustment programme for Greece, fifth review* (European Economy, Occasional Paper No. 87). Brussels.

European Commission. (2011c). *The economic adjustment programme for Portugal* (European Economy-Occasional Paper No. 79). Brussels.

European Commission. (2011d). *The economic adjustment programme for Portugal* (European Economy-Occasional Paper No. 79). Brussels.

European Commission. (2012a). *The second economic adjustment programme for Greece* (European Economy-Occasional Paper No. 94). Brussels.

European Commission. (2012b). *The second economic adjustment programme for Greece-first review* (European Economy-Occasional Paper No. 123). Brussels.

European Commission. (2013a). *The economic adjustment programme for Portugal-seventh review* (European Economy-Occasional Paper No. 153). Brussels: Directorate General for Economic and Financial Affairs.

European Commission. (2013b). *The economic adjustment programme for Portugal, eighth and ninth review* (European Economy-Occasional Paper No. 164). Brussels.

European Commission. (2013c). *The second economic adjustment programme for Greece-second review* (European Economy-Occasional Paper No. 148). Brussels.

European Commission. (2014a). *The economic adjustment programme for Portugal, tenth review* (European Economy-Occasional Paper No. 171). Brussels.

European Commission. (2014b). *The second economic adjustment programme for Greece-fourth review* (European Economy-Occasional Paper No. 192). Brussels.

Eurostat. (2014a). *EU-SILC database.*

Eurostat. (2014b). *Labour market policy database.*

Featherstone, K. (2001). *The political dynamics of the Vincolo Esterno: The emergence of EMU and the challenge to the European social model* (Queen's Papers on Europeanisation No. 6/2001). Belfast: Queen's University Belfast.

Ferrera, M. (1996). The 'Southern Model' of welfare in social Europe. *Journal of European Social Policy, 6*(17), 16–37.

Hall, P. A. (1993). Policy paradigms, social learning, and the state: The case of economic policymaking in Britain. *Comparative Politics, 25*(3), 275–296.

Hall, P. A., & Soskice, D. (2001). An introduction to varieties of capitalism. In P. A. Hall & D. Soskice (Eds.), *Varieties of capitalism: The institutional foundations of comparative advantage.* Oxford: Oxford University Press.

Hope, K. (2012, October 17). Greece nears agreement with lenders. *Financial Times.* http://www.ft.com/intl/cms/s/0/8d8754ec-1849-11e2-80e9-00144 feabdc0.html?siteedition=intl#axzz35Sd6NuLp. Accessed 20 June 2014.

Hope, K. (2013a, April 15). Greece secures deal on 2.8bn euros aid tranche. *Financial Times.* http://www.ft.com/intl/cms/s/0/90f0e0da-a5b1-11e2-9b77-00144feabdc0.html#axzz35Sd6NuLp. Accessed 20 June 2014.

Hope, K. (2013b, December 8). Greece shows new assertive attitude to troika demands. *Financial Times.* http://www.ft.com/intl/cms/s/0/87291ba6-600c-11e3-916e-00144feabdc0.html#axzz35Sd6NuLp. Accessed 20 June 2014.

IMF. (2012). *World economic outlook: Coping with high debt and sluggish growth.* http://www.imf.org/external/pubs/ft/weo/2012/02/. Accessed 30 Sept 2014.

in t'Veld, J. (2013). *Fiscal consolidations and spillovers in the Euro area periphery and core* (European Economy Economic Papers No. 506). Brussels: European Commission-Directorate General of Economic and Financial Affairs.

Krugman, P. (2013, May 25) Europe's Keynesian problem. *The Conscience of Liberal blog.* http://krugman.blogs.nytimes.com/2013/05/25/europes-keynesian-problem/. Accessed 20 June 2014.

Ladi, S., & Graziano, P. R. (2014). Fast-forward' Europeanization and welfare state reform in Greece and Italy in light of the Eurozone crisis. In R. Coman, T. Kostera, & L. Tomini (Eds.), *Europeanization and EU integration: From incremental to structural change?* Basingstoke, UK: Palgrave Macmillan.

Leibfried, S., & Pierson, P. (1995). *European social policy: Between fragmentation and integration.* Washington, DC: Brookings Institution.

Matsaganis, M. (2013). *The Greek crisis: Social impact and policy responses.* Berlin: Friedrich Ebert Stiftung.

OECD (2004). *Employment outlook.* Paris: OECD.

OECD. (2005). Pension-system Typology. In *OECD pensions at a glance 2005.* Paris: OECD.

OECD. (2010). Rebalancing the economy towards sustainable growth. In *Economic surveys: Portugal 2010.* Paris: OECD.

OECD. (2013). Protecting jobs, enhancing flexibility: A new look at employment protection legislation. In *OECD Employment Outlook 2013.* Paris: OECD.

OECD (2014). *Society at a glance 2014 highlights: Portugal-the crisis and its aftermath.* Paris: OECD.

Petmesidou, M. (2010). *Pensions, health and long-term care-Greece.* ASISP Country Document 2010. http://socialprotection.eu/. Accessed 20 June 2014.

Petmesidou, M. (2013). *Pensions, health and long-term care-Greece.* ASISP Country Document 2013. http://socialprotection.eu/. Accessed 20 June 2014.

Pierson, P. (2001). Coping with permanent austerity: Welfare state restructuring in affluent democracies. In P. Pierson (Ed.), *The new politics of the welfare state.* Oxford: Oxford University Press.

Pisani-Ferry, J., Sapir, A., & Wolff, G. B. (2013). *EU-IMF assistance to Euro-area countries: An early assessment* (Bruegel Blueprint 19). Brussels: Bruegel.

Regan, A. (2013). *Political tensions in Euro-varieties of capitalism: The crisis of the democratic state in Europe* (EUI Working Paper MWP 2013/24). San Domenico di Fiesole: European University Institute.

Ribeiro Mendes, F. (2010). *Annual national report 2010: Portugal.* ASISP. http://socialprotection.eu/.

Ribeiro Mendes, F. (2012). *Annual national report 2012: Portugal.* ASISP.

Sapir, A., Wolff, G. B., de Souza, C., & Terzi, A. (2014). *The Troika and financial assistance in the Euro area: Successes and failures.* Brussels: European

Parliament, Study on the request of the European Parliament's Economic and Monetary Affairs Committee.

Stovicek, K., & Turrini, A. (2012). *Benchmarking unemployment benefit systems* (European Economy-Economic Paper No. 454). Brussels.

Theodoropoulou, S., & Watt, A. (2015). An evaluation of the austerity strategy in the Eurozone: Was the first Greek programme bound to fail? In G. Karyotis & R. Gerodimos (Eds.), *The politics of extreme austerity: Greece beyond the crisis*. Basingstoke, UK: Palgrave Macmillan.

Venn, D. (2009). *Legislation, collective bargaining and enforcement: Updating the OECD employment protection indicators* (OECD Social, Employment and Migration Working Papers No. 89). Paris: OECD.

Whelan, K. (2015). The Grexit mechanism: What it means for the future of the Euro. *Bull Market*. Accessed 17 Sept 2015.

Wise, P. (2013a, May 5). Portugal begins talks on further austerity measures. *Financial Times*. http://www.ft.com/intl/cms/s/0/6e1d5e72-b57d-11e2-a51b-00144feabdc0.html#axzz35Sd6NuLp. Accessed 20 June 2014.

Wise, P. (2013b, April 14). Troika to assess Portugal's austerity plans. *Financial Times*. http://www.ft.com/intl/cms/s/0/620f604a-a4fb-11e2-8777-00144feabdc0.html#axzz35Sd6NuLp. Accessed 20 June 2014.

Wren-Lewis, S. (2013, October 28). The 'official' cost of austerity. *Mainly Macro blog*. http://mainlymacro.blogspot.be/2013/10/the-official-cost-of-austerity.html. Accessed 20 June 2014.

Zartaloudis, S. (2014). The impact of the fiscal crisis on Greek and Portuguese welfare states: Retrenchment before the catch-up? *Social Policy and Administration, 48*(4), 430–449.

# 6

# From Austerity to Permanent Strain? The European Union and Welfare State Reform in Italy and Spain

Emmanuele Pavolini, Margarita León,
Ana M. Guillén, and Ugo Ascoli

## Introduction

Recent years and day-to-day chronicles from many European countries deeply affected by the economic crisis tell a story of potentially profound changes in the structure and nature of Welfare States. In particular Southern European Welfare States have reached dire straits since the advent of the economic crisis and the subsequent EU-driven policies targeted at attaining fiscal balances. This chapter aims to analyse comparatively the trajectories of change in Italy and Spain, the two largest south European countries, both strongly affected by the economic crisis and the austerity measures that ensued. Within such trajectories of change, the chapter prominently assesses the level of influence of the EU through not only formal instruments around the European Semester but also agreements with the Troika and the ECB. Since the advent of the crisis, the policymaking process in both countries has been altered: party politics, public and parliamentary debates and involvement of organized interests

E. Pavolini (✉) • M. León • A.M. Guillén • U. Ascoli
SPOCRI Department, Macerata University, Macerata, Italy

© The Author(s) 2016
C. de la Porte, E. Heins (eds.), *The Sovereign Debt Crisis, the EU and Welfare State Reform*, DOI 10.1057/978-1-137-58179-2_6

and other actors are losing relevance, while the European Commission (EC), the International Monetary Fund (IMF) and the ECB have tended to play an increasingly salient role in decision-making processes. The chapter is structured as follows. The analytical approach is spelled out in the following section. Section three consists of an in-depth analysis of the evolution of policy changes since the 2000s with the double purpose of, firstly, eliciting reform trajectories and, secondly, discussing the role played by the EU with the aim of assessing the degree of EU influence. An interpretation of the research results is offered in the concluding section.

## The Analytical Approach

To characterize policy change, our analysis uses two widespread concepts to assess what has happened since the end of the so-called golden era of social policy expansion (Pierson 1998): retrenchment and recalibration. Retrenchment is commonly used to describe policies that introduce cuts in social provision. Contrary to the well-known Pierson's welfare state resilience theory,[1] other scholars have argued that retrenchment can take place explicitly as well as implicitly through creeping forms of privatization (Streeck and Thelen 2005). When countries confront deep economic crises and very large budget deficits, politicians might argue that they are engaging in retrenchment not for its own sake but to save public finances and restore economic growth and employment. Apart from explicit retrenchment policies, a relatively large amount of the literature has argued that retrenchment policies can be based on more hidden and undeclared complex devices. Streeck and Thelen (2005) use the notion of 'gradual transformation' to refer to institutional change that is incremental in form but disruptive in the outcomes. In this form, the authors argue, far-reaching change can be accomplished through the accumulation of small adjustments. Adopting this perspective, Palier (2010) integrates Streeck and Thelen's concepts with Hall's typology on

---

[1] The interpretation of welfare policy changes based on retrenchment has been deeply criticized by Pierson (2001). Analyzing British and US social spending trends, Pierson found that it not only did not decline but rather grew at a faster rate than the economy as a whole. Thereafter welfare state resilience has become a relevant but also a contested concept.

first, second and third order change (1993) and explains the 'defreezing' process that has characterized the Bismarckian welfare systems in recent decades on the basis of the accumulation of small, incremental changes.

Along with the possibility of retrenchment, the concept of recalibration (Ferrera et al. 2000) has been introduced in the scientific literature as an extensive form of welfare state re-modelling. In particular 'functional' recalibration deals with the social risks covered by the welfare state, how they have evolved over time and how, increasingly, there are gaps in social protection. Functional recalibration is often associated with the concept of 'old' and 'new' social risks (Taylor-Gooby 2004) related to the transition from a 'male breadwinner' industrial society to a 'dual earner' post-industrial one, which is also affected by demographic aging and flexible labour markets. 'Distributive' recalibration concerns the re-balancing of social protection provisions across different policy beneficiaries.

The recalibration approach can be useful to assess policy change in European welfare states in so far as, in many cases, cost-containment and cuts in traditional social policy fields (pensions and unemployment benefits), together with (partial) deregulation of the labour market, have been matched by programmes concerned with new functions, such as helping people back into employment, integrating work income for the working poor, helping parents reconcile work and family life, promoting gender equality, supporting child development and human capital accumulation and providing long-term care for individuals with chronic health and dependency problems (Bonoli and Natali 2012). As a matter of fact, looking at public expenditure and needs' coverage, the story of the last two decades is not only of retrenchment or 'frozen landscapes' but also of expansion in social policies covering new social risks (Saraceno and Keck 2011; Ranci and Pavolini 2013). The notion of 'Social Investment' has been put forward to describe this approach potentially behind the functional reorientation of welfare states (Jenson 2008; Morel et al. 2012).

To evaluate if, overall, simple resilience, mainly retrenchment or some recalibration, has been taking place in a specific country, a broad view on changes in different social policy fields is needed. In particular, an important element to consider when analysing trajectories of policy change are the differences in the types of institutional design various policies might have. Following traditional welfare state typologies, we will distinguish between 'state corporatist' (pensions and labour market), 'universalistic' (healthcare and education) and 'targeted' (social assistance, social care and family policies) institutional designs.

Given the increasing relevance of the EU integration process during the last two decades, the question of how national welfare states change mingles with the role played by the EU in this process. Is it possible to argue that heightened EU integration (de la Porte and Heins, Chapter 2) is the main variable explaining what happened since the beginning of the last decade in Spanish and Italian social policies?

The EU uses a set of 'adjustment pressures' on national welfare states including, on the one hand, formal procedures and, on the other, a mix between conditionality and 'backroom' diplomacy. Formal procedures are those described by de la Porte and Heins in Chapter 2: monetary and economic, as well as social and labour market policy coordination through a set of instruments (the Stability and Growth Pact [SGP], the Six Pack and Fiscal Consolidation, the European Employment Strategy [EES] and Europe 2020). Conditionality consists of financial help provided by the EU in exchange for structural adjustments, and it has been used for those member states most in trouble from an economic and/or budgetary point of view. Usually conditionality has been matched by backroom diplomacy: informal negotiations used by the EU to convince domestic policymakers to introduce the reforms proposed by the EU.

To analyse the role of the EU, three sets of documents have been used: Commission recommendations and Council decisions in relation to EDPs, Commission country-specific recommendations based on the assessment of each country's plans for sound public finances (Stability or Convergence Programmes, or SCPs) and policy measures to boost growth and jobs (National Reform Programmes, or NRPs). These documents allow an analysis of the contents of formal adjustment pressures. Other documents and sources (including newspaper articles) have also been analysed to look at the role of conditionality and backroom diplomacy.

Whereas the expenditure and policy reforms analysis refers to a longer time span (late 1990s until 2014), that on EU adjustment pressures covers the period 2005–13 to grasp if changes took place before and after the onset of the economic crisis.

We argue that the Italian and Spanish welfare states have witnessed increasing EU intrusiveness in recent years that go beyond the new formalised EU procedures around economic and monetary union. The influence of the EU in national policymaking has taken place more via conditionality and backroom diplomacy than through formal procedures (although the latter have become more effective due to the former). While the core messages from the EC to Italy and Spain have substantially remained the same before and after the outset of the economic crisis, the level of detailed specification on actual policy reforms has increased significantly with a much tighter timing for their implementation.

The result of EU pressure, together with other factors at the domestic level, has been a substantial retrenchment of the Spanish and Italian welfare states in recent years, in which the facets of recalibration are hard to find. However, retrenchment has followed different paths depending on the institutional design of each social policy domain. In sum, with the advent of the economic crisis and the austerity measures that followed, the welfare states of these two countries seem to be converging again after a decade (2000–09) of diverging trajectories.

## Policy Changes in Southern Europe Since the Turn of the Century and the Role of the EU

An overview of social protection expenditure over time can provide a first hint of the general changes in the two welfare states (Table 6.1). Spain's investment in social policies increased quite strongly in the last decade when compared to the EU-15 and Italian trends: the average annual growth rate of expenditure between 2000 and 2009 was +4.7 per cent (respectively +2.5 per cent for EU-15 and +2.1 per cent for Italy). The higher growth rates in the last decade allowed the Spanish welfare state to reduce its distance from the average level of expenditure in the EU-15: in 2000 the per capita expenditure in Spain was 63 per cent of that of the EU-15; by 2009 it increased to 75 per cent. However, the impact of austerity measures, introduced mainly starting from 2010, can be traced by looking at what happened between 2009 and 2011: the average annual

**Table 6.1** Social protection expenditure in Spain and Italy compared to the EU-15

|  | Euro per inhabitant (at constant 2005 prices) | | | | | Purchasing power standard per inhabitant—distance from EU-15 = 100 % | | |
|  | 2000 | 2009 | 2011 | Average annual % var. 2000–09 | Average annual % var. 2009–11 | 2000 | 2009 | 2011 |
|---|---|---|---|---|---|---|---|---|
| EU-15 | 6670 | 8151 | 8049 | +2.5 | –0.6 | 100.0 | 100.0 | 100.0 |
| Spain | 3683 | 5236 | 5107 | +4.7 | –1.2 | 62.9 | 75.3 | 74.0 |
| Italy | 5874 | 6982 | 6855 | +2.1 | –0.9 | 93.4 | 92.9 | 91.9 |

*Source*: Eurostat-ESSPROS database (2013)

**Table 6.2** Changes in social needs in Spain and Italy compared to the EU-15 during the crisis

|  | People at risk of poverty or social exclusion (%) | | | Unemployment rate (15–64) (%) | | |
|  | 2007 | 2011 | Variation in the absolute number of people | 2007 | 2013 | Variation in the absolute number of unemployed |
|---|---|---|---|---|---|---|
| EU-15 | 21.6 | 22.6 | +6.6 % (+2.5 %)[a] | 7.1 | 9.6 | +38.8 % (+14.0 %)[a] |
| Spain | 23.3 | 27.7 | +23.3 % | 8.3 | 21.7 | +172.6 % |
| Italy | 26.0 | 28.2 | +11.0 % | 6.1 | 8.4 | +40.0 % |

*Source*: Eurostat-ESSPROS database (2013)
[a]Value referred to EU-15 without Spain and Italy.

growth decreased by 1.2 per cent. This reduction was twice as strong as in the EU-15 (–0.6 per cent).

Italy is a slightly different story. Total social protection expenditure increased at a slightly slower pace than the average EU-15 until 2009 (+2.1 per cent vs+2.5 per cent); after 2009 the decrease was also more pronounced than in the EU-15 (–0.9 per cent vs –0.6 per cent). The result is that, between 2000 and 2011, the distance from the EU-15 has increased.

These expenditure changes in recent years have taken place at a time when the social demand dramatically increased in Spain and Italy more than in western Europe in general (Table 6.2). If, in the EU-15, people at risk of poverty or social exclusion represented 21.6 per cent of the population in 2007 and they reached 22.6 per cent in 2011, the same figures for Spain and Italy were, respectively, from 23.3 per cent to 27.7 per cent and from 26.0 per cent to 28.2 per cent. The changes in need in absolute numbers are even more dramatic: the population at risk of poverty increased in western Europe by 6.6 per cent, whereas in Italy by 11 per cent and in Spain by 23.3 per cent. An important part of social demand concentrated in the two Southern European countries: between 2007 and 2011, there was an increase of around 5.5 million at the poverty level in western Europe—around 4.1 million of these were concentrated in Spain and Italy.

If we look at unemployment, the figures for Spain were skyrocketing in terms of rates (from 8.3 per cent to 21.7 per cent) and even more in absolute numbers (+172.6 per cent unemployed between 2007 and 2011). In Italy the increase in absolute numbers was +40 per cent. In the rest of western Europe, excluding Spain and Italy, it was +14 per cent. Again, as for the case of social exclusion, out of 5.1 million new unemployed between 2007 and 2011 in the EU-15, around 3.8 million were from Spain and Italy.

Spain and Italy have a similar overall structure of their welfare state. The institutional design changes depend on the policy field, and it takes mainly three different forms: a predominantly state corporatist model in pensions, unemployment and labour market policies; a universalistic form in healthcare and education; and a targeted model in social assistance, social care and family support.

Nonetheless, two different paths of institutional change may be ascertained in the two countries in the 2000s, whereas a new convergence seems to emerge in more recent years after the onset of austerity.

## The 2000s

The Italian welfare state in the 2000s can be best described as an almost 'totally frozen' landscape (Naldini and Saraceno 2008; Maino and Neri 2011). The main paradigmatic reforms were introduced in the 1990s. Those related to the state corporatist pillar had a direct cost-containment goal (especially those in the pensions field in 1992–93 and 1995, which radically changed and rationalized the system; see Natali 2011), whereas those related to the universalistic pillar were mainly focused on changing the government and governance model of healthcare and education (with the introduction of decentralization and new public management; Pavolini and Guillén 2013). At the same time, the reforms of the 1990s did not really touch the issue of a better and more appropriate coverage of 'new social risks', which remained 'targeted' and quite residual. Italy missed a minimum income scheme, and it presented a relatively low level of needs' coverage also in the main social care fields, namely, childcare and elderly care (Ascoli and Pavolini 2012). According to Eurostat data, still in 2007, Italy spent an amount of per capita resources equal to 57 per cent of the average EU-15 level on family and children. More awkward in the international perspective was the social exclusion expenditure (13 per cent of the EU-15 average).

Therefore, the 2000s were a time when no relevant policy reform was implemented. Cost-containment policies in traditional state corporatist welfare state fields coupled by no real 'functional' recalibration toward new social risks has meant that an overall retrenchment process took place in the country.

In this setting, the role of EU institutions was small, both in terms of coordination of public finances and of recalibration of social and labour market policies. Also, if the EES and Lisbon Strategy goals were not taken too much into consideration in the Italian debate, the enforcement of instruments aimed at the sustainability of public finances (in particular the tools related to the SGP, such as the EDP) was limited. *De facto* there was a medium level of enforcement, as indicated by de la Porte and Heins in Chapter 2. Substantially, Italy felt that, once entered in the European Monetary Union ( EMU), the risks of being sent out for lack of strict compliance to EMU rules were low. Financial sanctions were never levied, and the SGP, in particular the deficit rule, was weakly enforced (de Haan et al. 2004).

Until 2010, the effectiveness of EU formal procedures to foster adjustment pressures on the Italian welfare state was limited. Commission recommendations and Council decisions in relation to the EDP (Italy was under the EDP from 2005 to 2013), as well as Commission country-specific recommendations based on the assessment of the Italian SCP and NRP, are generic. In the pension field the leitmotiv was the same until the 2011 reform: appreciation for previous reforms as well as the need to fully implement them or to introduce new elements (e.g., the gradual increase of the retirement age for female civil servants in 2009). Also, worries were expressed about the fact that pension expenditure as a share of GDP remained among the highest in the EU. As regards the labour market, until 2011 the EU recommendations were mainly related to the 'need to strengthen unemployment strategies in key areas' (years 2005–07), to give the highest priority to 'the operation of employment services, within a flexicurity approach' (year 2008) and 'to reallocate social expenditure so as to put in place a more comprehensive and uniform unemployment benefit system that ensures appropriate work incentives and effective activation policies' (years 2009–10). In general, from 2005 to 2010 the recommendations promoted, in very general terms, a flexicurity approach. Overall, apart from the increase in the retirement age for female civil servants, none of the recommendations influenced the Italian debate in any substantial way.

The 2000s were an almost totally different story in Spain, both in terms of reforms and the role of the EU. In the pension field, rationalisation reforms (of a comparatively less imbalanced and more equal system than the Italian one) had already started in the mid-1980s; further reforms aimed at a combination of rationalisation and enhanced re-distribution took place in 1996, 2003 and 2007. Cuts in the state corporatist pillar were matched by growing public investments in the universalistic form (healthcare and education; Pavolini and Guillén 2013) and, perhaps even more importantly, in policies addressing new social risks (Guillén and León 2011). Up until 2011, expansion took place (in terms of access and funding) in childcare services, paid parental leave, financial support for working mothers, minimum pensions, means-tested unemployment benefits and long-term care. Regarding the latter, the 2006 Law on Dependency became the first normative framework for long-term care granting a universal subjective right to be cared for. In March 2011, applications had reached 1.5 million, and over 800,000 services and economic transfers had been conceded (Consejo Económico y Social [CES] 2011).

These policy innovations can be seen as important path departures from a tradition of weak state involvement in the sphere of care, thus challenging the underpinnings of familialistic assumptions. Trends for expenditure witness these changes over time, as Eurostat data show. In 2000, Spain was starting from a relatively low level of per capita expenditure both in family and social exclusion policies (respectively, 38.2 per cent and 36.3 per cent of the EU-15 average). In 2007, the situation had strongly improved (per capita expenditure was respectively 56.8 per cent and 63.9 per cent of the average for western Europe). The result was obtained thanks to very high yearly growth rates (+7.8 per cent in family policies and +19.8 per cent for social exclusion).

The EU has contributed to this result, especially in terms of the effects of EU 'interference' through the instruments aiming at re-calibrating social and labour market policy (the EES and the Lisbon Strategy).

The Spanish reforms in long-term care, childcare and active labour market policies were all influenced by the EU debate and tools such as the open method of coordination (OMC); the Spanish literature describes this process as the 'Europeanization' of social policies (Guillén and León 2011). These were developed through soft governance tools and the diffusion of ideas, which had had little impact in Italy.

Also in the Spanish case, formal instruments aimed at the sustainability of public finances did not put a strong indirect pressure on welfare state policies until 2010, although Spain came under an EDP in 2009. The level of excessive deficit was, however, not so high as to prompt immediate action, and the recommendation of the Commission was that, given special circumstances—that is, the sharp economic downturn and the size of the required budgetary adjustment—the correction of the excessive deficit should be undertaken in a medium-term time frame (EC 2009a). At this stage, and pretty much in contrast to what would happen a year later, the EC was granting Spain two years (until 2012) to follow the reduction of government deficit in a gradual manner therefore giving a green light to the intentions of the Spanish government as outlined in the 2009 NSP, which combined 'mild' austerity with spending. Moreover, in November 2009 the Commission reviewed the actions taken by the Spanish government, and in its recommendation to the Council (EC 2009b), it concluded that, although Spain's fiscal outlook worsened during the course of 2009, the blame is thus not placed on the Spanish government, which 'has taken effective action in compliance with the Council recommendations of 27 April 2009' (ibid., p. 7). The EC is still endorsing the medium-term path to limit risks to the required medium-term fiscal adjustment. At the same time and in the same document, the Commission asked Spain to implement the necessary reforms to its old-age pension and healthcare systems to contain and reduce the budgetary costs of aging populations, without specifying, however, what kind of measures should have been taken to ensure the sustainability of the two systems.

## The Onset of the Economic Crisis

Until 2009, Spain and Italy came under EU pressures asking for reforms, both countries being under EDP, but these pressures came mainly via formal instruments (EC Recommendations). Moreover, as described earlier, the contents of such pressures were relatively general (asking for reforms in broad terms) and not rigid in terms of the reforms' time schedule. Neither country reacted immediately, but they were more concerned with the mounting economic crisis than answering Brussels' requests.

After 2009, EU action was enhanced, firstly, via 'recommendations' through formal instruments that became very specific and detailed and with a tight time schedule; secondly, pressures became more intrusive through a mix between conditionality and backroom diplomacy.

The change in the level of EU influence, in the mechanisms used and its efficacy in transforming the Spanish and Italian welfare states (as described later) are related to the phenomenon of the 'sovereign debt crisis'; due to the perseverance of the recession, the difficulties in re-financing debt became a huge problem both for Italy and Spain (paying increasingly high interest rates) and the EMU as a whole, given their economic size and their relevance in the functioning of the Euro.

The reforms and the austerity plans starting since 2010–11 have taken place inside this environment; tremendous pressure from financial markets with the crisis of the state debt financing and, connected to it, the increasing conditionality in the EU institutions support to face it. All three dimensions of EU integration, that is, interference, surveillance and enforcement, were at work. They also had a potential immediate effect through various tools, the most important being the possibility for the ECB to stop purchasing public debt bonds.

Moreover, in the case of Spain, another source of conditionality came into play. In June 2012, the Spanish Government requested external financial assistance in the context of the ongoing restructuring and recapitalization of the Spanish banking sector. The Troika approved a loan from the European Financial Stability Fund (EFSF) of an estimated €100 billion for the duration of 18 months. The Memorandum of Understanding (MoU) on financial-sector policy conditionality that was adopted on 23 July 2012 details the policy conditions as embedded in the Council Decision (EC 2012). The conditionality established by the MoU is all financial-sector specific with all 33 measures referring to monitoring different aspects of the banking sector. In other words, its main objective is to restore and strengthen the Spanish banking sector. However, the MoU granted financial assistance to Spain subject to harsh conditionality. This implies high intrusiveness of the EU. The degree of integration is very high in terms of objectives to the extent that the targets require far-reaching structural policy reforms also in the context of the EDP and the Macro-economic Imbalance Procedure (MIP), which includes taxation and labour market policies. The degree of enforcement is also very high to the extent that the loan from the EFSF is subject to treaty-based corrective action and strict conditionality.

If EU integration has been enhanced, national welfare state change took different shapes depending on the institutional design of each policy field, as shown in Table 6.3 and in the text.

## The 'State Corporatist' Pillar: Explicit Retrenchment with Few Hints of Recalibration in Pensions and Labour Market Policies

Even if positive results were obtained with the 1990s reforms, the need for 'austerity' invoked since 2010 to counter the financial crisis and to reduce the public debt pushed for new interventions in Italian pensions policy. The pension reform, passed at the end of 2011 by the Monti Government,

**Table 6.3** National welfare state policies in Spain and Italy, EU pressure and its character

| Welfare state pillar | EU mechanisms for 'adjustment pressures' | EU explicit reference to the need of reforms by Spain and Italy | Character of EU recommendations |
|---|---|---|---|
| *State corporatist* (pensions and labour market) | Formal procedures + conditionality | Explicit reference to cuts | Explicit retrenchment ('credit claiming') |
| *Universalistic* (healthcare and education) | | Implicit reference to cuts (EDP and MIP) | Implicit retrenchment ('policy drift') |
| *Targeted* (social assistance, social care, family policies) | | Implicit reference to cuts; explicit reference to recalibration | Implicit retrenchment; no recalibration |

*Source*: Own elaboration

sped up the shift to a 'pay-as-you-go' system with a contribution-related method applying to everyone. There was also a drastic reduction in the possibility of accessing 'seniority pensions'. To qualify for this type of pension in 2012, men will have to have worked for at least 42 years and women for 41 years. To benefit from the traditional 'old-age pension', it will be necessary to have at least 20 years' contributions. The retirement age has also been raised considerably; from 2018, the required age for all workers will be 66 years and 7 months, and this will increase automatically on the basis of life expectancy trends. Finally, the contribution rates for the self-employed were raised to move more quickly toward a homogenization with employees' rates. Thanks to the previous reforms (especially those in the 1990s) and the most recent, the Italian pension system has adopted one of the least 'generous' institutional frameworks in Europe, if one looks at forecasts for the expenditure level in the years to come.

The first retrenchment measures in Spain, the freezing of pensions for 2011, were announced by the Socialist (Partido Socialista Obrero Español, or Spanish Socialist Workers' Party, or PSOE) Government in 2010. The reform of the pension system was then enacted in August 2011. This entailed the postponement of the official retirement age from 65 to 67 years of age and a further 10 years expansion (from 15 to 25) of the number of salaried years used to calculate the initial pension (to be phased out from 2013 to 2026), thus lowering the replacement rate in the medium term. The new law also tightened access to early retirement. The newly elected Conservative Government (Partido Popular, or People's Party, or PP) discontinued the freezing of pensions for 2012, although the increase was only of 1 per cent. In March 2013, new measures were enacted to restrict pre-retirement and partial retirement conditions.

Both labour markets were largely affected by reforms. More specifically, reforms in both countries after 2010, for the first time after decades, were not 'at the margins'. They tried to reshape the overall functioning of the labour market and, especially, the positions of the 'insiders', allowing easier dismissals for permanent full-time contracts.

In Italy, the reform had four main goals. The first was by an unemployment benefits scheme, with a broader range to cover part of the atypical workers. The third goal consisted of strengthening active labour market policies. Finally, the reform aimed at fostering women's employment through new forms of reconciliation, but it was scarcely innovative.

In Spain, the labour market reform was passed in early 2012. Among other flexibility measures, most prominently, the cost of dismissals was drastically reduced for permanent full-time contracts, so that, in a way, all workers have become 'outsiders'. Unemployment subsidies consisting of €400 per month (a programme running after unemployment contributory transfers are exhausted) have been protracted temporarily (six months) several times after the advent of the crisis. The aim is to alleviate those social groups most affected by the crisis, or, in other words, people within active ages, especially young families. The costs are massive, though, amounting to around €40 billion per year.

In sum, explicit retrenchment reforms took place in both countries in the fields of pensions and labour market policies in 2011 and 2012.

Unemployment protection saw attempts at improvement in Italy and remained unchanged in Spain, where several temporary protection programmes were approved and the expenditure went skyrocketing. EU pressure played an increasing and strong role, both in terms of the effect the recommendations had and the mechanisms adopted to implement such pressure on Italy and Spain.

In the Italian case, recommendations became more precise and detailed after 2010, but their real impact was stronger from 2011, when the financial crisis hit Italy and the EU institutions found other, more effective ways to influence reforms than 'simple' EC recommendations, which were drowned by domestic politics.

In August 2011, Jean-Claude Trichet, the President of the ECB, and his designated successor Mario Draghi wrote a firm letter to Prime Minister Silvio Berlusconi asking him to take incisive measures regarding growth, competition and liberalizations. The letter was very specific in its requests, asking for a review of the rules regulating the hiring and dismissal of employees (flexibility) and the establishment of an unemployment insurance system (to combat segmentation), as well as more stringent eligibility criteria for seniority pensions and a rapid alignment of the retirement age of women in the private and public sectors. As Sacchi (Chapter 7) underlines, this letter marked a turning point, practically indicating the actions to be implemented quite precisely and explicitly requiring the Italian government to resort to an urgent decree to implement such actions. The letter came in the heat of the financial markets turmoil, when the financing of the Italian debt was becoming more difficult by the minute. The yield differential between the German and Italian bonds had reached 4 percentage points (since the introduction of the EMU, it had never before risen above 2 percentage points).

As eloquently expressed by Sacchi (Chapter 7), the ECB was clearly proposing an exchange. It would commit to easing the pressure on the Italian bonds by making purchases on the secondary market, and, in turn, the Italian Government would follow the strict conditionality despite not being formalized in a memorandum as in other European countries, such as Spain, requesting financial aid.

Berlusconi was unable[2] to fulfil the letter's request, and the policy package introduced by his government was unable to convince either international investors or EU institutions.[3] The financial markets' turmoil and the growing pressure from the EU that followed in autumn 2011 put his government under heavy strain. At the beginning of November 2011, on the one hand, the European Commission asked for very specific clarifications on the welfare reforms promoted by Berlusconi (a total of 39 detailed remarks), asking for a response within a week (!). On the other hand, the ECB Governing Council threatened to stop purchasing Italian bonds if the Italian government failed to implement the promised reforms. Given this situation, Berlusconi resigned and a new government led by the former EU Commissioner Mario Monti was formed. It was this Monti Government that passed the two reforms on pensions and the labour market.

Following the reforms, the EU influence through enhanced EU integration kept its pace mainly in relation to the labour market regulation. In 2011, recommendations were issued proposing quite precise changes in the collective bargaining system.

Recommendations for 2012–13 followed similar lines. In 2012, the EC requested a more extensive use of firm-level contracts. A few months later in November 2012 a 'programmatic agreement between the Italian Governments and the Social Partners promoting productivity and competitiveness in Italy' was signed[4] (only one of the main trade unions refused it), fostering firm-level contracts.

This pressure from the EU level can explain why reforms were implemented so fast by the Monti Government and why no real negotiations with social partners took place (the delivery of reforms would otherwise

---

[2] Berlusconi's weak position was the result of an increasing loss of legitimacy in the domestic arena due to scandals and the difficulties with his main ally in government, the Northern League, which was against a pension's reform (de la Porte and Natali 2014).

[3] In the two European Council meetings and in the summit of the heads of state and government of the Eurozone in autumn 2011, the EU institutions and various governments (especially the French and German) insistently asked Italy to make further efforts in implementing structural reforms, expressing at the same time skepticism over Berlusconi's capacity to deliver them.

[4] http://www.ilsole24ore.com/art/notizie/2012-11-21/linee-programmatiche-crescita-produttivita-214548.shtml?uuid=Ab8CnE5G&refresh_ce=1 as reference for the agreement between the government and the social partners. The link gives the full text of this agreement.

have been delayed and would have likely been watered down by potential opponents). However, it should not be forgotten that some of the problems had been pressing for a long time. Internal worries about mounting labour market dualism, unemployment and the pension system sustainability in the long run were already present but had only been partially addressed due to the domestic Italian political game. Monti presented his reforms from a double perspective: [W]e need to do it to "save Italy from the abyss" of the financial turmoil in the short term (words pronounced by the Prime Minister); we need to do it in order to restore some basic macro-economic conditions in order to help Italy grow again. In fact, between 2000 and 2007 (before the crisis), the Italian GDP grew by only 1.6 per cent yearly on average, and its public debt was on average 106 per cent of the GDP—in both cases the worst figures in the whole EU-28.

A similar general pattern developed in Spain. On the one hand, recommendations became more stringent and precise. In 2010, the Council adopted the recommendations from the Commission and issued the deadline of 2 June 2010 (few months) for the Spanish Government to take effective action to implement deficit-reducing measures. On the other hand, the turmoil in the financial markets put Spain under severe pressure through the financing of its debt: the ECB agreed to intervene but asked for strong budgetary cuts in exchange for European protection from speculative attacks (see *Romero* 16/5/2010). In May 2010, the Spanish government was forced to announce the biggest cuts in public spending since the beginning of democracy, meaning a U-turn in respect to what Prime Minister Zapatero had been defending even a few weeks before— that is, there would not be any drastic cuts in spending and that deficit reduction would take place gradually within a medium-term framework. In June 2010, the Communication from the Commission to the Council (EC 2010), published a month after the reforms were introduced, implied a change in the 'tone' of the assessment; the measures might have not sufficed to reach the revised targets for 2011. The Commission prompted the Spanish government to enact labour market and pension reforms 'without further delay' (EC 2010, p. 49). The reform on pensions was introduced just a month later (August), and the labour market reform— via Royal Decree on urgent measures—was introduced in September 2010.

## The Universalistic Pillar: Hidden Retrenchment in Education and Healthcare

Contrary to what occurred in pensions and labour market regulations, since 2010 no relevant explicit reform took place in healthcare or education. However, if the formal institutional universalistic design has remained untouched, the same cannot be said for the level of public expenditure.

From 2010, cost-containment in the Italian National Health Service (NHS) became the primary goal. The 2011 budget-planning bill stated that expenditure cuts equal to around €8 billion had to be introduced for the years 2012–14. Also, the law introduced a substantial freeze on new hiring in the NHS and, from 2014, a robust new set of co-payments on healthcare services (Jessoula and Pavolini 2012). In expenditure terms, whereas the yearly public expenditure dropped on average by 2.2 per cent between 2009 and 2011, the distance in respect of the EU-15 has grown. Italian per capita public healthcare expenditure in 2000 was equal to 85.5 per cent of the EU-15 average; in 2011 it dropped to 77.1 per cent (Eurostat 2012–2014).

The crisis has not reduced nominal access to healthcare to the Spanish NHS, with the exception of illegal immigrants. However, when regional deficits became fully apparent in 2011, regions were obliged to cut budgets severely and to negotiate bailouts with the central government. The only out-of-pocket payment in place (introduced in the early 1970s) is on pharmaceuticals, consisting of 40 per cent on over-the-counter drugs for all people except those persons over retirement age. Moreover, the salaries of all public employees (including health professionals) have been significantly reduced, while working hours have increased. The effects of these changes can be seen also in terms of public expenditure, with an average annual cut of 4.3 per cent between 2009 and 2011, even stronger than in the Italian case. The first result of these new trends is that the distance with the rest of western Europe has started to increase again: Spanish per capita expenditure fell to 70.1 per cent of the EU-15 average in 2010, whereas it was 79.6 per cent in 2007 (Eurostat 2012–2014).

Education policies have followed a very similar path: absence of reform and/or formal restrictions of universal access but rather budgetary reductions. In Italy, very low growth took place since 2000 and cuts began with the crisis, as Eurostat (2012–2014) shows. National data on 2011 tell us that the freeze became even more pronounced with a –3.4 per cent decrease in expenditure between 2010 and 2011 and a more general –5.5 per cent between 2007 and 2011 (Istat 2013b).

In Spain, expenditure grew up to 2010 and then fell drastically. Budgets have been so severely cut to the extent that the reduction between 2012 and 2013 in the education budget was 14 per cent. The strongest reductions occurred in secondary education and vocational training (MINHAP 2013). Also, the salaries of teachers have been significantly reduced while working hours have increased. Moreover, within the public compulsory education system, the maximum number of children in classrooms has increased by law.

The recent developments in the universal pillars of the Italian and Spanish welfare states make one wonder for how long it will be possible to preserve universal access to healthcare and education and how much the quality of such services will be affected in the medium term. What seems to be at work is a potential 'policy drift' or 'gradual transformation' mechanism (Streeck and Thelen 2005). Formally, no explicit reform dismantling universalism has been promoted, but severe cuts in public expenditure (in countries already spending less on a per capita base than in western Europe), changes in the rules concerning (increasing) co-payments and (freezes) hiring professional personnel can, in the medium term, undermine their substantial universalistic functioning.

In the case of these policies, EU influence was relevant but took a different form. Formal procedures and conditionality were at the basis of the cuts, but, unlike the case of pensions and labour market reforms, rarely did EU institutions' documents ask explicitly for retrenchment in healthcare and education. Instead, the more general reference to fiscal consolidation and a strict control of public expenditure growth was the basis to intervene in these two sectors that represent by far the two most important sources of welfare state expenditure after pensions. In other terms expenditure after pensions. In other terms, the EU request to reduce public deficits has been translated at the national level in cutting expenditure in two of the most prominent sources of state spending, without the need for naming healthcare and education explicitly. At the same time when, since 2010, Spanish and Italian governments introduced severe cuts to both these policy areas, they clearly stated that it was to respect EDP rules.

## The 'Targeted' Pillar: (Even More) Residual Policies in Social Assistance, Social Care and Family Policies

As described earlier, the 2000s represented a period of differentiation between Spain and Italy. Until the 1990s, both countries shared a common familialistic and residual approach to social assistance, social care and family policies. During the last decade, Spain began to innovate and recalibrate its welfare state through policies designed to cope with new social risks and started a path of reform toward a more Continental and Northern European welfare state institutional design, whereas Italy remained more a 'frozen landscape'. The onset of the economic crisis, and especially austerity plans, since 2010 was a sort of 'cold shower' for Spain, and the trajectories of the two countries have started to converge again.

In Italy, austerity plans hit hard also in this field. Italy did not develop any real minimum income protection programme, although the number of individuals at risk of poverty or unemployment rose significantly in recent years (see Table 6.2). Recent budget planning laws (2010–11) have deliberated quite draconian expenditure cuts. For example, the central state financing for social care and social assistance between 2008 and 2012 was cut by 91 per cent (from €2.5 billion in 2008 to €0.2 billion in 2012; Basile 2011). Furthermore, between 2009 and 2012 social care and social assistance expenditure dropped by 3.5 per cent; part of this expenditure consisted in state transfers to regional and local authorities, which found themselves in even greater dire straits to cope with the crisis (Istat 2013a). Public expenditure for family and children contracted between 2009 and 2011 on a yearly average by 2.7 per cent. The result was that, in 2011, this expenditure was around 56 per cent of that for western Europe and the social exclusion expenditure remained down at 15 per cent, even if the economic situation of many households has deteriorated dramatically (Eurostat 2012–2014).

The consequences of austerity were even more pronounced in Spain. Since the mid-2010s, measures have placed implementation at odds because of drastic budgetary cuts at the central state level. The regional budgets have also been drastically reduced for the sake of stability, which is forcing them also to cut minimum income and social exclusion programmes. Trends on expenditure witness these changes over time, as Eurostat data (2012–2014) show. In 2000, Spain was starting from a relatively low level of per capita expenditure both in family and social exclusion policies (respectively 38.2 per cent and 36.3 per cent of the EU-15 average). Until 2009, the situation had strongly improved (per capita expenditure was respectively 58.0 per cent and 49.6 per cent of EU-15 average). This result was obtained thanks to very high yearly growth rates during the 2000s and due to a whole set of new programmes, for example, in long-term care and activation. However, since 2009, the situation has changed dramatically; between 2009 and 2011 the expenditure dropped on a yearly base by –6.9 per cent for family and children policies and by –8.8 per cent in social exclusion. The distance from western Europe has widened again; in 2011 family and children per capita expenditure was equal to 51.3 per cent to the EU-15 average, and the expenditure for social exclusion was down to 39.6 per cent.

What has been the role of EU institutions in these policy changes? EU influence has taken two forms: on the one hand, implicit retrenchment was requested to obtain fiscal consolidation, following the same line as healthcare and education and, on the other hand, recommendations repeatedly asked for recalibration and a broader capacity to cope with new social risks. For example, in the 2011 Recommendations it was clearly stated that Italy should 'take steps to promote greater participation of women in the labour market, by increasing the availability of care facilities throughout the country and providing financial incentives to second earners to take up work in a budgetary neutral way' (EC 2011, p. 7). However, the EU institutions seem to be asking for a very difficult mission: to cut down quickly on social expenses in general and, at the same time, to improve some specific programmes (such as reconciliation). The result so far has been that national governments have concentrated mainly on the first (and more stringent) goal, with the result that broad recalibration is becoming less and less an aim in the short term.

# The EU and National Welfare State Changes: A Conclusion

The EU role on national welfare states in the 1990s was perceived by a vast majority of Italian and Spanish policy actors, and by public opinion, as an external 'beneficial constraint'. Economic and social reforms were launched to join the EMU. The EU (also with its strict requirements) was perceived as a 'solution' to many national problems. In 2000, around 67 per cent of Spaniards and 60 per cent of Italians thought that their country's membership of the European Community was a good thing. In 2003, 57 per cent of Spaniards and 60 per cent of Italians had a positive image of the EU.

In recent years, the EU has started to be perceived in a more critical manner. In 2011, the percentage of Spaniards and Italians thinking that EU membership was a good thing for their country dropped respectively to 55 per cent and 41 per cent, and in 2013 only one citizen out of four in both countries had a positive image of the EU[5].

When the EU put increasing pressure on Italy and Spain, starting in 2010, it was interpreted by different policy actors both as a constraint and as an opportunity to reform their welfare states. However, in comparison to what happened in the 1990s, the 'external constraint' in the most recent years has been perceived less as something 'beneficial by a larger part of the public opinion (and political parties; see León et al. 2015). This situation makes reforms harder to sustain in the medium term. If, in the 1990s, Europe was seen as a potential solution to deadlocks and problems arising from the nation political and economic domain, in recent years it is increasingly perceived as a part of (if not) the problem.

In terms of policy reform, in the case of Spain more than Italy, an attempt to recalibrate the whole system took place up to the years of the crisis. A reduction of coverage in traditional fields (e.g., pensions) has been partially compensated by new (social) investments in policy fields such as education, care, active labour market and social exclusion poli-

---

[5] The data on public opinion were retrieved from the 'Eurobarometer interactive search system' on the European Commission web site (http://ec.europa.eu/public_opinion/index_en.htm).

cies. In Italy, a recalibration approach was considered in the 1990s but then never implemented during the following decade.

What has been the impact of the crisis, understood as a two-way street? It has not led to a reconfiguration of welfare policies in either country, implying a paradigmatic change of the welfare state so far. From mid-2010 onwards, mounting EU integration and, not least, 'intrusiveness' led to reforms adopted with extreme haste and an absence of parliamentary debate, agreements or social pacts to support them, leading to a retrenchment phase. The pressure exercised by EU institutions has been all but negligible.

In Italy and Spain, the crisis phase, clearly dominated by contraction and retrenchment to face the imperatives of cost containment, can be termed as a new '*age of permanent strain*' in the sense of being much more acute than 'the age of permanent austerity' initiated by the Maastricht Treaty in the early 1990s. The age of permanent strain also goes beyond the concept of 'pervasive austerity', this being the outcome of political choices made at the EU level regarding the original construction of the EMU and the response to the aftermath of the 2008–09 crisis (see Theodopoulou, Chapter 5) affecting all Member States in general. The new age of permanent strain entails a decision-making process characterized by extreme haste, intense tensions, growing anxiety among the population and growing public unrest. This situation has not been shared by all EU countries.

From mid-2010, reforms have been dominated by rising taxation and freezes or reductions in salaries, quickly followed by drastic attempts to contain public deficits through budgetary cuts, restrictive social policy reforms and even more severe budgetary cuts since the latter months of 2011, coinciding with the change of government in both countries and the intensification of pressure by the EU.

Still, even if the two countries share these common elements, the different trajectories in which the austerity plans set in should be recalled. In Spain, the changes in 2010–13 represent a shock not only because of the size of cuts involved but also because they entail a dramatic change after more than a decade of welfare state recalibration, put forward both by Conservative and Socialist governments. In Italy, instead, the austerity measures taken in 2011–12 follow a similar reform path to the pre-existent one, even if, of course, much more severe in terms of cuts to that started already in the 1990s.

As hypothesized in the beginning of this chapter, the types of institutional design do matter in terms of how retrenchment is introduced. Both in Italy and Spain, governments have enacted explicit reforms in State Corporatist welfare state programmes (e.g., contributory income maintenance policies, etc.) than universalistic (e.g., healthcare and education) or targeted policies. While State Corporatist policies, especially pensions, have been phased out, universalistic and targeted policies are suffering from mere retrenchment. The universalistic and (already weak) targeted pillars are the easiest to cut by mere budget reductions. However, what is most likely happening (the near future will tell us if it is so) is a 'gradual transformation' and a 'hidden retrenchment' (Streeck and Thelen 2005) with governments formally declaring that they do not intend to reduce universal coverage, but, in fact, to adopt severe expenditure cuts and first and second order policy changes à la Hall (1993; e.g., in terms of co-payments, waiting lists, etc.) that increasingly hinder the access to services.

All in all, it is too early to say if the actual austerity plans have changed the face of the Italian and Spanish welfare states. What seems clear is that Spain has interrupted its path toward a recalibration of its welfare system, while Italy has chosen a retrenchment approach. Some recalibration took place in both countries, with the attempt to improve the coverage for the traditional outsiders (those with fixed-term contracts, etc.) of the two systems, and there was an expansion in expenditure on unemployment. However, it seems that what took place is what Ferrera (2012) defines as 'subtractive recalibration' Differences between outsiders and insiders have decreased, not mainly because the former started to be better treated by the new welfare state regulation but because the latter started to be less protected. Naturally 'distributive recalibration' is important, and 'subtractive recalibration' may be considered one of its facets. However, the freezing of any real 'functional recalibration' (between policies and needs) makes the whole welfare change weaker in terms of coverage.

# References

Ascoli, U., & Pavolini, E. (2012). Ombre rosse. Il sistema di welfare italiano dopo 20 anni di riforme. *Stato e Mercato, 94*(3), 429–464.

Basile, R. (2011). Tagli al welfare. C'è un futuro per le politiche sociali? *Rivista delle Politiche Sociali, 12*(3), 543–558.

Bonoli, G., & Natali, D. (Eds.). (2012). *The politics of the new welfare state.* Oxford: Oxford University Press.

CES, Consejo Económico y Social. (2011). *Memoria sobre la situación socioeconómica y laboral.* Madrid: CES.

de la Porte, C., & Natali, D. (2014). Altered Europeanization of pension reform during the Great Recession: Denmark and Italy compared. *West European Politics, 37*(4), 732–749.

European Commission. (2009a). *Recommendation for a Council Decision on the existence of an excessive deficit in Spain SEC (2009) 561 final, 24 March.* Brussels: European Commission.

European Commission. (2009b). *Recommendation for a Council Recommendation to Spain with a view to bringing an end to the situation of an excessive government deficit SEC (2009) 562, 24 March.* Brussels: European Commission.

European Commission. (2010). *Communication from the Commission to the Council. Assessment of the action taken by Belgium, the Czech Republic, Germany, Ireland, Spain, France, Italy, the Netherlands, Austria, Portugal, Slovenia and Slovakia in response to the Council Recommendations of 2 December 2009 with a view to bringing an end to the situation of excessive government deficit, 15 June.* Brussels: European Commission.

European Commission. (2012). *Memorandum of understanding on financial-sector policy conditionality, 20 July 2012.* Brussels: European Commission.

Eurostat. (2012–2014). *EESPROS database.* Brussels: European Commission.

Ferrera, M. (2012). Verso un welfare più europeo? Conclusione. In M. Ferrera, V. Fargion, & M. Jessoula (Eds.), *Alle radici del welfare all'italiana* (pp. 323–344). Venice, Italy: Marsilio.

Ferrera, M., Hemerijck, A., & Rhodes, M. (2000). *The future of Social Europe.* Oeiras, Portugal: Celta Editora.

Guillén, A. M., & León, M. (Eds.). (2011). *The Spanish welfare state in European context.* Farnham: Ashgate.

de Haan, J., Berger, H., & Jansen, D. (2004). Why has the stability and growth pact failed? *International Finance, 7*(2), 235–260.

Hall, P. (1993). Policy paradigms, social learning, and the state: The case of economic policymaking in Britain. *Comparative Politics, 25*(3), 275–296.

Istat. (2013a). *Spesa per la protezione sociale.* Rome, Italy: Istat.

Istat. (2013b). *Spesa delle Amministrazioni pubbliche per funzione.* Rome, Italy: Istat.

Jenson, J. (2008). Children, new social risks and policy change: A Lego future? *Comparative Social Research, 25*(1), 357–382.

Jessoula, M., & Pavolini, E. (2012). Italy annual national report 2012: Pensions, health and long-term care. In *Annual ASISP report for DG employment, social affairs and equal opportunities.* Brussels: European Commission.

León, M., Pavolini, E., & Guillén, A. M. (2015). Welfare rescaling in Italy and Spain: Political strategies to deal with harsh austerity. *European Journal of Social Security, 17*(2), 182–201.

Maino, F., & Neri, S. (2011). Explaining welfare reforms in Italy between economy and politics: External constraints and endogenous dynamics. *Social Policy & Administration, 45*(4), 445–464.

MINHAP. (2013). Presupuestos Generales del Estado 2013. In *Informe Económico-financiero.* Madrid: MINHAP.

Morel, N., Palier, B., & Palme, J. (Eds.). (2012). *Towards a social investment welfare state? Ideas, policies and challenges.* Bristol: The Policy Press.

Naldini, M., & Saraceno, C. (2008). Social and family policies in Italy: Not totally frozen but far from structural reforms. *Social Policy & Administration, 42*(7), 733–748.

Natali, D. (2011). Le politiche pensionistiche. In U. Ascoli (Ed.), *Il welfare in Italia* (pp. 57–77). Bologna: Il Mulino.

Palier, B. (Ed.). (2010). *A long good–bye to bismarck: The politics of welfare reforms in continental welfare states.* Amsterdam: Amsterdam University Press.

Pavolini, E., & Guillén, A. M. (Eds.). (2013). *Health care systems under austerity.* Basingstoke: Palgrave Macmillan.

Pierson, P. (1998). Irresistible forces, immovable objects: Post-industrial welfare states confront permanent austerity. *Journal of European Public Policy, 5*(4), 539–560.

Pierson, P. (Ed.). (2001). *The new politics of the welfare state.* Oxford: Oxford University Press.

Ranci, C., & Pavolini, E. (Eds.). (2013). *Reforms in long-term care policies in Europe. Investigating institutional change and social impacts*. New York: Springer.

Saraceno, C., & Keck, W. (2011). Towards an integrated approach for the analysis of gender equity in policies supporting paid work and care responsibilities. *Demographic Research, 25*(4), 371–406.

Streeck, W., & Thelen, K. (Eds.). (2005). *Beyond continuity. Institutional change in advanced political economies*. Oxford: Oxford University Press.

Taylor-Gooby, P. (2004). *New risks, new welfare. The transformation of the European welfare state*. Oxford: Oxford University Press.

# 7

# Conditionality by Other Means: European Union Involvement in Italy's Structural Reforms in the Sovereign Debt Crisis

Stefano Sacchi

## Introduction

The aim of this chapter is to show the relevance of implicit conditionality within the range of instruments deployed by the EU in the Eurozone crisis. Contrary to conditionality that requires formalized, explicit covenants based on Memorandums of Understanding (MoUs), as in the aid packages crafted for Ireland (Dukelow, Chapter 4), Greece and Portugal (Theodoropoulou, Chapter 5), this sort of conditionality is based on an implicit understanding of the stakes and sanctions involved, underlain by some measure of power asymmetry. Since the terms of the exchange are relatively indeterminate, compliance is an issue of distinctive relevance for the effectiveness of implicit conditionality, making monitoring all the more important. Pervasive monitoring coupled with external mechanisms of enforcement, such as the sheer power of market discipline, can, however, make implicit conditionality very consequential and a powerful source of EU involvement in domestic social sovereignty.

S. Sacchi (✉)
University of Milan, Milan, Italy

© The Author(s) 2016
C. de la Porte, E. Heins (eds.), *The Sovereign Debt Crisis, the EU and Welfare State Reform*, DOI 10.1057/978-1-137-58179-2_7

Following Sasse (2008), conditionality is understood here as a process, rather than a static arrangement locked in at a given point in time. Process-tracing is therefore used to elucidate how implicit conditionality operates and unfolds over time. This will be done through the analysis of Italy's acute sovereign debt crisis between July 2011 and June 2012. During this period, as a consequence of contagion risks in the Eurozone, the government led by Silvio Berlusconi faced a severe market confidence crisis. To obtain support from EU institutions—most notably the European Central Bank (ECB)—Italy committed to an array of structural reforms. The inability to deliver led to increasing pressure on the government, which was finally replaced by a new one-headed government, led by Mario Monti. Requests from the EU to introduce structural reforms, particularly in pensions and labour market policy, became the new government's roadmap, and their implementation was carefully monitored and scrutinized. Actual or potential access to EU financial support, carried out through the purchase of Italy's bonds to alleviate market tensions on its debt, was the implicit carrot. The threat of having to enter formalized, explicit conditional lending programmes with the IMF to avoid default, thereby explicitly yielding Westphalian sovereignty (Krasner 1999) to non-EU institutions, was the implicit stick. Market discipline was the operating mechanism that made implicit conditionality effective.

The aim of this chapter is not to explain Italy's structural reforms and their outcomes. The goal is a more modest one: to highlight the power of implicit conditionality as a source of EU involvement in domestic matters and cast light on the way it operates. This chapter testifies to a quantum leap in EU's involvement in policymaking of Eurozone members: even without formally prescribing this through MoUs, intervention of EU officers in domestic policymaking escalated to a degree of pervasiveness previously unimaginable. While the bearing of this for democratic processes at the national level is not a concern addressed here, developments described in this chapter seem to support a revitalization of the fusion hypothesis between EU and member states (Wessels and Rometsch 1996a)—at least in the Eurozone.

The chapter is structured as follows. The concept of implicit conditionality is defined and is rendered applicable to the analysis of Italy's sovereign debt crisis in the following section. In the next section, an account of the crisis, laying bare the mechanisms at the core of implicit conditionality in the Italian case, is provided. The process of adoption of structural reforms in pensions and labour policy by the Monti government is traced in the fourth section. The final section concludes, taking stock of the evidence.

## Implicit Conditionality and Its Features

Conditionality can tentatively be defined as the granting of some good by a party (or a coordinated group of parties) to a second party that deems such a good valuable, linked to the latter party's compliance with some behaviour valued by the former party. This definition comprises the various forms of conditionality that can be empirically observed, such as ex ante or ex post, financial, macroeconomic or structural, private or official, membership, cross-based and so forth.[1] It accommodates various types of goods and envisaged behaviour, as well as sanctions for non- or partial compliance and reinforcement by punishment, support or reward (Schimmelfenning and Sedelmeier 2004).

In all its forms, even when it is framed in terms of "ownership" (Khan and Sharma 2003), or what Dyson (2006) calls the "good servant" narrative, conditionality implies an underlying asymmetry of power. In other words, the stakes for the receiving party are higher than for the granting party, although the latter must of course have an interest in the behaviour of the former, otherwise the overall arrangement would have no raison d'être.

Irrespective of definitional issues, conditionality has been widely analysed in macrocomparative politics in two different realms: the provision of financial aid by the International Financial Institutions (IFIs), such as the IMF and the World Bank, and EU accession for central and eastern European countries (CEECs). With the Eurozone crisis, the former type of conditionality, that is, "the placement of policy conditions on the disbursement of financial resources to national governments" (Babb and

---

[1] See Babb and Carruthers (2008) for a review.

Carruthers 2008, p. 15), has been adopted for some Eurozone members, most notably Ireland, Greece and Portugal.

Although instances of conditionality are usually embodied in formalized agreements, and their terms—including the sanctions for non-compliance—explicitly specified through detailed covenants, this chapter argues that this is not necessary for conditionality to be operational and effective in influencing a party's behaviour. Conditionality can be based on an implicit understanding between the two parties involved that a particular behaviour is expected for the good to be made available, even in the absence of detailed covenants. This will be called *implicit conditionality*, and its operational capacity will be illustrated through detailed process tracing of Italy's structural reforms in the sovereign debt crisis.

Comparative politics and political economy literature does not provide much help to "seize the object" (Sartori 1984, p. 26) of implicit conditionality. In one of the very few times the concept is mentioned, it "refers to the requirement by private investors and lenders that recipient nations follow certain kinds of policies in order to be deemed 'credit-worthy'. Such requirements are rarely laid out in the explicit form assumed by agreements with the IFIs" (Griffith-Jones and Stellings 1995, p. 169). In the empirical reconstruction to follow, implicit conditionality is used by the EU institutions rather than by private parties; however, it will become apparent that financial markets play a fundamental role, as market discipline functions as the key operating mechanism for implicit conditionality to be effective.

Although they offer no guidance on implicit conditionality per se, discussions of EU conditionality in enlargement to the CEEC provide insight by their treatment of neighbouring concepts. Hughes et al. (2004, p. 526) distinguish between formal conditionality, "which embodies the publicly stated preconditions as set out in the broad principles of the Copenhagen criteria and the legal framework of the acquis", and informal conditionality, "which includes the operational pressures and recommendations applied by actors within the Commission to achieve particular outcomes during interactions with their CEEC counterparts". Moreover, they argue that the "concept of conditionality should be seen less as a generic tool for applying pressures for rule adoption [...] and more as a process which involves a tool bag of shifting prescriptive norms, and a variety of institutional formats" (p. 547). Although—as will be seen in the empirical analysis—the deployment of implicit conditionality resonates with their concept of informal conditionality, the latter is embedded in a formalized, explicit assertion of the terms of the covenant. A distinction between formal and informal conditionality is also made by Dyson (2006), although with a different meaning: analysing enlargement of the Eurozone, he argues that the request to comply with the acquis, in particular on central bank independence and convergence to Maastricht criteria (formal conditionality) is "reinforced by a tightly defined informal conditionality" (p. 13) that "functions at the deeper ideational level of background policy paradigms" and "takes the form of two complementary sets of policy beliefs": the optimal currency area theory and the sound money and finance paradigm (pp. 19–20). Again, informal conditionality is rooted in formalized, explicit arrangements. However, the meaning attached to it by Dyson helps us understand the type of behaviour requested from Italy: structural reforms, particularly labour market liberalizations, as functional equivalents to the missing preconditions of the EMU as an optimal currency area (Hemerijck 2014).

Finally, the concept of soft conditionality has been introduced in the literature on IFIs' conditional aid. According to Caraway et al. (2012, p. 42), soft conditions "refer to policy steps that the IMF would like to see but that have no explicit conditionality attached to them". They are written in the letters of intent (the MoUs) but "are not included in the loan contract".[2] Soft conditions "contained in the letters of intent can be ignored with few, if any, consequences" (p. 50). Whereas conditions explicitly mentioned in the loan contract entail sanctions for non-compliance, soft conditionality does not. Conversely, in the case that follows, implicit conditionality does entail implicit, but harsh, sanctions. These include the withdrawal of financial support—through sovereign bond purchases—to face severe and, at some points, almost unsustainable market conditions, with the implication of being forced to agree to explicit conditionality, entering a (presumably more constraining and certainly more humiliating) financial aid programme. Thus, the envis-

---

[2] Caraway et al. (2012) show the relevance of looking also at the actual content of loan contracts, rather than only at MoUs.

aged sanction is the denial of further support, so that the conditioned party (Italy) would have to formally relinquish sovereignty, or default on its sovereign debt. Structural asymmetry of power is pervasive: while the conditioning party (the EU) certainly had a deep-seated interest in helping Italy regain market's confidence, as its default could have entailed the wreck of the Eurozone with dire consequences for all, Italy would have lost its access to markets altogether.

While in-depth case analysis shows that implicit conditionality can be consequential and effective, this is not meant to deny that it may suffer from compliance problems as compared to formalized, explicit conditionality. In a situation in which determinacy of conditions (Schimmelfennig and Sedelmeier 2004) is low, however, certainty of incentives and sanctions (Grabbe 2006) can be enhanced by monitoring (Kahn-Nisser 2013). The role of EU monitoring to ensure Italy's compliance with the prescribed behaviour will be analysed in the next two sections.

## At the Roots of Implicit Conditionality: Italy and the Sovereign Debt Crisis

Italy was hit by the financial storm in the summer of 2011 as a consequence of risks of contagion through the European banking system. This was due to the interplay of several exogenous factors, from the EU mismanagement of the second aid package to Greece, to the necessity for Portugal, after Greece and Ireland, to get conditional financial aid in May 2011, to the an "unconvincing" second round of stress tests conducted by the European Banking Association and published in July 2011 (Jones 2012, p. 89). Institutional reforms in the governance of the Economic and Monetary Union (EMU) failed to reassure the markets (Hodson 2012), as repeatedly did signals coming from EU summits (Smeets and Zimmermann 2013). The new European Stability Mechanism (ESM) was established by a treaty in July 2011 with a lending capacity of €500 billion , a sum that according to the US Treasury "would need to be doubled or tripled to provide an effective backstop for the rest of the eurozone" (Geithner 2014, p. 473).

In all this, Italy, with the fourth largest sovereign debt in the world after Japan, the United States and Germany, hovering at €1.9 trillion or 1.2 times the GDP in 2011, started to scare the investors. As a matter of fact, more fine-grained considerations would suggest that Italy's gigantic public debt needs not constitute a fundamental threat in a country where net households' wealth was at €8.6 trillion in 2011, about 5.4 times the GDP (Bank of Italy 2012), and considerable primary budget surpluses have been run since 1991 with the sole exception of 2009 (–0.7 % despite a GDP plunge of 5.5 %) and 2010 (an immaterial –0.1 %). But when fears of contagion rose, structurally low growth even before the Great Recession (with real GDP growth rate at 1.3 % per year on average between 1995 and 2008) and policy stalemate (with the Berlusconi government incapable of making tough decisions due to internal cabinet rifts and a divided majority) did nothing but contribute to the flight from Italy's sovereign debt.

In July 2011, the heads of state and government of the Eurozone eventually agreed on a second aid package to Greece, while emphasizing private sector involvement. Despite their reassurances that this was due to the fact that "Greece requires an exceptional and unique solution" (Council 2011a), fears of contagion exploded. Some days later, the *Financial Times* disclosed that Germany's biggest lender, the Deutsche Bank, had reduced its net exposure to Italy's debt by a stunning 88 % in the first six months of the year, from €8 billion to less than one (Milne and Wilson 2011). From April to early July Italian credit default swaps had tripled, and the yield differential between 10-year Italian and German government bonds, which had been lower than 200 basis points since the introduction of the euro in 1999, reached 400 basis points at the beginning of August. This occurred only a month after the June European Council had endorsed a budget-correction package aimed at reaching a balanced budget in 2014, then passed in parliament in mid-July.

Italian sovereign debt became a matter of immediate concern for the survival of the Eurozone. On 4 August 2011, the ECB governing council decided to resume purchases of sovereign debt paper on the secondary market—the Securities Markets Programme launched in May 2010—to ease tensions on the financial markets. This decision was, however, taken by majority vote, as German, Dutch and Luxembourg members of the council voted against any resumption of the programme. Purchases started while the ECB President, Jean-Claude Trichet, was briefing the press, but much to everyone's surprise, they only involved Irish and Portuguese bonds, thus adding even more pressure on the Italian bonds. In the same press conference, Trichet repeatedly emphasized the role of structural reforms, in particular "the removal of labour market rigidities" (ECB 2011a).

The following day, a confidential letter was sent to the Italian government, signed by Trichet and the president-elect of the ECB, Mario Draghi, at the time still the governor of the Bank of Italy. Later in the day, the Italian government announced that it would hasten the achievement of a balanced budget by one year, to 2013. A new meeting of the ECB governing council was called two days later (on a Sunday), after which the ECB issued a statement where it announced it would now "actively implement its Securities Market Programme" (ECB 2011b). Between 8 and 12 August 2011, the ECB purchased on the secondary market sovereign paper for €22 billion (ECB 2011c).[3]

To bring forward a balanced budget from 2014 to 2013 was a request set out in the letter from the ECB, alongside incisive specific measures regarding growth, competition and liberalizations. Among these, "a thorough review of the rules regulating the hiring and dismissal of employees should be adopted in conjunction with the establishment of an unemployment insurance system and a set of active labour market policies".[4] Moreover, the letter asked the Italian government to "intervene further in the pension system, making the eligibility criteria for seniority pensions more stringent and rapidly aligning the retirement age of women in the private sector to that established for public employees" (already harmonized with the male age following a decision of the European Court of Justice).

The letter sent by Trichet and Draghi never mentioned the Securities Market Programme (SMP). Still, the sequence of events is rather eloquent. Although not explicitly embedded in a formalized conditional aid programme, the letter imposed a policy agenda on the Italian government, going as far as to indicate the specific actions to be implemented

---

[3] At the end of 2012, the ECB held Italian government bonds worth €102.8 billion, out of a total of €218 billion of bonds purchased between 2010 and 2012 through the programme (ECB 2013).
[4] The letter was leaked to the Italian daily Corriere della Sera, where it was published in late September, see Draghi and Trichet (2011). All quotations from there.

and the policy alternatives to be selected (Kingdon 1984). Moreover, it clearly specified the regulatory instrument to implement such actions, requiring the Italian government to resort to an urgent decree, to be ratified by parliament in September.

In short, while acting to ease the pressure on the Italian bonds by making purchases on the secondary market, the ECB imposed certain conditions that, despite not being formalized in MoUs, were nonetheless stringent and pervasive, as the ECB was setting the policy agenda, alternatives and instruments to be adopted in exchange for its support.

An emergency package was introduced by decree in mid-August and approved by Parliament in September, as per the ECB's request. It aimed at reaching a balanced budget in 2013 through austerity measures worth €45.5 billion overall (€20 billion in 2012 and €25.5 billion the following year, to be realized mostly after the general elections envisaged in 2013). It brought about elements of retrenchment in pensions, adding to the ones already implemented in the two previous years. What the government could not agree on was a thorough reform of seniority pensions, mainly due to the opposition of the Northern League (the bulk of seniority pensions going to workers in the manufacturing north). As for the reform of individual dismissals, an issue that despite various attempts had proved intractable for the Berlusconi governments since the early 2000s, a provision was passed that allows for collective agreements at the plant or local level to derogate from national collective agreements and also from the law in various areas, including employment protection, paving the way for plant-level concessions against the will of the unions at the national level.[5]

Skewed towards savings to be realized in the future, the August policy package failed to convince the international investors. In the last days of August, the yield differential with the Spanish bonds became positive. Under attack on the financial markets, Italy became "the most important focus for concern in the eurozone" (Jones 2012, p. 93).

At the European Council of 22–23 October 2011 the EU institutions insistently asked Italy to make further efforts in implementing structural

---

[5] The decree disregarded completely the issue of income protection in case of unemployment, mentioned in the ECB letter.

reforms. Berlusconi promised new reforms, promises met with scepticism from other EU governments and institutions.[6] An informal summit of the European Council members was then called on 26 October 2011. In the days between the two meetings, Berlusconi desperately tried to convince the Northern League of the necessity to reform seniority pensions, to no avail. Then, with the international reputation of the Italian government irremediably compromised, he sent a letter to the presidents of the European Council and of the European Commission (EC) announcing a set of reforms, to be better specified by November 15. In particular, the Italian government committed itself to approving, by May 2012, a "reform of labour legislation (…) functional to a greater propensity to hiring and to the companies' need for efficiency also through new regulations concerning dismissal for economic reasons in open-ended labour contracts" (Berlusconi 2011, own translation). As for pensions, Berlusconi could do nothing more than mention Italy's success in reforming its pension system and making it financially sustainable, increasing the retirement age for old-age pensions to a threshold higher than that of many of its European partners. The government committed itself to setting the statutory retirement age at 67 years for all citizens (both men and women, in both the public and private sector) by 2026, but it did not mention any new actions concerning seniority pensions besides the measures already adopted.

Worried by what sounded like a plan about future plans, in an unprecedented step with a country that had not signed any MoU, the heads of state and government of the Eurozone entrusted the EC with the task of providing "a detailed assessment of all the measures and monitoring their implementation", inviting "the Italian authorities to provide in a timely way all the information necessary for such an assessment" (Council 2011b). Then, the EC—in the person of the Commissioner for Economic and Monetary Affairs, Olli Rehn—pushed again for a quicker transition for women employed in the private sector as well as the abolition of seniority pensions and asked for clarifications on Italy's

---

[6] At the end of the summit, the President of the France, Sarkozy, and the Chancellor of Germany, Merkel, made clear that they did not trust Berlusconi to keep his word. The President of the European Council, Van Rompuy, declared that he had asked the Italian government for reassurance that the measures announced would actually be enacted.

commitment to reform the labour market (as well as on several other aspects of Berlusconi's letter). This was done in a letter sent to the Italian Treasury Minister, Tremonti, on 4 November 2011, making no less than 39 detailed remarks for which it elicited a response within a week.

Monitoring of the implementation of announced reforms would also come from the IMF. At the G-20 summit in Cannes, on November 3–4, Italy was offered to enter an IMF precautionary credit line worth €85 billion . Despite forceful pressures to sign up, the Italian government refused, accepting, however, IMF surveillance without financial aid, so as not to enter a formal conditional lending programme.

On this backdrop, with Italy haunted by the outright lack of credibility, the only lifeline could come from ECB purchases. However, at the beginning of November, members of the ECB governing council discussed (and disclosed) the possibility of stopping the purchase of Italian paper if the Italian government failed to implement the promised reforms.[7]

At the end of October, a bond auction was covered less than 1.3 times, at yields above 6 % that was previously considered the redline before serious default risks. In just a handful of days, the yield spread between 10-year Italian and German government bonds increased by 150 basis points. It reached 553 basis points on 9 November when a major clearing house announced it would increase the cost of using Italian paper as collateral (Jones 2012). Two days later, after the budget law for 2012 was passed in Parliament, Berlusconi resigned, followed by a technocratic government formed under the aegis of the President of the Republic Napolitano and led by the former EU Commissioner Monti. The three main parties in Parliament supported the Monti government: the centre-left Democratic Party, the centrist Union of the Center and the centre-right People of Freedom, Berlusconi's own party.

---

[7] In an interview to the Italian daily La Stampa, ECB governing council member Yves Mersch said, "If we observe that our interventions are undermined by the lack of effort on the part of national governments, we have to pose ourselves the problem of incentives", and replying to the interviewer's question if this meant that ECB would stop purchasing Italian bonds if the government failed to implement promised reforms, he stated "If the ECB governing council reaches the conclusion that the conditions that led it to take a decision are no longer there, it is free to change such decision at any time. We discuss this all the time" (Mastrobuoni 2011, own translation).

# The Monti Government and Its Structural Reforms

The government led by Mario Monti quickly adopted the ECB letter—and the structural reforms it prescribed—as its roadmap. The government identified pension and labour policy as the stage in which to show commitment to reform and acquire a reputation by successfully tackling issues that had daunted the previous governments. It also did nothing to conceal blatant distaste for the trade unions, perceived and portrayed as forces for the preservation of the status quo and partly responsible for the country's dramatic situation. This also meant the introduction of reforms that would deeply affect categories of workers ("insiders") largely untouched by previous reforms.

Actually in his keynote speech to the Italian Senate on 17 November 2011, asking for the Parliament's confidence, Monti had sounded much more cautious and keener on accepting compromise than what would then be the case. About the labour market reform, he stated that it would be introduced "with the agreement of the social partners" and, most notably, "the new system to be designed shall be applied to new labour relationships (…), while already existing regular and stable labour relationships shall not be modified"—words to be later contradicted by the actual realization of the reform. As for pensions, he praised the reforms introduced over the previous two decades, "which have led the Italian pension system to be among the most sustainable in Europe". However, he then framed the issue in terms of inter-generational and horizontal equality, so as to pave the way to a new reform: "Yet, our pension system remains characterized by wide disparities in treatment across different generations and categories of workers, as well as by unjustified privileged areas" (Monti 2011, own translation).

The pension issue was tackled immediately, also to secure financial savings. A reform was introduced in December 2011 within a budget package that included an array of interventions worth €30 billion , 3 % of the GDP, made of €13 billion in cuts and €17 billion in new taxes. The reform implemented with immediate effect some of the measures adopted by the previous Berlusconi government in its summer packages, in particular a system for an automatic retirement age increase based on increased life expectancy, entailing a projected minimum retiring age of 67 years by 2019 irrespective of gender, locked in by 2021, irrespective of any more favourable demographic trend. The retirement age for women employed in the private sector was rapidly equalized to that of the other categories. Further measures were introduced, but the most incisive changes concerned seniority pensions, which were abolished and replaced by early-drawn pensions, following new conditions that were made more stringent with immediate effect. Overall savings were estimated in 0.2 % of the GDP in 2012, 0.9 % in 2015 and 1.4 % in 2020 (Jessoula 2012).

The Monti government implemented the pension reform unilaterally, without negotiating with the social partners but merely informing them of the decisions taken. Negotiations with the social partners took place instead on the labour market reform, starting in January 2012. The planned reforms were mainly aimed at two policy goals, both stemming from the ECB letter.[8] The first was to reduce segmentation in the Italian labour market through the (mainly re-)regulation of non-standard contracts, on the one hand, and, on the other, the (de-)regulation of individual dismissals of open-ended workers, especially of economic dismissal (i.e., for economic motives). The second was to reform income support for the unemployed, an issue mentioned by the ECB letter, which the Berlusconi government had chosen to ignore completely but on which both the Eurozone leaders and Commissioner Rehn had insisted.

The contentious issue was obviously that of the regulation of economic dismissal. This quickly became the focus of attention of financial media and analysts, as well as of European institutions and international economic organizations in their monitoring of Italy's reforms. Monti was determined to get fast approval of a reform that had become the litmus test for the capacity of the government to deliver. The commitment made by Berlusconi in his letter to introduce a reform by May 2012 was written on the wall. In February the Spanish government led by Rajoy had approved an important labour reform, reducing protection

---

[8] For a reconstruction of the decision-making process and a discussion of the main contents of the reform, see Sacchi (2013).

for open-ended workers and making economic dismissal easier (Berton et al. 2012). This was making Italy look behind the curve in the implementation of structural reforms, all the more so after a bill to liberalize services and professions (another request from the ECB letter) had been watered down by Parliament after pressure from economic lobbies (Mattina 2013). Relief of tensions on Italian debt as a consequence of Long-Term Refinancing Operations (LTRO) performed by the ECB in December 2011 and February 2012 was taking urgency away and risked delaying the reform process.

Therefore, in a meeting between the government and the social partners in late March, Monti—who had not previously participated in the negotiations—decided to push the unions to the wall. He asked them to agree on a proposal he made that no longer envisaged reinstatement in their job for workers whose dismissal for economic motives was later declared illegitimate by a judge. Only monetary compensation was envisaged, determined by the judge within a predefined range.[9] Monti was about to leave for the Far East to meet potential investors in Italian debt securities at a road show in China, which was seen as a crucial opportunity for Italy's financial viability.

All of the social partners, except the left-wing trade union, the Italian General Confederation of Labour (CGIL), agreed to the government's reform proposal that included also interventions in the field on nonstandard work and an overhaul of the unemployment benefit system. However, the opposition of CGIL created serious problems to the Democratic Party, in which the wrench made by the prime minister risked causing an internal rift, with unpredictable repercussions on the support given to the government. Indeed, the reform was being opposed not only by the CGIL but also by the rank and file of the other trade unions, which, at the local and plan level, sided with the CGIL despite the stance taken by their national representatives.

The EU, for its part, sided with Monti and warned him not to retreat. In a confidential note on Italy's financial situation prepared for a Eurogroup meeting in late March, the EC (or rather, its Economic and Financial

---

[9] It is to be recalled that there is no severance payment in Italy.

Affairs Directorate) gave a positive assessment of the reform, urging the government not to water it down:

> The Commission has been closely following the debate between the government and the social partners on the content of labour market reform. ... The momentum of reform must be maintained. The responsibility for a quick adoption of an effective reform now rests with the parliament. While it is very positive that the draft reform proposal by the government builds on a constructive dialogue with the social partners, it is crucial that the objective and degree of ambition of the reform remain commensurate to the challenges of the Italian labour market, in line with the Council recommendation.[10]

The government itself, however, was not all of one mind about the matter at hand. At the same time, the CGIL showed its willingness to reach a reasonable agreement that could allow it to bring home some bacon, thus eroding support for the hard-line internal opponents of its reformist leadership. A compromise was brokered by the leaders of the three coalition parties, and Monti had to swallow it. It gave judges power to order the reinstatement of workers in case of proven "manifest non-existence" of the alleged grounds for economic dismissal, as an exception to the general rule of monetary compensation and no reinstatement.

The reform bill introduced to the Senate in early April was acceptable to all parties involved. All of the political forces, as well as the trade unions, knew that the discussion in Parliament could lead to some changes being made with regard to other issues, but the compromise reached on individual dismissal regulations could not be challenged. All of the actors were aware of the fact that, by showing acceptance of the agreement, a clear message was being sent to the European institutions, the other member states, international economic organisations and the markets. The development of parliamentary work was constantly and closely monitored by EU institutions and international economic organizations, which had regular contacts with the decision makers involved. After being approved under a motion of confidence in the Senate at

---

[10] Cited in Spiegel (2012).

the end of May 2012, thus showing that the commitment made by the Berlusconi government was being honoured, the reform bill entered the House. There, for reasons related to domestic politics, its advancement was at risk of delay (Sacchi forthcoming), despite resumed tensions on the Italian bonds, whose yields surpassed again 6 % with a spread against German ones hitting again 400 basis points.

As already seen when Monti left for China, the process of the reform was influenced by another circumstance, which he exploited as an external constraint to get the bill approved—that is, the European Council planned for 28–29 June. As a matter of fact, that was a summit of paramount importance for Italy, as the implementation of the ESM was to be discussed. Italy and Spain, backed by France (now with a Socialist government), were trying to curb the resolute opposition of Germany to accept Eurozone support facilities to take pressure off the sovereign debt of a member state through government bond purchases by the ESM (what the media called "anti-spread shield"). In particular, Monti insisted that such facilities could be accorded on the grounds of fulfilling standard conditions written in the EU budgetary and economic surveillance rules, with no stricter conditionality and without any involvement of the IMF in the drawing up of the MoU. To secure this outcome, which Monti considered vital to pre-empt speculative attacks against Italy, his government had to show that homework had duly been done and commitments made had been honoured, hence the urge to get the labour market reform passed by the House before the summit. This occurred on 27 June. The law was signed by the President of the Republic the next day, with the approval of the EU, international economic organizations and rating agencies.

## Conclusions

EU involvement in member state policymaking has clearly escalated as a consequence of the Eurozone crisis, after recognition of interdependencies within the EMU. Changes in EMU governance, from the introduction of the European Semester to the adoption of new treaties such as the Fiscal Compact to buttress the diptych "sound money and finance" paradigm and "optimal currency area" theory (including their most immediate consequence, the ubiquitous cry for structural reforms) testify to this development. De la Porte and Heins (Chapter 2) identify three dimensions of such renewed involvement: objectives, or policy aims, that refer to "how precisely and with which magnitude policy change is suggested" (p. 19); surveillance of national policy by EU actors; and, finally, enforcement, which refers "to the type of measures EU actors have at their disposal to ensure implementation and/or corrective action in the case of non-compliance" (p. 20).

In terms of objectives, it seems fair to say that the abolition of seniority pensions can be deemed a relevant departure from Italy's policy legacy, although not completely path-breaking. What is certainly path-breaking is the new discipline of individual dismissal, with the removal, if not in very particular cases, of reintegration of the unfairly dismissed workers in their previous jobs, even in large firms. Another important bit of the labour market reform involves the reform of unemployment benefits that, contrary to the usual European trend, extends coverage and increases protection (Sacchi 2013). As seen, although mentioned in the ECB letter, this issue had been obstinately dodged—for financial concerns as well as for its policy beliefs (ibid.)—by the Berlusconi government, despite EU's insistence on it.

Where EU involvement in domestic politics and policymaking really looms up, however, is on the surveillance dimension. EU institutions carried out frequent and pervasive monitoring of Italy's commitment to the agreed structural reforms, from adoption to implementation. Policy prescriptions that would then constitute the roadmap of Monti's government had long been advocated for by EU institutions, particularly as concerned labour market segmentation and a reform of dismissal rules, but not having teeth, they had been sidestepped.[11] This time was different, however, as such prescriptions were now written in the ECB letter, the unofficial covenant—as it were—of implicit conditionality. The Council mandates the Commission to monitor the implementation of Berlusconi's commitment, an unprecedented step vis-à-vis a country not

---

[11] See, for instance, the 2011 country-specific recommendations issued in the context of the European Semester just a few weeks before the ECB letter (Council 2011c).

under formalized, explicit conditionality. Commissioner Rehn commands the Italian treasury minister to answer an array of detailed points he fastidiously raises, and to do that within a week. The labour market reform is monitored at every juncture, its contents thoroughly scrutinized, warnings are issued in a way that could easily make defenders of old-school democracy raise an eyebrow and the parliamentary process is followed day by day.

While monitoring is fundamental in a context marked by low determinacy of implicit conditions, the empirical analysis has clearly highlighted how enforcement crucially hinged on market pressures. Market discipline emerged as the operating mechanism that made implicit conditionality effective. The whole process was driven by Italy's vital necessity to maintain access to markets, with over €400 billion of refinancing needs between July 2011 and the end of 2012.[12] This is why benefiting from the Securities Markets Programme was of paramount importance for a country that, despite formidable pressures by some of its Eurozone partners, staunchly refused to relinquish sovereignty to the IMF. The same can be predicated about the extension of the ESM to purchases of sovereign debt without having to undergo Troika conditionality (that is, including the IMF).

The importance of implicit conditionality as a source of involvement of the EU in domestic policymaking has been shown in this chapter. The empirical evidence about labour policy reform would seem to point out an extreme case of vertical—and to a large extent horizontal, across member states—integration of the policy arena, which goes well beyond what is generally meant by Europeanization and cannot be captured through multilevel governance heuristics. As a matter of fact, the image that could most aptly represent this transformation seems to be that—introduced by Wessels and his associates almost two decades ago—of a fusion "of national and European institutions in the policy cycle, i.e. the common sharing of responsibilities for the use of state instruments and the increasing influence of the E[U] arena on the vertical and horizontal interaction of national and European institutions" (Wessels and Rometsch 1996b, p. 328). "This means for national institutions that they increasingly share

---

[12] *Source*: Bloomberg.

responsibilities with other institutional actors outside their own control, be they national actors from other member states or from independent bodies" (Wessels 1996, p. 36). Whether this will result in any institutional convergence in the foreseeable future does seem a question of some practical relevance for over 300 million Eurozone citizens.

# References

Babb, S. L., & Carruthers, B. G. (2008). Conditionality: Forms, function, and history. *Annual Review of Law and Social Science, 4*(2008), 13–29.

Bank of Italy. (2012). La ricchezza delle famiglie italiane, Supplementi al Bollettino Statistico, n. 65, Rome, Banca d'Italia.

Berlusconi, S. (2011, October 26). Letter to the President of the European Council and to the President of the Commission. Retrieved from http://blogs.ft.com/brusselsblog/files/2011/11/BerlusconiLetter.pdf

Berton, F., Richiardi, M., & Sacchi, S. (2012). *The political economy of work security and flexibility*. Bristol: Policy Press.

Caraway, T. L., Rickard, S. J., & Anner, M. S. (2012). International negotiations and domestic politics: The case of IMF labor market conditionality. *International Organization, 66*(Winter), 27–61.

Council. (2011a, July 21). *Statement by the heads of state or government of the Euro area and EU institutions*. Brussels.

Council. (2011b, October 26). *Eurosummit statement*. Brussels.

Council. (2011c). Council Recommendation of 12 July 2011, 2011/C 215/02. In *Official Journal of the European Union C 215, 21.7.2011* (pp. 4–7).

de la Porte, C., & Heins, E. (2016). 'A new era of European Integration? Governance of labour market and social policy since the sovereign debt crisis', pp. 15–42.

Draghi, M., & Trichet, J. C. (2011). Letter to the Prime Minister of Italy. Retrieved from http://www.corriere.it/economia/11_settembre_29/trichet_draghi_inglese_304a5f1e-ea59-11e0-ae06-4da866778017.shtml

Dyson, K. (2006). Euro entry as defining and negotiating fit: Conditionality, contagion, and domestic politics. In K. Dyson (Ed.), *Enlarging the Euro area* (pp. 7–43). Oxford: Oxford University Press.

ECB. (2011a). Introductory statement to the press conference (with Q&A), 4 August. Frankfurt am Main.

ECB. (2011b). Statement by the President of the ECB. Press Release, 7 August.

ECB. (2011c). Consolidated Financial Statement of the Eurosystem as at 12 August 2011. Press Release, 16 August.

ECB. (2013). Details on securities holdings acquired under the Securities Markets Programme. Press Release, 21 February.

Geithner, T. F. (2014). *Stress test*. New York: Crown.

Grabbe, H. (2006). *The EU's transformative power*. Basingstoke: Palgrave Macmillan.

Griffith-Jones, S., & Stellings, B. (1995). New global financial trends: Implications for developments. In B. Stellings (Ed.), *Global change, regional response: The new international context of development*. Cambridge: Cambridge University Press.

Hemerijck, A. (2014). Fault lines and (still too few) silver linings in Europe's social market economy. In D. Natali (Ed.), *Social developments in the European Union 2013*. Brussels: OSE-ETUI.

Hodson, D. (2012). The Eurozone in 2011. *Journal of Common Market Studies (Annual Review), 50*, 178–194.

Hughes, J., Sasse, G., & Gordon, C. (2004). Conditionality and compliance in the EU's eastward enlargement: Regional policy and the reform of sub-national government. *Journal of Common Market Studies, 42*(3), 523–551.

Jessoula, M. (2012). *Like in a skinner box: External constraints and the reform of retirement eligibility rules in Italy* (Working Paper No. 4/2012). Centro Einaudi–LPF.

Jones, E. (2012). Italy's sovereign debt crisis. *Survival, 1*(54), 83–110.

Kahn-Nisser, S. (2013). Conditionality communication and compliance: The effect of monitoring on collective labour rights in candidate countries. *Journal of Common Market Studies, 51*(6), 1040–1056.

Khan, M. S., & Sharma, S. (2003). IMF conditionality and country ownership of adjustment programs. *The World Bank Research Observer, 18*(2), 227–248.

Kingdon, J. W. (1984). *Agendas, alternatives, and public policies*. Boston: Little, Brown.

Krasner, J. D. (1999). *Sovereignty: Organized hypocrisy*. Princeton: Princeton University Press.

Mastrobuoni, T. (2011, November 6). La BCE può smettere di comprare bond italiani. *La Stampa*.

Mattina, L. (2013). Interest groups and the "amended" liberalizations of the Monti government. *Italian Politics, 28*(1), 227–248.

Milne, R., & Wilson, J. (2011, July 26). Deutsche Bank hedges Italian risk. *Financial Times*.

Monti, M. (2011, November 17). *Testo delle dichiarazioni programmatiche consegnato dal Presidente del Consiglio dei ministri, senatore Mario Monti*. Rome: Senato della Repubblica.

Sacchi, S. (2013). Italy's labour policy and policymaking in the crisis: From distributive coalitions to the shadow of hierarchy. In H. Magara & S. Sacchi (Eds.), *The politics of structural reforms social and industrial policy change in Italy and Japan* (pp. 192–214). Cheltenham: Edward Elgar.

Sartori, G. (1984). Guidelines for concept analysis. In G. Sartori (Ed.), *Social science concepts: A systematic analysis* (pp. 15–88). Beverly Hills: Sage.

Sasse, G. (2008). The politics of EU conditionality: The norm of minority protection during and beyond EU accession. *Journal of European Public Policy, 15*(6), 842–860.

Schimmelfenning, F., & Sedelmeier, U. (2004). Governance by conditionality: EU rule transfer to the candidate countries of Central and Eastern Europe. *Journal of European Public Policy, 11*(4), 661–679.

Smeets, D., & Zimmermann M. (2013). Did the EU summits succeed in convincing the markets during the recent crisis? *Journal of Common Market Studies, 51*(6), 1158–1177.

Spiegel, P. (2012, April 2). More leaked warnings, this time for Italy. *Brussels Blog, Financial Times*.

Wessels, W. (1996). Institutions of the EU system: Models of explanation. In W. Wessels & D. Rometsch (Eds.), *The European Union and member states* (pp. 20–36). Manchester: Manchester University Press.

Wessels, W., & Rometsch, D. (Eds.). (1996a). *The European Union and member states*. Manchester: Manchester University Press.

Wessels, W., & Rometsch, D. (1996b). Conclusion: European Union and national institutions. In W. Wessels & D. Rometsch (Eds.), *The European Union and member states* (pp. 328–365). Manchester: Manchester University Press.

# 8

# Still the Sound of Silence? Towards a New Phase in the Europeanization of Welfare State Policies in France

Patrick Hassenteufel and Bruno Palier

## Introduction

The impact of the EU on French public policies is often discussed in the literature (Rozenberg 2013). In the social policy area, this influence is obvious in new fields such as anti-discrimination and disability, where new actors have been actively mobilizing European legal resources (especially directives) and successfully changing the field's principles and instruments (Caune et al. 2011). In most of the traditional domains (pensions, employment, and healthcare) that we will examine here, the picture is more ambiguous. Decision-makers have tended to deny European influence, but there are several indications that important reforms following European-defined guidelines or ideas were adopted since the end of the 1990s (Caune et al. 2011).

Regarding the impact of EU integration and policies on national welfare state reforms the consensus in the literature before the crisis

P. Hassenteufel (*)
Department of Law and Political Science, University of Versailles, France

B. Palier
Centre for European Studies, Sciences Po, Paris, France

© The Author(s) 2016                                              **181**
C. de la Porte, E. Heins (eds.), *The Sovereign Debt Crisis, the EU and Welfare State Reform*, DOI 10.1057/978-1-137-58179-2_8

was that the EU's ability to impose specific welfare state reforms was very limited (for a survey, see Jacquot 2008). The EU was perceived as having no direct competence on the core of social protection but merely "subsidiary competence provisions" under which intervention is possible only if considered functional to market integration (Hantrais 2007). Research has shown that the Europeanization of Continental welfare state reforms has historically been channelled through economics: it was in order to be competitive in the single market and to protect the strength of the single currency that certain welfare reforms aimed at retrenchment were seen as necessary (Palier 2000). If the channel of influence is merely an economic one, the fact that the European Commission's (EC) power in economic and budgetary issues has recently been enhanced (as demonstrated by de la Porte and Heins, Chapter 2) may reinforce its capacity to weigh in on national welfare state reforms through the budgetary angle. In that regard France offers a very interesting case for the analysis of EU influence from a comparative standpoint. France did not experience a sovereign debt crisis (contrasting with the Southern European countries, France continues to be able to borrow on international markets at very low rates of interest) but was put twice under the excessive deficit procedure (EDP) since 2009.

Therefore, our main question is, to what extent have the new rules adopted since 2010 (the European Semester, Fiscal Compact, Six Pack) changed this ambiguous relationship between France and Europe in the field of welfare policies? In this chapter, we will analyse these changes at three levels: first, the level of the content of welfare state reforms and of EU recommendations; second, the level of political discourses related to these reforms and recommendations; and third, the level of policy decision processes, looking at the different national actors involved. To test whether the tightening of EU economic instruments is followed by greater EU influence on social policy than in the past, we will compare the role played by the EU in French welfare state reform before and after 2010, that is, before and after the changes in the EU rules, focusing on the three policy domains most targeted by EU guidelines and representing the heaviest financial burden: pensions, healthcare and employment policies.

Our analytical perspective is based on the concept of Europeanization[1] to catch the different channels of influence of the EU on French welfare state policies. We are firstly particularly interested in harder budgetary constraints, requested by the EC through new tougher instruments (see de la Porte and Heins, Chapter 2) but where competitiveness and market confidence also comes into the picture. Secondly, we are interested in cognitive diffusion of policy orientations, in which discourses can be used by the French actors in different ways (on the notion of usage of Europe, see Jacquot and Woll 2003, 2010; Graziano et al. 2011). Third, the political dimension of reforms is very important in the case of France because of the high level of politicization of welfare issues (especially pensions) and the deep political polarization on EU conceptions, as shown by the 55 per cent of 'no' votes in the referendum on the European Constitutional Treaty in 2005. Since the 2005 ballot, French governmental actors are very cautious with references to Europe, which is often used by political opponents to delegitimize reform proposals. It partly explains the importance of 'silent Europeanization' and the political limits of EU impact in the French case, at least prior to the crisis and prior to the development of new and tougher EU instruments in the area of budgetary control. In this paper, we will therefore analyse whether the recent re-enforcement of the EU budgetary competences has led to a stronger capacity of the EU to prescribe reforms in France and whether this has led to certain evolutions in the national actors' behaviour towards EU pressure for change.

We will first analyse long-term trends in French welfare reform since the early 1990s until 2009. We will underline a strong consistency between EU recommendations and French reforms, despite an absence of explicit reference to EU guidelines when French politicians are presenting the reforms. At the time, governments were afraid that referring to Europe would reinforce opposition to already unpopular welfare reforms. Second, we will focus on the reforms adopted when France has been subjected to the EDP (in 2009 and since 2013). French authorities have (re)-discovered that the EU has gained two means of pressure: first, the need for deficit reduction is now explicitly integrated into French political discourses and policies (thus having a strong impact on control over social

---

[1] On the notion of Europeanization, see Featherstone and Radaelli (2003).

spending) and, second, the EU is able to demand evidence of reform. Finally, we will show that France has maintained some flexibility on the timing and content of the reforms. Yet, because, on the one side, welfare state reforms need to be negotiated domestically and, on the other side, of growing market concern about public debt, it remains difficult to claim that Brussels is the main driver of welfare state reform (as it is for pension reforms in Denmark and Italy, see de la Porte and Natali 2014).

# Welfare Reforms Before the Crisis: Going Silently in the EU-defined Direction

Welfare reform since the 1990s goes to the heart of France's paradoxical relationship with Europe. Since the 1990s, specific policy measures have led to a shift in social policies in France. This re-orientation of social policies is in line with the main ideas promoted at the EU level. However, there are also great gaps between practice and discourse, because when governments justified reforms they hardly ever linked the reform of traditional social policies to EU development. In this section, we will underscore the coincidences between EU guidelines and the direction of French social policy development, particularly for pensions and employment policies.

## Employment: Lowering the Cost of Labour, Developing Activation Measures

French labour market policy has experienced many reforms since the mid-1990s. One of the main themes in the 1990s was the negative effects of social protection on employment, with the cost of labour supposedly preventing job creation in France (Palier 2005, chapter 7). The argument was two-pronged: first, labour costs were supposedly too high for companies, preventing them from hiring; and second, welfare payments were too passive and thus created a disincentive for the unemployed to return to active employment. Two new typically supply-side sets of policies were developed to address this: policies to lower the cost of labour and activation policies. These reforms marked a break with the French conservative-corporatist model of social protection (Palier 2010).

In the 1990s, France made lowering "social charges" a primary objective of its employment policies. Policies were at first very specifically targeted and then later applied to all lower wages. Despite the lack of an explicit reference, one cannot help but notice that this change echoed the Commission's *White Paper on Growth, Competitiveness and Employment,* as well as the criteria set in Maastricht.

Since the 1980s, there has been a paradigm shift in employment policies, away from a vision of involuntary unemployment, and towards an analysis of voluntary unemployment resulting from individual behaviour. In light of these new conceptions, new policies have gradually been developed based on the will to activate social policies (Barbier 2002). Policy measures started to focus on unemployment insurance in 1992. The *allocation unique degressive* (AUD) reduced both the level of unemployment benefits and their duration. Activation was implemented across the board with the 2001 reform of unemployment insurance schemes. The allowance paid was changed from an unemployment benefit to a job-seeking allowance (*allocation pour la recherche d'emploi*, ARE), which was necessarily accompanied with a return-to-employment action plan signed by the beneficiary (*plan d'action pour le retour à l'emploi*, PARE). In addition, a new measure aiming to foster employment was introduced in 2001, the "employment bonus" (*prime pour l'emploi*) which aimed to 'make work pay'.

Following this trend, a new benefit was created in 2008, the *revenu de solidarité active* (RSA), replacing the minimum benefit payment created in 1988, the Revenu Minimum d'Insertion (RMI). The RSA sought to benefit anyone taking a low-income job with a state-financed subsidy that guaranteed its beneficiaries a better income than on the RMI (Palier 2010). Also here, the national actors who implemented these policies (mainly the social partners for unemployment insurance and the government for minimum income schemes) did not refer to the EU discourses on activation or the European Employment strategy (de la Porte and Jacobsson 2012).

## Pensions: Returning to Work, Remaining on the Labour Market

The pension reforms in the 1990s have been few and remained partial. The Balladur reform, adopted in 1993, only concerned private sector employees. The principle measure was the lengthening of the contribution record to be entitled to a full pension from 37.5 years to 40 years. It also involved a change in the way the base for calculating the level of pension was calculated, and pensions were indexed on inflation rather than on wage (Palier 2000).

After the re-election of French President Jacques Chirac in 2002, Prime Minister Jean-Pierre Raffarin set pension reform on the agenda. The principal initiative was the alignment of public sector employees with private sector regimes. Measures were enacted in an attempt to significantly curb the rise in early retirements, once viewed as the preferred instrument to complement economic reorganization. Despite a big social movement and major strikes in May 2003, the government obtained the agreement of the employers' organisations and of two trade unions, the *Confédération Française Démocratique du Travail* (CFTD) and the *Confédération Générale des Cadres* (CGC), to adopt the reform. A strong majority of the Parliament supported the reform bill, which was adopted in July 2003. A voluntary regime of pensions, financed through capitalisation for private sector employees, was also accepted by Parliament (Palier 2010).

This reform followed the main policy prescriptions of the EU: ensuring the financial sustainability of the pension system, introducing some parametric measures (lengthening the period of contribution), and developing some supplementary private pension plans to compensate for the diminution of the public pension. It also follows the EU's policy prescriptions concerning active aging, to encourage people to work longer and to close the early retirement schemes. Finally, the EU's orientation to the principle of equity and alignment between the public and private sector pension regimes is also taken into account (Mandin and Palier 2004). Here again, despite being in line with EU recommendations, the French government did not refer to the EU.

## Healthcare: The Agenda Setting of Cost Containment

For healthcare, the connection with the ideas promoted at the European level is far more limited than in the social policy sectors analysed previously. However, the Maastricht criteria were a strong agenda-setting factor of cost containment measures in the 1996 Juppé reform and the 2004 Law on Health Insurance.

In the 1990s, the EC, in line with other international organizations (especially the Organisation for Economic Co-operation and Development [OECD]), promoted the ideas of 'organized competition' and 'quasi-markets' in healthcare, mainly referencing the 1991 British reform (Hassenteufel et al. 2000). Because of the characteristics of the French health insurance system, especially the already existing competitive elements (based on free choice of doctors and hospitals by patients), these policy reform orientations were not really discussed. Some proposals, inspired by the American health maintenance organization (HMO) model, were made by liberal think tanks to introduce competition between health insurers (especially between the publicly funded sickness funds and private insurers) but were not adopted by the French government (Benamouzig 2012). The main structural reform adopted during that period concerned the role of general practitioners (GPs) in the healthcare system. The 1996 reform made it possible for GPs to act as gatekeepers for patients who agree to contract with them (*médecins référents*). This system was replaced by another (*médecin traitant*) in 2004, geared to making GPs the 'drivers' of patients in the health system. All insured French citizens had to choose their *médecin traitant*. The EU dimension seems not to play any role here (except through comparisons of different healthcare systems). Rather, it was mainly the result of the creation of a new GP organization (MG France) and of negotiations with doctors' organizations (Hassenteufel 2010).

The main European impact on French healthcare was the orientation towards cost containment. Even if cost-containment policies started in the 1980s, the Maastricht criteria had a direct impact on the agenda setting of new cost-containment policies in 1996 and 2004. The 1996 reform aimed to curb growth in health spending to tackle the social security system's large deficit (€6.05 billion deficit for health insurance in 1995), which was threatening the adoption of the euro in France. It introduced capped budgets for all health insurance expenditures based on National Health Insurance Spending Objectives (ONDAM, *Objectif National de Dépenses d'Assurances Maladie*) for ambulatory and hospital care, voted every year by the Parliament. Nevertheless, health expenditures continued to grow very fast and the deficit still deepened. The target of ONDAM was temporarily reached in 1997 but never again in subsequent years (until 2010). These budgets were ineffective because of insufficient sanction mechanisms. Doctors led a successful legal battle against penalties, which were finally abandoned (Hassenteufel 2003).

In 2003, the deteriorating finances of the health branch of the social security system (which amounted to a €10.6 billion deficit in 2003) contributed to the violation of the Stability and Growth Pact (SGP) criteria and led to the drafting of a new health insurance legislation adopted by the French Parliament in August 2004. This reform marked a clear shift in cost-containment policies, favouring industry over consumers (Hassenteufel 2008). The policy of capping health budgets, introduced by the Plan Juppé in 1996, was *de facto* withdrawn because the law made no mention of penalties on doctors if they exceeded expenditure objectives. At the same time, the law required patients to increase their own financial contribution to their healthcare costs via increased hospital co-payments and discontinued reimbursement for a number of expensive drugs. This trend was followed in 2005 with the introduction of a payment of €18 for acute medical procedures. In 2008, prescription charges were introduced under President Nicolas Sarkozy. By the end of 2008, the health insurance deficit decreased to €4.4 billion. The other consequence was that coverage by the public health insurance system has decreased from 77 per cent in 2004 to 75.5 per cent in 2008. While chronic diseases and hospital care are still well covered, non-acute care coverage has been reduced to 55 per cent (Tabuteau 2010, p. 88).

The main European impact on the French healthcare policy reforms of 1996 and 2004 was exerted by the Maastricht Criteria that demanded cost containment. While the 2009 healthcare reform contained many of the same policy objectives as those included in the open method of coordination (e.g., better geographical distribution of doctors to improve equality of access, improved coherence and consistency of health policies, better coordination between ambulatory and hospital care, improved prevention, etc.), compared to the policy areas of employment and pensions, the content of healthcare reforms was much less influenced by European orientations. Instead, healthcare reforms were shaped and countered by other, more domestic, considerations, such as elections and fear of street protests. At the same time as cost-containment measures were introduced, other reforms created new rights and benefits, for example, allowances for frail elderly and specific health insurance schemes for the poorest were adopted in 2000. As a result, France's level of social expenditure continued to become one of the world's highest, and its governments continually flaunted Economic and Monetary Union (EMU) budgetary rules. Thus, the tightening of these rules following the crisis introduced a major challenge.

## Since 2010: France under Surveillance

At his start of term, President Nicolas Sarkozy justified several pre-financial crisis reforms, like the adoption of the RSA, the decrease in employer contributions or the introduction of prescription fees, as fulfilment of campaign promises made in 2007 (Hassenteufel 2012a).

The dominance of the domestic policy agenda over European influences continued through 2009 regarding welfare reforms, in line with Sarkozy's discourse at the time when he was defending the French social model. A major change occurred in 2010 with the deterioration of the French financial situation coinciding with stronger European pressure. French authorities were afraid of being unable to refinance their debt on acceptable terms and becoming the next Greece or Italy. Under these acute financial conditions, French actors have been more willing to listen to the EC, partly because they may need its support should refinancing become difficult and partly because the EC can help reassure international bond markets that France is on the right path, hence reassuring lenders about France's capacity to re-pay.

This shift in attitude is very visible with the passage in 2010 of a new pension reform, clearly linked to EU recommendations and financial market demands. In contrast to the previous pension reforms, which were negotiated with the trade unions and involved substantial give and take, the post-2009 reforms have conceded almost nothing to the trade unions. The case of pension reform illustrates the significant shift in French government behaviour since 2010, which is more than in the past taking into account the EC's recommendations. Therefore, we will analyse France as a test case to show how the European Semester and the new criteria under the reinforced SGP are having an impact on a country that is under an EDP and, more generally, affected by the crisis, but without being at its centre: unlike the other countries studied in this volume, France has not been put under a bailout.

Table 8.1 shows that France has long been under EU scrutiny, mostly because deficits have frequently been higher than the 3 per cent public deficit criterion stipulated by the SGP. Even if the formal 60 per cent for public debt had been overpassed in 2003, it is mainly since 2009 that the debt ratio has also gone far beyond the SGP rules.

Since 2009, France has clearly operated far from meeting the European criteria, and the EU has replied with multiple warnings and actions. On 27 April 2009, the European Council published a 'recommendation to France with a view to bringing an end to this situation of an excessive government deficit'. The Council recognised the existence of special circumstances and therefore allowed the correction of the excessive deficit to be set in a medium-term framework. The Council placed France under enhanced surveillance and required it to explain every six months the type of decisions it has taken to reduce the excessive deficit. In the Council's recommendation, the intrusion into French welfare state reforms remains relatively limited though. The only explicit reference to the content of reforms appears when the Council 'recommends to swiftly implement the planned measures and reforms to contain current expenditure over the coming years, especially in the areas of healthcare and local authorities'.[2]

On 11 November 2009, the EC reported that France needed to make further policy changes to end its excessive deficits. More precise contents of the reforms were proposed since the EC suggested that the Council recommends to French authorities to implement reforms with a view to improve the general budget balance and the growth potential of the economy.

---

[2] COM(2015) 115 final (http://ec.europa.eu/transparency/regdoc/rep/1/2015/FR/1-2015-115-FR-F1-1.PDF)

**Table 8.1** French public deficit and debt as calculated by the EU

| | 2001 | 2002 | 2003 | 2004 | 2005 | 2006 | 2007 | 2008 | 2009 | 2010 | 2011 | 2012 | 2013 |
|---|---|---|---|---|---|---|---|---|---|---|---|---|---|
| Public deficit (as a percentage of GDP) | −1.5 | −3.1 | −4.1 | −3.6 | −2.9 | −2.3 | −2.7 | −3.3 | −7.5 | −7.1 | −5.3 | −4.8 | −4.3 |
| Public debt (as a percentage of GDP) | 56.9 | 58.8 | 62.9 | 64.9 | 66.4 | 63.7 | 64.2 | 68.2 | 79.2 | 82.4 | 85.8 | 90.2 | 93.5 |

*Sources: 2001–2012 Eurostat, 2013 INSEE*

Increased enforceability of expenditure control, notably in the areas of healthcare and local authorities, and the reduction of the multiple existing tax exemptions would improve the quality of public finances. In addition, France should improve the overall competition framework, with particular emphasis on the network industries [...], further reform the pension system, modernise employment protection and enhance life-long learning to enhance potential GDP growth.[3]

In December 2009, after President Sarkozy communicated to the Council that France planned policy changes in the regulation of labour market and a pension reform for 2010, the Council adopted a text that soft pedalled these issues and was much less detailed than what the EC proposed.

On June 2010, after strong lobbying from national governments, in which France played a big role along with Spain and Italy, the EU decided to step back from overtly harsh pressures for fiscal adjustments that endangered the tenuous economic recovery. In its assessment of national policy making, the Commission decided that France along with 11 other countries required no further procedure to reduce their excessive deficit. The assessment of the French case, however, was rather ambiguous. The Commission noted positively that France was reducing its recovery plan but voiced concern that France had been increasing its public spending. The Commission recommended that France should specify more deficit-reduction reforms and make sure that the previously announced pension reform would be indeed implemented.

Between 2010 and late 2012, the EC did not put France under any specific scrutiny, but in February 2013 it issued an analysis of the French budgetary situation. It called for putting France again under an EDP. Remarkably, in this analysis, the EC extensively detailed the decisions (called *discretionary measures*) that France had already taken, including healthcare, labour market and pension policy changes. In this case, it was to show that more efforts had been done than were visible if only looking at the gross numbers such as the public deficit or the debt ratio.

---

[3] http://ec.europa.eu/economy_finance/eu/forecasts/2013_spring_forecast_en.htm

Despite the acknowledgement of these measures, according to the Commission services' 2013 Spring Forecast, 'France is not expected to correct its excessive deficit by the deadline established in the Council recommendation of 2 December 2009'. Consequently, the Commission recommended a new procedure for France to end its excessive deficit. The French government asked for an extended deadline to reach the defined goal without threatening the first signs of economic recovery. At the end of May 2013, the Commission granted France two additional years for correcting its excessive deficit because of the negative impact that a long-lasting economic recession in France could have on the EU as a whole. This extended deadline was presented by the French Finance Minister, Pierre Moscovici, as an illustration of the capacity of the French government to influence the Commission's policy: 'France is not alone. It is a general measure. It is a new doctrine for the Commission: it has been aware that structural deficits are more important than nominal deficits. It is a discussion that I had with Olli Rehn for one year. It shows the necessity to reorient the European policy' (Ricard 2013).

In the Recommendation that followed this negotiation, published on 18 June 2013, the Council decided to put France again under a procedure to end its excessive government deficit but with a two-year extended deadline. In exchange for this extension, the Council recommended that the budgetary measures the French government announced must be effectively implemented. The Council concluded in very explicit and detailed points that the French government's announced pension reforms were necessary to meet the extended deadline: '[T]he French authorities should strengthen the long-term sustainability of the pension system by further adjusting all relevant parameters. In particular, the planned reform, as currently envisaged, should be adopted by the end of this year, and bring the system into balance in a sustainable manner no later than 2020 while avoiding any further increase in the cost of labour'. Consequently, in January 2014 France adopted a new pension reform law, with a very small majority in the Parliament. The Council's recommendation also concerned labour market reforms: lower labour costs, better integration of the youngest and oldest workers, the reduction of the segmentation of the labour market and more flexibility in the firing and hiring regulation.

# Pension Reforms to Satisfy Brussels

This review of the recent history of France under European scrutiny shows a relatively strong connection between the excessive deficit procedures, the negotiation of a delay and pension reforms in France (in 2010 and 2013). However, France has enacted pension reforms in the past (notably in 1993, 2003 and 2007) that were not closely related to the European procedures. To see whether the recent procedures have changed the relation of French welfare state reforms to the EU, we need to look more closely at the content of the most recent pension reforms from a political discourse point of view (Were the reforms justified by the necessity to comply with Brussels?) and from a content point of view (Do they seem to fit more than in the past with EU orientations?).

## The European Dimension of the 2010 Pension Reform

In compliance with the April 2009 EDP, President Sarkozy announced in June 2009 that the government would seek to reform statutory pension schemes in 2010. He did not mention this type of reform during his presidential campaign or during the subsequent legislative campaign in 2007. This new reform had been justified in French national discourse largely because of the sharp increase in the pay-as-you-go (PAYG) schemes' deficits following the financial crisis. The government made it clear that the main aims of the reform were to deal with these deficits, to demonstrate to the EU France's commitment to reduce its budget deficit and to improve its credibility in the international financial markets.

The government presented its draft bill in June 2010, which the Parliament adopted in autumn. It included an increase in the minimum statutory retirement age from 60 to 62 years by 2018, an increase in the minimum age to get a full pension without a penalty from 65 to 67 years by 2023, an increase in the minimum contribution period to 41.5 years by 2010, the harmonisation of contribution rates between public-sector and private-sector statutory schemes within 10 years[4], additional

---

[4] Contribution rates were traditionally higher in private-sector schemes. Public-sector contribution rates were thus increased from 7.85 per cent to 10.55 per cent.

resources of €3.7 billion through an increase in the highest income tax bracket from 40 to 41 per cent, and increased taxes on dividends, stock options and final-salary supplementary pensions offered mostly to senior executives in private companies. The government also maintained the early retirement schemes for long careers and introduced a right to retire at the age of 60 years instead of the age of 62 years for workers employed in 'hard working conditions' who would have a 'rate of incapacity to work' of 20 per cent (Naczyk et al. 2011).

The implementation of the reform was accelerated in autumn 2011 because of the enduring deficit of the pension system (€8.9 billion in 2010). In November 2011, the government announced it would increase the minimum retirement age to 62 years by 2017 instead of 2018, as planned by the 2010 reform. This measure was taken after the credit rating agency, Moody's, announced at the end of October that it would re-assess and possibly downgrade France's credit rating. The government's decision to accelerate the increase in the retirement age was thus clearly a reaction to this threat, although it did not prevent another agency, Standard & Poor's, to lower France's credit rating in January 2012 (Naczyk et al. 2011).

Broadly speaking, the 2010 pension reform and its acceleration in 2011 are in line with the goals set by the EU 2020 strategy, the 2011 Annual Growth Survey and the country- specific recommendations of the Commission and the Council published in July 2011. With the 2010 reform and its November 2011 decision to increase its pace, France's priority has been to ensure the long-term sustainability of the pension system by increasing the statutory retirement age. In the National Reform Programme it submitted in spring 2011 (http://ec.europa.eu/europe2020/pdf/nrp/nrp_france_en.pdf), the French government emphasized the fact that the 2010 reform bill would reduce the public deficit by 0.5 per cent of GDP by 2013 and 1.25 per cent by 2020, resulting in a reduction of public debt by 10 per cent of GDP in 2020 (p. 13). This would mean an improvement in the financial sustainability of the pension system.

## The EU Strikes Back: The 2013 Pension Reform

In July 2012, the new socialist government made good on its election campaign promise to revert the retirement age back to 60 years for those people who started working before the age of 20. It also extended the types of non-working situations that are taken into account in the calculation of workers' contribution record (two additional semesters of maternity leave and unemployment). However, slow economic growth and the forecasts made by the Pension Orientation Council (*Comité d'orientation des retraites, COR*) in December 2012 have again put the pension reform in front of the political agenda, despite the fact that this was not at all announced by François Hollande during his presidential campaign. COR announced that the deficit would grow by up to more than €18 billion in 2017 and more than €20 billion in 2020 if no new measures were taken.

In the meantime, the Commission prepared a recommendation for putting France under an EDP again (adopted in spring 2013, as shown earlier). The pension reform was explicitly encouraged by the EC. In its recommendations made in May 2013 (twice as long as those made one year before), the Commission insisted that the French government had to tackle the roots of the public finance deficit in exchange for a two-years' delay (up to 2015) for the return to the 3 per cent of the GDP public deficit threshold. This would require, again, reforming the pension system, which was not considered financially sustainable after 2018.

Despite François Hollande's declaration that 'the European Commission does not dictate us what to do. We have to respect our European commitments for public deficits. Concerning structural reforms we are the only one to decide what the right way to achieve the goal is' (Roger 2013), the content of the reform presented in spring 2013 was in line with the recommendations. The main aspects were the increases in contributions (+0.3 percentage point for employees and employers from 2014 to 2017) as well as length of contributions (one trimester more every three years from 2020) and the decision to postpone by six months the revalorization of pensions. It also created a 'hard working conditions account' (*compte pénibilité*) for workers with difficult working conditions and included measures aimed at improving pension adequacy for women, youths and workers employed in non-standard forms of employment (Naczyk et al. 2013). However, in November 2013, the EC criticized this reform for not being ambitious enough. The EC argued this was the case because the reforms maintained the legal retirement age and lacked measures harmonizing the different pension systems, especially the 'special regimes' for public service employees. The reform has, however, been adopted in Parliament on 18 December 2013, with the content planned by the government and some adjustments made to obtain the votes of the more left-leaning members of Parliament (MPs; hence, going in the other direction than the one supported by the EC).

The case of the 2013 pension reform shows that French governments are still reluctant to explicitly accept and defer to EU constraints. This is a matter not only of political legitimization but also of the political necessity to negotiate welfare reforms with the social partners.

## National Translation through Negotiation: Reforms *à la française*

The conflictual character of French welfare state reforms is often highlighted, especially for pensions, with the strong mobilizations against the Plan Juppé in 1995, the 2003 Fillon Reform and in 2007 against the special regime reform. From this point of view, the 2010 Pension reform did not differ. Most unions as well as the left-wing opposition were opposed to an increase in the retirement age, arguing that it would not solve the problem of a low employment rate of older workers. Unions also strongly criticised the increase in the minimum age for a full pension without a penalty, arguing that it would most strongly harm women, whose pensions are usually lower because of broken career records. Due to their opposition to the reform, unions organised demonstrations in the spring and the summer of 2010. Strikes continued through the autumn while Parliament debated the bill. In response to the union mobilisation, the government made some concessions at the beginning of September. It agreed to decrease from 20 to 10 per cent the 'rate of incapacity to work' that would allow workers employed in 'hard working conditions' to retire from the age of 60 instead of the age of 62. Before the reform bill progressed to the Senate, the government announced another concession, agreeing to maintain the right to a full pension without penalty at the age of 65 for around 130,000 mothers born before 1956. However, no concession was made on the flagship measure of the increase in the statutory minimum retirement age.

In 2013, the French government criticized the EC's recommendations and remarks, arguing that they would hamper negotiations with its social partners. The negotiation of pension reform was put strongly forward by the new government in line with the 'social-democratic' line favoured by newly elected President Hollande: the reform was announced at the end of August 2013 after two days of consultations with all social partners. This highlights the importance given to the negotiation process in domestic politics, not only for pensions but also, more generally, for any welfare reforms. This way of doing is also obvious for employment and healthcare policies.

## Negotiated Reforms in Employment and Healthcare Policies

The most important negotiated change in employment policies, in line with European concepts, is the combination of flexibility and social security. This turn to 'flexicurity' was first tried before the crisis, under Nicolas Sarkozy's presidential mandate with the agreement on the securization of professional tracks (*sécurisation des parcours professionnels*), which was negotiated by the social partners (but not signed by the CGT) and then enacted by law in 2008. During the parliamentary debates, the government and the MPs from the right-wing majority used frequently the expression *flexicurité à la française* to stress the translation of the Scandinavian model by the French policy actors (Caune 2013, pp. 454–456). However, it had limited effects because it concerned mostly qualified workers (Cahuc and Zylberberg 2010, p. 58).

A new negotiation, launched by the new socialist government, took place during autumn 2012. The national agreement (*Accord National Interprofessionnel*) signed between the social partners (but not by the CGT) in January 2013 is clearly a deal brokering more flexibility (companies can more easily sign an agreement with salary or working time

**Table 8.2** Health insurance deficit and spending, France 2009–2013

|  | 2009 | 2010 | 2011 | 2012 | 2013 |
|---|---|---|---|---|---|
| Health insurance deficit (billion euros) | −10.6 | −11.4 | −8.6 | −5.9 | −6.8 |
| Development of health insurance spending (%) | +3.6 | +2.6 | +2.7 | +2.3 | +2.4 |

*Source: Les Comptes de la Sécurité Sociale* (2014)

decreases to protect jobs and force their employees to change jobs in the same company; laying off workers is also facilitated) and new securities (complementary health insurance for all employees in the private sector, reloadable rights to unemployment benefits, higher taxation of short time contracts, bottom level of weekly working hours for part-time contracts, personal accounts for training). Like in 2008, the social partners and political actors supporting the agreement used the expression *flexicurité à la française* and mentioned the 'German model' to legitimize it (Caune 2013). Parliament passed the law enacting this agreement a few weeks later despite strong opposition from the Communist Party and the Left Party, supported by the two trade unions that did not sign the agreement Confédération Générale du Travail (CGT), Force Ouvrière (FO). At the end of 2013, it was followed by a new negotiation on professional training concluded by a national agreement between business associations and trade unions, creating the 'individual training account' for the whole professional career (including unemployment periods) and reforming the complex training financing system.

In healthcare, the cost-containment policies adopted since 2004 were not able to prevent the rise of the health insurance deficit from €4.4 billion in 2008 to €10.6 billion in 2009 (Hassenteufel 2012b). This enormous deficit (see Table 8.2), contributing to the general deterioration of French public finances and to closer European scrutiny as we have seen, led to the adoption of new measures in the financing of social security since 2010: mainly price reductions for drugs and medical procedures (especially radiology), an increase in the proportion of generic prescription and efficiency gains in hospitals and sickness funds. The amount of the annual evolution of the ONDAM has been progressively trimmed from 3.6 per cent in 2009 to 2.4 per cent in 2013 and respected since 2010.[5]

---

[5] This evolution cannot only be related to these measures: the decrease of the number of doctors and the absence of new pharmaceutical "blockbusters" are two main factors to take into account

Also in the field of healthcare, negotiations between the social partners, namely the national sickness fund organization (UNCAM, created
by the 2004 reform and tightly controlled by the government) and the
organizations representing doctors in the ambulatory sector have taken
place since the crisis. First, they concerned the creation of a new payment
system inspired by the British 'payment by results' system (Hassenteufel
2012b). In 2009, 'contracts for enhancing doctors' individual practice'
(*Contrats d'amélioration des pratiques individuelles*, CAPI) were introduced on a voluntary basis. According to this target-based scheme, doctors are paid €7 for completing 16 healthcare objectives for each patient
(including, for example, flu vaccinations for persons over 65 years, breast
cancer screening for women over 50 years, increased use of generic prescriptions and better monitoring of chronic diseases). In a national agreement signed in July 2011 between the UNCAM and the main doctors'
organizations, this performance-related payment system was extended
and its remuneration increased. In 2012, the new socialist government
put pressure on the UNCAM to negotiate with doctors' organizations to
regulate overbilling. The agreement signed in October 2012 creates a new
contract limiting the amount and proportion of overbilling for doctors
(in exchange for lower social contributions). Like another proposal by the
Health Ministry to attract doctors in under-served areas, it is a voluntary
contract. Thus, the effectiveness of these new policy tools depends on the
good will of doctors: the successive health ministers, since the failure of
the implementation of the Plan Juppé at the end of the 1990s, are reluctant to see direct confrontation with doctors' organizations and therefore
avoid using more constraining policy tools.

A last illustration of the importance of the national negotiations is
the Responsibility Pact announced by Hollande in January 2014 aiming to reduce labour costs for companies (by reducing social contributions, especially those aimed at financing family policy) to boost
competitiveness in exchange for job creation and financed by a €50
billion cut in public spending over three years. In March 2014, three
trade unions and the two business associations agreed to open negotia-

---

(Tabuteau 2013, p. 195) as well as the broader context of the crisis. Health expenditure is stabilised
or in decrease in almost all OECD countries since 2010.

tions in every branch on the job creation objectives and to participate in a tripartite observatory for the implementation of the Pact. The Pact became the core element of the economic policy and public finance strategy presented to the EC by the new Prime Minister Manuel Valls in spring 2014.

## Conclusion

Our analysis of recent French welfare state reforms clearly shows that France is more and more obliged to follow EU recommendations. As far as pension reforms and healthcare cost containment are concerned, the timing shows how much the EU pressures now seem to (really) matter in France. France-implemented pension reforms in 2010 and 2013 and since 2010, the national targets for health insurance expenses, fixed more tightly, were reached, showing a stabilisation of the development of health insurance costs. The pension reforms were not announced during the 2007 or 2012 electoral campaigns as part of the policy programme of the winning candidates (on the contrary, for Hollande the promise was to undo the Sarkozy pension reform). However, both Sarkozy and Hollande have implemented pension reforms when the EU placed France under an EDP.

When looking at the political discourse and content of these pension reforms, French authorities continue, as in the past, to deny that they act 'because of Europe' and justify the reforms with reference to the economic and demographic situation. Moreover, they try to find political room for manoeuver in the content of the reform for it to be accepted (in the last pension reform, especially the 'hard-working conditions account'). However, the French government is now obliged to show to EU authorities that reforms are decided and implemented. Moreover, France is now in permanent welfare reform stress. After the pension and labour markets reforms in 2013, in 2014 health insurance was at the top of the welfare policy reform agenda.[6] Importantly, the contents of these

---

[6] In the €50 billion reduction of public spending planned for the 2015–2017 period, €10 billion concern health insurance and €11 billion other social policies (mainly based on the freeze of the amount of social benefits).

reforms are similar to those adopted since 2010 in the countries under MoUs analysed in other contributions to this volume.

A traditional French strategy to avoid excessive EU pressure and interference on domestic social and economic reforms is to find allies in Europe, as did President Chirac in German Chancellor Schroeder in 2003 and again President Sarkozy in 2010 in Chancellor Merkel. But after his election in 2012, François Hollande had not been able to the re-negotiate the Fiscal Compact, although it was a strong and loud promise made during his electoral campaign.[7] The only concession obtained, in 2013, was the two-year additional delay to reach the 3 per cent public deficit level.

Since 2009, French authorities are more constrained in a second way. The Great Recession has revealed the alarming erosion of France's competitiveness, especially in manufacturing. Consequently, French governments, of left and right alike, are convinced that they must provide more support for business. The French government is under heightened 'surveillance' not only from the Commission and bond markets but also from French employers, and both sets of actors are making demands that threaten or crowd out French social protection. If concerns about sovereign debt make the government prioritize deficit reduction, concerns about competitiveness push in the opposite direction. Perhaps the biggest reason why the Hollande government is having so much trouble bringing down France's budget deficit is that the government is simultaneously providing €30 billion in tax breaks to French corporations in the hope of improving competitiveness and hiring.

Finally, if the Europeanization of French welfare policies since 2010 is louder than before, the crisis does not mean a radical shift; most of the measures adopted since 2010 are rooted in long-term reform paths that already started in the 1990s: retrenchment in pensions, control of healthcare expenditures, activation of unemployment policies and so forth. Therefore, French social security reforms continue to reinforce the separation of the two 'worlds of welfare' (Palier 2010) within the French social protection system.

---

[7] Already in 1997 Lionel Jospin, the new Prime Minister after the victory of the left parties at the parliamentary election, did not succeed to renegotiate the Amsterdam treaty

# References

Barbier, J.-C. (2002). Peut-on parler d'"activation" de la protection sociale en Europe? *Revue française de sociologie, 43*(2), 307–332.

Benamouzig, D. (2012). Du grand soir au clair obscur. Expertise économique et privatisation bureaucratique de l'assurance maladie. *Actes de la recherche en sciences sociales, 193,* 56–73.

Cahuc, P., & Zylberberg A. (2010). *Les réformes ratées du Président Sarkozy* (2nd ed.). Paris: Flammarion.

Caune, H. (2013). *Les États providence sont aussi des États membres. Comparaison des logiques nationales de l'européanisation des politiques de l'emploi en France et au Portugal.* PhD thesis, Sciences Po, Paris.

Caune, H., Jacquot, S., & Palier, B. (2011). Boasting the national model: The EU and welfare state reforms in France. In P. Graziano, S. Jacquot, & B. Palier (Eds.), *Europa, Europae. The EU and the domestic politics of welfare state reforms* (pp. 48–72). Basingstoke: Palgrave Macmillan.

de la Porte, C., & Jacobsson, K. (2012). Social investment or recommodification? Assessing the employment policies of the EU member states. In N. Morel, B. Palier, & J. Palme (Eds.), *Towards a social investment welfare state? Ideas, policies and challenges* (pp. 117–150). Bristol: Policy Press.

de la Porte, C., & Natali, D. (2014). Altered Europeanization of pension reform during the Great Recession: Denmark and Italy compared. *West European Politics, 37*(4), 732–749.

Featherstone, K., & Radaelli C. (Eds). (2003). *The politics of Europeanization.* Oxford: Oxford University Press.

Graziano, P., Jacquot, S., & Palier, B. (Eds.). (2011). *Europa, Europae. The EU and the domestic politics of welfare state reforms.* Basingstoke: Palgrave Macmillan.

Hantrais, L. (2007). *Social policy in the European Union* (3rd ed.). Basingstoke and New York: Palgrave Macmillan and St. Martin's Press.

Hassenteufel, P. (2003). Le premier septennat du plan Juppé. In J. de Kervasdoué (Ed.), *Carnet de santé de la France 2003* (pp. 21–147). Paris: Dunod.

Hassenteufel, P. (2008). Welfare policies and politics. In A. Cole, P. Le Galès, & J. Levy (Eds.), *Developments in French politics* (pp. 227–242). Basingstoke: Palgrave Macmillan.

Hassenteufel, P. (2010). La difficile affirmation d'un syndicalisme spécifique aux generalists. In G. Bloy & F. X. Schweyer (Eds.), *Singuliers généralistes. Sociologie de la médecine générale* (pp. 403–418). Rennes: Presses de l'EHESP.

Hassenteufel, P. (2012a). La Sécurité sociale entre ruptures affichées et transformations silencieuses. In J. De Maillard & Y. Surel (Eds.), *Les politiques publiques sous Sarkozy* (pp. 341–360). Paris: Presses de Sciences Po.

Hassenteufel, P. (2012b). Les sources intellectuelles des réformes du système de santé français. La prédominance des forums et des acteurs administratifs. In J. de Kervasdoué (Ed.), *Carnet de santé de la France 2012* (pp. 161–183). Paris: Dunod.

Hassenteufel, P., Delaye, S., Pierru, F., Robelet, M., & Serré, M. (2000). La libéralisation des systèmes de protection maladie européens. Convergence, européanisation et adaptations nationals. *Politique Européenne, 2,* 29–48.

Jacquot, S. (2008). *National welfare state welfare reforms and the question of Europeanization: From impact to usages. REC-WP 01/2008.* Working Papers on the Reconciliation of Work and Welfare in Europe. Edinburgh: RECWOWE Publications, Dissemination and Dialogue Centre. Retrieved July 10, 2014, from http://www.socialpolicy.ed.ac.uk/recwowepudisc/working_papers/01-08

Jacquot, S., & Woll C. (2003). Usage of European integration – Europeanisation from a sociological perspective. *European Integration online Papers (EIoP), 7,* 12. Retrieved April 7, 2014, from http://eiop.or.at/eiop/texte/2003-012a.htm

Jacquot, S., & Woll C. (2010). Using Europe: Strategic action and multi-level politics. *Comparative European Politics, 8*(1), 110–126.

Mandin, C., & Palier, B. (2004). The politics of pension reform in France: The end of exceptionalism? In G. Bonoli & S. Toshimitsu (Eds.), *Ageing and pension reform around the world* (pp. 74–93). Cheltenham: Edward Elgar.

Naczyk, M., Morel, N., & Palier, B. (2011). Annual national report 2011: Pensions, health care and long-term care France. ASISP (Assessing the socio-economic impact of social reforms). Retrieved March 28, 2014, from http://socialprotection.eu/

Naczyk, M., Morel, N., & Palier, B. (2013). Country document 2013: Pensions, health care and long-term care France. ASISP (Assessing the socio-economic impact of social reforms). Retrieved March 12, 2014, from http://socialprotection.eu/

Palier, B. (2000). 'Defrosting' the French welfare state. *West European Politics, 23*(2), 113–136.

Palier, B. (2005). *Gouverner la Sécurité sociale.* Paris: PUF.

Palier, B. (2010). The dualizations of the French welfare system. In B. Palier (Ed.), *A long good bye to Bismarck? The politics of welfare reforms in continental Europe* (pp. 73–100). Amsterdam: Amsterdam University Press.

Ricard, P. (2013). Bruxelles donne deux ans de plus à Paris pour réduire son deficit. *Le Monde, 4*(May), 3–4.

Roger, P. (2013). Hollande brandit la souveraineté de la France face aux demandes de Bruxelles. *Le Monde, 31*(May), 1–2.

Rozenberg, O. (2013). France: Genuine Europeanization or Monnet for nothing? In C. Lequesne & S. Bulmer (Eds.), *The member states of the European Union* (pp. 57–84). Oxford: Oxford University Press.

Tabuteau, D. (2010). La métamorphose silencieuse des assurances maladies. *Droit social, 1*, 85–92.

Tabuteau, D. (2013). *Démocratie sanitaire: les nouveaux défis des politiques de santé*. Paris: Odile Jacob.

# 9

# Depleted European Social Models Following the Crisis: Towards a Brighter Future?

Elke Heins and Caroline de la Porte

## Introduction

This book has analysed welfare reforms in those Eurozone countries most severely hit by the Great Recession and has teased out the causal influence of the EU in that process. The financial crisis in Europe has first and foremost been framed as a sovereign debt crisis, which rapidly, pervasively and with little democratic debate, led to an EU policy response focused almost exclusively on reducing public debt and deficits (Laffan 2014). Politically, the EU and international levels of governance have been extremely influential in welfare state reform, especially in countries with high Economic and Monetary Union (EMU) vulnerability—that is, when the whole Eurozone is threatened by one country's economic and

E. Heins (✉)
School of Social and Political Science, University of Edinburgh, Edinburgh, UK

C. de la Porte
Department of Business and Politics, Copenhagen Business School, Copenhagen, Denmark

© The Author(s) 2016
C. de la Porte, E. Heins (eds.), *The Sovereign Debt Crisis, the EU and Welfare State Reform*, DOI 10.1057/978-1-137-58179-2_9

budgetary conditions (de la Porte and Natali 2014). However, the level of EU involvement has varied, both across policy areas and countries, and there is still a degree of choice afforded by governments when it comes to the implementation of EU policy recommendations (Dukelow, Chapter 4; Pavolini et al., Chapter 6; Theodoropoulou, Chapter 5; Sacchi, Chapter 7). In other countries, where the economic and budgetary conditions were not a threat to the whole EMU, the decisive level of governance in the two-level game of EU and Member States was the domestic one (de la Porte and Natali 2014; Hassenteufel and Palier, Chapter 8).

The involvement of the supranational actors in severely crisis-ridden countries has rightly been criticized for lacking democratic legitimacy. Indeed, the scope of public policy reform that has been required in these countries is extensive (Schmidt 2015). However, this critique begs the counter-factual: had the EU not been involved, then how would the EMU cirsis have played out? Nevertheless, the lack of democratic legitimacy in the imposition of EU-IMF austerity policy has had a boomerang effect—embodied in the electoral outcome in Greece and the subsequent refusal to comply with austerity-driven EU/IMF programme requirements and exacerbated the economic and budgetary conditions to the brink of bankruptcy in the summer of 2015. 'Grexit' was avoided, but the social and political consequences of years of austerity has left deep wounds (see Theodoropoulou, Chapter 5). Despite this, the EU/IMF has not fundamentally changed its approach, since austerity is still dominant in the reform conditionality of the programmes. Also, the EU Council has not seriously considered alternatives, such as significant debt relief, despite the extreme severity of the budgetary constraints on the Greek economy, welfare state and society at large.

# Welfare Societies in Europe Following the *Great Recession*: Less Secure and More Unequal

While this book has shown that the reforms in the countries that were most severely affected by the sovereign debt crisis have been drastic, it is important to bear in mind that the welfare state has been reformed in all EU countries during the past decade (Farnsworth and Irving 2012).

While the core of the various social models is resilient, there are developments at the margins of welfare states leading to new inequalities. EMU membership does limit possibilities for responding to crises, but while non-EMU countries have benefited, to an extent, from adjusting currencies and interest rates, the paths of growth, employment and equality are not unambiguously better. Inequality has been rising everywhere; this is problematic for future growth prospects, since rising income inequality is hampering economic growth (OECD 2015).

Recovery from the Great Recession has been is now picking up across the EU, although at different paces and still leaving welfare states. with deep scars The composition of the workforce has changed, with a larger share of workers in vulnerable jobs. Countries where temporary employment is increasing have a greater share of low-paid workers in the labour force (Dølvik and Martin 2015). It is also notable that the average unemployment rate in the EU is still higher in 2015 than in the years before the crisis. Young people have been particularly affected by the crisis, reflected by higher rates of youth unemployment—sometimes reaching rates of over 50 per cent (Eurostat 2015) - and sometimes more than double overall employment rates. These trends are worrying, as they may become permanent features of the European economy, especially in the context of weakened unions and the breakdown of social partnership (Dukelow, Chapter 4; Erne 2015). Future research will need to look at not only the economic and social impact of such a 'lost generation', but also at the political consequences resulting from a disappointed youth.

## The Casual Impact of Europe on Welfare State Reform

As the single and comparative country studies in this book have shown, EU involvement in social and labour market policy has increased during this past decade. However, direct and clear causal impact of the EU has been through extraordinary measures, that is, the formally institutionalised Memorandums of Understanding (MoU) (Dukelow, Chapter 4; Theodoropoulou,Chapter 5) and Chapter 4; Theodoropoulou,Chapter 5) and more informal measures (Sacchi,Chapter 7).

There is a clear correlation between the intensity of EU-led intervention and crisis severity, especially when a country's economic and budgetary situation put the whole of the EMU at risk. The Spanish and Italian cases show that EU pressure for (welfare) reform prior to the crisis was present in excessive deficit procedures (EDPs). However, the lack of urgency at the time put the prescribed policies in the EDPs on the back-burner. The EU pressure became stronger and specific (in labour market policy and pensions as well as in healthcare) following the crisis. Finally, in both countries, EU pressure was effective only through backroom diplomacy and informal bargaining (Pavolini et al., Chapter 6; Sacchi, Chapter 7).

Among the three countries officially seeking full bailout from the IMF and EU/European Central Bank (ECB), there are notable variations in reforms as well as in how domestic elites responded to reform pressure by the Troika. In Ireland, the welfare reforms prescribed by the lenders had a high fit with the domestic reform paradigm among the political elite. By contrast, the overall perception of intrusiveness of reforms prescribed by the EU/IMF in Greece and Portugal was high. However, the starting points of Greece and Portugal were dissimilar, they responded differently to the EU/IMF reform demands, and their economies did not react the same way to austerity measures. Prior to the MoU, Portugal had already introduced reforms to the unemployment benefit system and made its labour market more flexible, thus EU/IMF pressure in this area was not as strong as it had been for Greece. Overall, degrees of EU involvement mainly varied with the difficulty of implementing the MoU reform recommendations. Theodoropoulou (Chapter 5) documents in her in-depth analysis of MoU implementation in the two countries that the weaker the results regarding fiscal or competitiveness indicators turned out, the stronger EU surveillance and enforcement became. It is striking that the austerity-laden reform requirements, framed in a neoliberal paradigm, were considered the only way forward by the Troika. There was virtually no scope, at the time, for re-thinking the EU strategy if a reform did not yield the expected results. This is a very relevant insight, especially since the reform demands often had a contradictory character due to the tension between social and fiscal aims. On the one hand, a string of modernising reforms in the form of extended social security coverage to previously disadvantaged groups or protection of the most vulnerable were demanded, while on the other hand the pressure to cut public expenditure made investment into the necessary policies impossible.

Yet it is noteworthy that the tightening of the SGP and the integration of economic and social policies within the European Semester also increases the indirect pressure on all Member States, particularly those in the eurozone, to reform their welfare states (Pavolini et al., Chapter 6; Hassenteufel and Palier, Chapter 8). Whereas the financial markets before the crisis did not react adversely to the frequent breaches of the SGP, even when an EDP initiated by the Commission did not manage to discipline a Member State in violation of the SGP criteria, this has changed dramatically with the crisis. The successive credit status downgrading of several heavily indebted Member States during the crisis has signalled that countries in the eurozone can be punished in case of important imbalances and become vulnerable on the international bond markets. The preventive arm of the SGP has been tightened through stricter and more encompassing budgetary criteria as well as more monitoring, while the corrective arm has been strengthened to ensure EDP procedures are launched with more ease and that they can be better enforced. This resulted in a great focus on macro-economic imbalances at the EU level, with negative repercussions on social policy (de la Porte and Heins, Chapter 2). The involvement of the EU-level is more prevalent across the EU, compared to before the crisis, although in countries that are not under MoUs, the impact on social policy is still only indirect through the emphasis on balanced budgets. It continues to be actors at the domestic level that decide on reforms, as elucidated by the case study by Hassenteufel and Palier on France (Chapter 8). On this basis, we develop the hypothesis, to be tested by future research, that, in the context of the Great Recession, domestic actors are more likely to make 'usage' of Europe to implement difficult reforms (Woll and Jacquot 2010), especially since there is more EU-domestic level interaction compared to the period before the financial crisis. In the following sections, we discuss how domestic and EU factors have influenced reform outcomes in two key welfare areas, namely, pensions and labour market policy.

## Pensions: Economic Stabilization Reached, but Adequacy Remains a Challenge

Before the onset of the 2007 financial crisis, the EU exerted pressure on pension reform through the EMU and the open method of coordination (OMC) with regard to cost containment, intergenerational fairness and adaptation to the pressure of aging populations (European Commission 2015b). The direct impact on national reforms was limited, although the ideational impact is not to be under-estimated. The EU's agenda-setting in pension policy has become particularly relevant since the Great Recession (Natali 2008; de la Porte and Natali 2014). The Commission notes that '[i] n the context of large budget deficits and a reinforced economic governance framework at EU level, Member States have adopted many pension reforms to control the increase in spending on public pensions' (European Commission 2015b, p. 2). Reform efforts can finally be detected in long-term projections of age-related spending: the Commission *does not* expect an increase in public spending on pensions at the end of its current projection period (2060).

Reforms to make pensions economically sustainable in the context of aging populations have been ongoing for several decades across the EU. While the various European systems are built up in different ways, there have been common trends in the reform processes: the restriction or abolition of early retirement schemes, an increase in statutory pension ages, and a reduction of replacement rates in statutory and mandatory occupational pensions. In the current crisis, in which markets have been deemed risky for long-term pension investments, privately managed pension schemes have no longer been promoted by member states.

There have also been policies equalizing retirement ages for men and women as well as for developing pension schemes for low income earners or those with a weak employment history (European Commission 2015b; Hinrichs and Jessoula 2012). However, this still remains a challenge. The gender pension gap is on average 40 % in the EU, which will require a combination of equal opportunity policies prior to pensionable age. Indeed, the lowering of benefit levels that has been pursued during the crisis imply that women are a group at risk when they reach pensionable age unless comprehensive policies are pursued to improve their situation. Younger workers, migrants and low-skilled and low-wage workers are identified as groups for which measures need to be adopted to ensure adequate pensions in old age (European Commission 2015b).

The dominant reform picture in the crisis countries under investigation in this book was not surprisingly one of pursuing cost containment, although some initiatives were planned to prevent poverty in old age. With the exception of Ireland, where pensions were exempt from the otherwise significant social protection cuts for political reasons (Dukelow and Heins forthcoming), the common themes were adjustments in the form of reductions in replacement rates, increasing retirement ages and contribution demands. The MoUs for Portugal and Greece identified the fragmentation of the pension system and the resulting inequities amongst beneficiaries as a problem, and recent reforms have addressed this. Another reform requirement detailed in the MoUs was the introduction of a means-tested minimum pension in Greece. However, this was not implemented, while the overall focus of cost containment was strongly enforced (Theodoropoulou, Chapter 5). In Spain, a comprehensive pension reform was enacted in August 2011 that entailed delaying the retirement age, increasing the number of years required to receive a full pension and decreasing the use of partial and early retirement, as well as lowering the replacement rates. In Italy, the reform measures were strikingly similar: extension of working lives, decrease of replacement rates and a shift to a defined contribution system. Finally, the contribution rates for the self-employed were raised to move more quickly towards a homogenization with employees' rates. The Italian case is notable, as the pension system has changed from being one of the most generous in Europe to becoming the least generous. This was due not only to the reform implemented in the context of the crisis but also to multiple reforms during the last three decades (Pavolini et al., Chapter 6). Given the increased demands being put on balanced budgets throughout the Eurozone and the expected increases in pension expenditure due to population aging—a common European problem with heightened significance in the Southern European countries—such focus is, however, hardly surprising.

## Unemployment Benefits and Labour Market Policies: Less Generosity, More Flexibility

Similar to pension systems, unemployment schemes were already significantly reformed in the decades prior to the crisis. As unemployment rates in Europe compared unfavourably to the situation of the EU's main economic competitors around the early 1990s, Europe's relatively strict labour market regulations, generous unemployment benefits and egalitarian wage policies came to be seen as the underlying causes of so-called Eurosclerosis (Boeri and Garibaldi 2009). At the same time there were high inactivity rates due to the widespread use of 'exit routes' through invalidity or early retirement benefits, while existing job creation schemes mainly functioned as a revolving door between benefit receipt and temporary work on a secondary labour market. A policy turn away from 'passive' benefits towards 'activation' was the main prescription to cure this ailment, but demands for the deregulation of labour markets also became stronger. The more systematic use of active labour market policies (ALMPs) to integrate the unemployed (as well as various other categories of working-age 'non-employed' people) into the regular labour market was recommended by the OECD (1994) and the European Employment Strategy (EES), focusing on policies to increase employment levels (Casey 2004; de la Porte and Heins, Chapter 2). The OECD Jobs Study and the European Employment Strategy (EES) identified work as the best way out of poverty and social exclusion, together with the aim to reduce welfare spending on working-age people to make social protection systems more financially viable. The EES became a powerful tool for policy learning and consensus-building on what constitutes appropriate labour market policies and acted as an efficient disseminator of key new concepts such as employability, 'making work pay' or flexicurity (Jacobsson 2004; Viebrock and Clasen 2009). These policies have been characterized by increased 'conditionality' for the receipt of benefits and called for the reduction of welfare spending more explicitly. As a vast comparative literature has shown, a suite of new labour market instruments were introduced in many European countries. These included 'enabling' or human capital-focused measures in the form of training and upskilling as well as 'demanding' elements in the form of increased conditionality for benefit receipt, the supplementation of low wages through tax credits or wage subsidies, or the exemption from social insurance contributions to integrate increasing proportions of working-age people into the labour market by 'making work pay' (Eichhorst and Konle-Seidl 2008; Clasen and Clegg 2011).

Following the crisis, reforms in the area of unemployment benefits were featuring prominently in 'Programme Countries' that had to seek bailouts from the Troika. While there was definitely room for catch up regarding the integration of activation and benefit services, the reform requirements stipulated in the MoUs were mainly driven by cost considerations. Everywhere reductions in benefit generosity and duration were imposed, although levels of generosity in the crisis countries were not high to begin with. Due to the absence of economic recovery, temporary unemployment assistance programmes had to be prolonged several times, exemplified by the Spanish and Italian cases (Pavolini et al., Chapter 6).

In Greece and Portugal, the MoUs prescribed a targeted extension to the self-employed, but this was not achieved in either country. Similarly, a Minimum Income Guarantee with the aim of enhancing poverty alleviation was stipulated in the Greek MoUs but has not been enforced so far (Theodoropoulou, Chapter 5). The MoU signed in August 2015 (the latest at the time of this writing) contains another provision for a national roll-out of a minimum income by the end of 2016, but it remains to be seen if and how it is implemented (Laterza 2015). Notwithstanding notable differences between the two countries' experience of EU/IMF conditionality, as elaborated by Theodoropoulou (Chapter 5), in both Portugal and Greece the adequacy of benefits was reduced, flexibility ambitions trumped security concerns and the already frail systems of social partnership has been further undermined.

Similarly, in Italy precise changes in the collective bargaining system have been demanded. Also, here, a new unemployment benefit scheme now links benefits more closely to contributions and slightly increased coverage to some categories of atypical contracts (Iudicone and Arca Sedda 2015). However, part of the recalibration in this field that did take place was in the form of labour market measures that weakened the dismissal protection for former 'insiders' on open-ended contracts . In Spain there were major labour reforms in the context of the financial crisis, whereby workers on fixed-term and open-ended contracts have come closer together in terms of anti-discrimination. The reforms of 2010 and 2012 enhanced flexibility for workers on open-ended contracts, particularly with regard to dismissals. There were, however, no changes for workers on fixed-term contracts, despite demand by unions for improving their conditions (and for incentives to reduce this type of contract). (Pavolini et al.,Chapter 6).

Also in France flexicurity-type reforms, combining some improvements for atypical workers with increased flexibility regarding wages and dismissal regulations pertaining to standard employment contracts, were introduced (Hassenteufel and Palier, Chapter 8; Clegg 2011). Whether these reforms finally tackle the long-standing problem of labour market dualization in these countries is an open question. Future research should examine whether a process of 'subtracted recalibration' (Pavolini et al, Chapter 6) is happening throughout Europe—that is, whether differences have decreased because formerly well-protected social groups have lost many of their privileges while the position of so-called outsiders has hardly improved.

## Recent Developments and Future Outlook

The empirical chapters in this book concentrated on the years from 2008 to 2013. In the meantime, a lot has happened both politically and economically: governments in crisis-hit countries changed (most prominently in Greece after the clear victory of the anti-austerity party Syriza), a new EU Commission was appointed in 2014 and the main media and public attention has shifted from the Euro crisis to the refugee crisis while the economic situation in some countries (but clearly not in all) improved. Ireland's economy returned to positive growth rates in 2011 and Portugal's in 2014, whereas Greece is still struggling (see Table 9.1).

Subsequently, Ireland (in December 2013) and Portugal (in June 2014) successfully exited their EU/IMF financial assistance programmes after 'investor confidence for the sovereign' was seen as 'restored'; however, these countries still remain under 'post-programme surveillance', and reform measures that are seen as being implemented too slowly or not comprehensively remain in the spotlight of the EU. Also, Spain stays under continued surveillance despite the completion of the EU's recapitalisation programme of its banks in January 2014.

Meanwhile, the EU-IMF Economic Adjustment Programme for Cyprus (not discussed in this book) continues, whereas Greece signed a new three-year European Stability Mechanism support programme in August 2015. The political turmoil around the Grexit referendum and early new elections that accompanied the prolongation of EU-IMF financial support for Greece captured the attention of the political elites, the media and wider public throughout the summer of 2015. While we do not want to go into these turbulent political developments as they are beyond our focus, it is interesting to briefly look at the new MoU. It once again spells out detailed policy conditions attached to the financial assistance to Greece. The demands placed on Greece are not new. For example, in the area of pension policy an increase of the retirement age, an integration of the fragmented social security funds, and the strengthening of the link between contributions and benefits has been recommended by experts for decades and were already included in previous MoUs. What is new in this latest agreement, however, is a clear recogni-

**Table 9.1** GDP growth rate (volume), percentage change on previous year, 2009–2016

|  | 2009 | 2010 | 2011 | 2012 | 2013 | 2014 | 2015 | 2016 |
|---|---|---|---|---|---|---|---|---|
| Euro area | −4.5 | 2.1 | 1.6 | −0.8 | −0.3 | 0.9 | n.a. | n.a. |
| Ireland | −5.6 | 0.4 | 2.6 | 0.2 | 1.4 | 5.2 | 3.6 | 3.5 |
| Greece | −4.3 | −5.5 | −9.1 | −7.3 | −3.2 | 0.7 | 0.5 | 2.9 |
| Spain | −3.6 | 0.0 | −1.0 | −2.6 | −1.7 | 1.4 | 2.8 | 2.6 |
| Italy | −5.5 | 1.7 | 0.6 | −2.8 | −1.7 | −0.4 | 0.6 | 1.4 |
| France | −2.9 | 2.0 | 2.1 | 0.2 | 0.7 | 0.2 | 1.1 | 1.7 |
| Portugal | −3.0 | 1.9 | −1.8 | −4.0 | −1.1 | 0.9 | 1.6 | 1.8 |

*Sources*: 2009–2014 growth rates from Eurostat main database, accessed 21 October 2015; 2015 and 2016 estimates based on DG ECFIN (2015)

tion by the EU Commission of the need for social fairness, which appears from the very beginning of the document. This is perhaps a small victory for the anti-austerity Greek government elected in January 2015 that refused to comply with the austerity-laden MoUs. Still, it is to be mentioned that reform requirements of the present MoU are by no means light, but perhaps more realistic.

It is a welcome change that social fairness considerations are more clearly acknowledged and that a 'Social Impact Assessment', in addition to fiscal sustainability assessments, now accompanies the latest MoU to guide the monitoring of its implementation. However, the agreement itself is still formulated in the spirit of the EU's ordoliberal paradigm, requiring austerity policy to exit the crisis. The Social Impact Assessment explores the employment and growth considerations of the main reforms and the social distribution of the costs of reforms and assesses the resilience and efficiency of social protection systems (European Commission 2015a). Whether any action will follow if the social costs of reform are found to be unacceptably high remains to be seen. In the future it would be relevant to analyse whether and, if so, how the involvement of the EU alters in terms of both governance and policy prescriptions in response to emerging evidence on negative effects of austerity.

The overall neglect of a social investment perspective in the various crisis responses so far is extremely regrettable, not least from an evidence-based policy perspective. In general, those countries that have been the source of social investment policies, in particular the Nordic countries, have emerged better from the crisis, due to the institutional foundation of welfare state universalism and their extensive high-quality social services (see Chapter 3 by Kvist). More recent research emphasises the important role that education has to play in preventing a further increase in inequality and in stimulating economic growth (OECD 2015). Generally, it seems absurd not to consider spending on education and training as a productive investment (in contrast to spending on road infrastructure, for example) and thus not to exempt it from the strict budgetary rules set by the new economic governance instruments. The Six Pack and other EU instruments have more recently started to consider broader social indicators, but more needs to be done if economic growth and fairer societies in the EU are to be achieved.

In relation to the questions of how to make the EMU more resilient against future recessions and how to build a genuine economic union in symmetry with the monetary union, new prospects on the issue of the constrained EU fiscal capacity are being discussed. So far, it is mainly limited to the European Social Fund and a few *ad hoc* instruments. While the term 'fiscal capacity' is used differently by various actors—for example, some Member States understand it as redistribution, while the *Five Presidents' Report* (Juncker et al. 2015) refers to it mainly in the sense of macro-economic stabilization—interesting policy suggestions emerge from this debate. There is, for example, some focus on increased risk sharing through better integrated financial and capital markets and a banking union. In the medium term, mechanisms of fiscal stabilization for the Eurozone as a whole are demanded (Juncker et al. 2015). A more radical suggestion is to introduce a European unemployment insurance that would act as a Eurozone-wide automatic stabilizer (Claeys et al. 2014). This would also have the potential of providing a foundation for a strengthened political union, as it might make the benefits of the EU more tangible and thus strengthen democratic legitimacy. However, the convergence of extremely diverse labour market institutions and existing unemployment benefit systems that would come with it is controversial and renders the idea fairly unrealistic at the moment (Clegg forthcoming). At a time when EU intervention in national welfare states has mainly led in order to retrenchment to correct public debt and budget deficits, such forms of positive integration through guaranteeing social rights would be a tremendous step towards a European *Social* Union, which has been much neglected since the onset of the sovereign debt crisis.

# References

Boeri, T., & Garibaldi, P. (2009). Beyond eurosclerosis. *Economic Policy, 24*(58), 409–461.

Casey, B. (2004). The OECD jobs strategy and the European employment strategy: Two views of the labour market and the welfare state. *European Journal of Industrial Relations, 10*(3), 329–352.

Claeys, G., Darvas, Z., & Wolff, G. B. (2014). Benefits and drawbacks of European unemployment insurance. In *Bruegel Policy Brief 2014/06*, Brussels: Bruegel.

Clasen, J., & Clegg, D. (Eds.). (2011). *Regulating the risk of unemployment: National adaptations to post-industrial labour markets in Europe*. Oxford: Oxford University Press.

DG ECFIN. (2015). *Spring 2015 economic forecast*. Retrieved from http://ec.europa.eu/economy_finance/publications/european_economy/2015/pdf/ee2_en.pdf

Clegg, D. (2011). France: Integration versus dualization. In J. Clasen & D. Clegg (Eds.), *Regulating the risk of unemployment: National adaptations to post-industrial labour markets in Europe* (pp. 34–54). Oxford: Oxford University Press.

Clegg, D. (forthcoming). Labour market policies in Europe. In P. Kennett & N. Lendvai (Eds.), *A handbook of European social policy*. Cheltenham: Edward Elgar.

de la Porte, C., & Natali, D. (2014). Altered Europeanization of pension reform during the Great Recession: Denmark and Italy compared. *West European Politics*, *37*(4), 732–749.

Dølvik, J.-E., & Martin, A. (2015). From crisis to crisis: European social models and labour market outcomes in the era of monetary integration. In J.-E. Dølvik & A. Martin (Eds.), *European social models from crisis to crisis: Employment and inequality in the era of monetary integration* (pp. 325–385). Oxford: Oxford University Press.

Dukelow, F., & Heins, E. (forthcoming). The Anglo-Saxon welfare states: Still Europe's outlier – or trendsetter? In P. Kennett & N. Lendvai (Eds.), *A handbook of European social policy*. Cheltenham: Edward Elgar.

Eichhorst, W., & Konle-Seidl, R. (2008). Contingent convergence: A comparative analysis of activation policies. In *IZA Discussion Paper* no. 3905. Retrieved from http://ftp.iza.org/dp3905.pdf

Erne, R. (2015). A supranational regime that nationalizes social conflict: Explaining European trade unions' difficulties in politicizing European economic governance. *Labor History*, *56*(3), 345–368.

European Commission. (2015a, August 19). Assessment of the social impact of the new stability support programme for Greece. Retrieved September 8, 2015, from http://ec.europa.eu/economy_finance/assistance_eu_ms/greek_loan_facility/pdf/assessment_social_impact_en.pdf

European Commission. (2015b). *The 2015 pension adequacy report: Current and future income adequacy in old age in the EU, Vol. 1*. Luxembourg: Publications Office of the European Union.

Eurostat. (2015). Unemployment statistics. Data up to September 2015. Retrieved November 9, 2015, from http://ec.europa.eu/eurostat/statistics-explained/index.php/Unemployment_statistics

Farnsworth, K., & Irving, Z. (2012). Varieties of crisis, varieties of austerity. *Journal of Poverty and Social Justice, 20*(2), 133–147.

Hinrichs, K., & Jessoula, J. (Eds.). (2012). *Labour market flexibility and pension reforms. Flexible today, secure tomorrow?* Basingstoke: Palgrave Macmillan.

Iudicone, F., & Arca Sedda, A. (2015). Italy: Reforms to system of unemployment benefits. Retrieved October 12, 2015, from http://www.eurofound.europa.eu/observatories/eurwork/articles/industrial-relations-law-and-regulation/italy-reforms-to-system-of-unemployment-benefits

Jacobsson, K. (2004). Soft regulation and the subtle transformation of states: The case of EU employment policy. *Journal of European Social Policy, 14*(4), 355–370.

Juncker, J.-C., Tusk, D., Dijsselbloem, J., Draghi, M., & Schulz, M. (2015). Completing Europe's Economic and Monetary Union. Retrieved from http://ec.europa.eu/priorities/economic-monetary-union/docs/5-presidents-report_en.pdf

Laffan, B. (2014). Testing times: the growing primacy of responsibility in the Euro area. *West European Politics, 37*(2), 270–287.

Laterza, V. (2015). Greece: Government to roll out a Guaranteed Minimum Income scheme. Retrieved October 12, 2015, from http://www.basicincome.org/news/2015/08/greece-government-to-roll-out-a-guaranteed-minimum-income-scheme

Natali, D. (2008). *Pensions in Europe, European pensions. The evolution of pension policy at national and supranational level.* Brussels: Peter Lang.

OECD. (1994). *The OECD jobs study. Facts, analysis, strategies.* Paris: OECD.

OECD. (2015). *In it together: Why less inequality benefits all.* Paris: OECD Publishing.

Schmidt, V. A. (2015). The forgotten problem of democratic legitimacy. In M. Mathijs & M. Blyth (Eds.), *The future of the Euro.* Oxford: Oxford University Press.

Viebrock, E., & Clasen, J. (2009). Flexicurity and welfare reform. *Socio-Economic Review, 7*(2), 305–331.

Woll, C., & Jacquot, S. (2010). Using Europe: Strategic action in multilevel politics. *Comparative European Politics, 8*(1), 110–126.

# Index

C. de la Porte, E. Heins (eds.), *The Sovereign Debt Crisis, the EU and Welfare State Reform*, DOI 10.1057/978-1-137-58179-2

Printed by Books on Demand, Germany